Praise for *Bones*:

'Tone digs deep into the colourful world of quarter-horse racing'
*New York Times*

'Riveting ... Working with rich material, Tone constructs a power-ful narrative that reveals tensions of class and race – and unbreak-able family bonds'
*National Book Review*

'Much of *Bones* reads like ... a colourful thriller. But this book is the result of reporting that took Tone from North Texas to tracks across the Southwest, as he explored how the murderous Zeta drug cartel came to be a major player in quarter-horse racing ... We highly recommend it'
*D Magazine*

'Throughout the book, Tone maintains a vivid and balanced narra-tive; he tells the story clearly, relatively objectively and without oversimplification'
*Kirkus Reviews*, starred review

'Tone's first foray into a book-length investigation is thorough and relentless. Painstakingly grounding this story in the misty beg-innings of quarter-horse racing, Tone carefully describes the modern art and science of the sport. He gives the same careful treatment to every aspect of this story as it gallops between racetracks in Texas, Oklahoma, New Mexico and California, chasing money and may-hem across the Mexican border. As José infiltrates the rarefied milieu of quarter-horse racing, Tone's fluid style and light touch reveal the detention, riches, obscurity, or horrifying death that awaits all the major players, including law-enforcement agents and collusive American ranchers. Tone's thoughtful coverage tells a tale of a borderland dream turned nightmare'
*Booklist*

'[*Bones*] stands out for its excellent reporting ... and for its up-to-date accounts ... [Tone succeeds] at tying the quarter-horse racing phe-nomenon to Miguel Treviño, the Zeta cartel, money laundering, Texas ranchers and, especially, the eventual surprising involvement of José Treviño'
*Dallas Morning News*

'What a cast of characters: a bloodthirsty Mexican drug lord, his unassuming blue-collar brother, a daring Texas rancher and an idealistic young FBI agent. And then there are the racehorses, as fast as the wind, competing for million-dollar purses on the quarter-horse tracks of the American Southwest. Through amazingly detailed research, Joe Tone has brought us a riveting tale about the pursuit of justice in the most dangerous of worlds'

SKIP HOLLANDSWORTH, author of
*New York Times* bestseller, *The Midnight Assassin*

# BONES

## A STORY OF BROTHERS,
## A CHAMPION HORSE AND
## THE RACE TO STOP AMERICA'S
## MOST BRUTAL CARTEL

# JOE TONE

WILLIAM
COLLINS

William Collins
An imprint of HarperCollins*Publishers*
1 London Bridge Street
London SE1 9GF

WilliamCollinsBooks.com

First published in Great Britain by William Collins in 2017
First published in the United States by One World, an imprint of
Penguin Random House LLC, New York, in 2017
This hardback edition published in 2018

Copyright © 2017 Joe Tone

Joe Tone asserts the moral right to be identified as
the author of this book in accordance with the
Copyright, Designs and Patents Act 1988

Book design by Jo Anne Metsch

Map copyright © 2017 David Lindroth Inc.

A catalogue record for this book is
available from the British Library

ISBN 978-0-00-820481-5

Printed and bound in Great Britain by
CPI Group (UK) Ltd, Croydon, CR0 4YY

MIX
Paper from
responsible sources
FSC™ C007454

This book is produced from independently certified FSC paper
to ensure responsible forest management

For more information visit: www.harpercollins.co.uk/green

FOR MELISSA

Every man suddenly became related to Kino's pearl, and Kino's pearl went into the dreams, the speculations, the schemes, the plans, the futures, the wishes, the needs, the lusts, the hungers, of everyone, and only one person stood in the way and that was Kino, so that he became curiously every man's enemy.

—JOHN STEINBECK, *The Pearl*

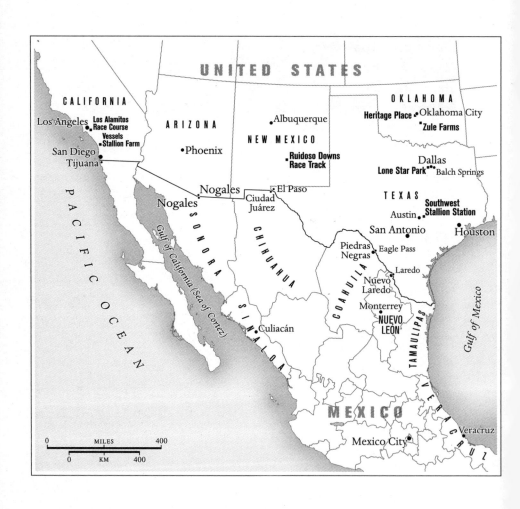

UNITED STATES

CALIFORNIA

Los Angeles
•Los Alamitos
Race Course
Vessels
•Stallion Farm

San Diego
Tijuana•

ARIZONA

•Phoenix

Nogales

Nogales

NEW MEXICO

•Albuquerque

•Ruidoso Downs
Race Track

El Paso
Ciudad
Juárez

OKLAHOMA

Heritage Place •Oklahoma City
•Zule Farms

Dallas
Lone Star Park••Balch Springs

TEXAS

Austin•
Southwest
Stallion Station

San Antonio

Houston•

Piedras
Negras •Eagle Pass

Laredo•
Nuevo
Laredo•

COAHUILA

Monterrey•

NUEVO
LEÓN

TAMAULIPAS

Gulf of Mexico

PACIFIC OCEAN

Gulf of California (Sea of Cortez)

SONORA

CHIHUAHUA

SINALOA

•Culiacán

MEXICO

Mexico City•

VERACRUZ

Veracruz•

0        MILES        400

0        KM        400

# BONES

# POCKET TRASH

NUEVO LAREDO,
TAMAULIPAS, MEXICO
June 2010

As he walked across the bridge that morning, approaching the invisible line that separated him from Texas, it wasn't hard for José to envision what would come next: the welcoming American half-smile, the face-down scan of his passport, the keyboard pecking, the faux-polite *please come with me, sir,* and the pat down, always a pat down, before a waterfall of questions about his brother. He'd be lucky to get out of there by lunchtime.

It was only eight in the morning, but already it was 80 on its way to 101, with the sun preheating the pedestrians on the Gateway to the Americas International Bridge. "Bridge One," as the U.S. Customs and Border Protection agents called it, was the span used by the thousands of people who crossed by foot each day between Nuevo Laredo, in northern Mexico's Tamaulipas state, and Laredo, Texas. José inched across, U.S. passport at the ready.

He was forty-three. He was thick through the chest and shoulders, soft in the middle, filling out his five-foot-seven frame. His black hair was thinning on top and fading at the temples; his round face was Etch-A-Sketched with proof of his status as lifelong laborer and father of four. He'd been trudging across this bridge for most of his four decades.

Crossing was once a breeze. Mexican or American, you could stroll across the bridge in either direction, the Rio Grande slogging beneath you, and through the checkpoint in a matter of minutes, often by just declaring yourself a citizen. It was the ease of crossing that made living on the border alluring: the ability to visit a favorite relative, attend a birthday celebration or quinceañera, play in a soccer game, or party in a country other than your own. You crossed the border the way people in other towns crossed a railroad track, so fluidly that residents referred to the two cities as one: Los Dos Laredos.

Over the years, though, the one-thousand-foot walk across had become excruciating, even for those who weren't yanked out of line the way José was. It started after the terrorist attacks of September 11, 2001, when more agents were dispatched to keep the cable-news nightmares at bay. Armed with scanners, X-rays, and political consensus, Customs and Border Patrol agents, soon to be rebranded as "Border Protection" agents, started scrutinizing every crosser, looking for reasons to turn someone away. The line into Texas could take hours now, even if your name didn't make the feds' hard drives spin.

José made his way between the chain-link fence that lined this section of the bridge and the metal barriers that protected him from cars inching past to his left. At around five after eight, he finally approached the kiosk and handed the agent his passport.

Do you have any weapons?

No.

Do you have more than ten thousand dollars to declare?

No.

For years his answers had been good enough. Lately, though, when the feds scanned José's passport, they got a notification from a proprietary security platform telling the agent there was some reason not to let José pass.

This time was no different. An agent escorted him into the fading beige U.S. Customs and Border Protection building. It was a maze of offices and interrogation rooms, connected by hallways with moldy tile and wheezy elevators that seemed forever on the verge of breaking down. The whole building smelled a little like a teenage boy's locker. There were holding cells for criminals caught crossing, furnished with nothing but metal toilets and wooden benches, handcuffs attached and waiting. There were rooms for counting currency, equipped with computer terminals and scales. There was an intake center for families, mostly Central American mothers and children who were fleeing gang violence and hoping for asylum. There were dog cages but usually no dogs. They were all outside sniffing.

An agent patted José down and escorted him into an interview room. They called this "secondary inspection" or "hard secondary." For José, a more apt name might have been a "We Know Who Your Brother Is, So Sit the Fuck Down for an Inspection" inspection. When José drove across, which was infrequent, they would comb his car and his person for guns, drugs, large amounts of cash, or anything else actionable. He had walked across this time, so they had to settle for what they called his "pocket trash": the contents of a bag he was carrying and the pockets of his clothes.

Agents moved in and out of the room. They didn't announce it, but José could guess what they were doing: making calls to whatever agency might have some questions about his little brother.

Thirty years before, when José was just a teenager, he had crossed this river on his way to lay bricks in Dallas. In time, people like him—Mexicans crossing north in search of work their homeland couldn't provide—would be weaponized and dragged to the front lines of America's culture war. But back then, for teenage José, it was as simple as crossing the bridge, driving seven hours north, finding a job, and going to work.

He laid his share of bricks in those early years. A few of his brothers did, too. They were constructing what could have been the foundations of a working-class American life. But before long, José was the only Treviño Morales brother left in Dallas. Now, as his wait on Bridge One stretched into its second sweaty hour, two of those brothers were dead. One was in an American prison. Another was enmeshed in Mexico's trafficking business.

Then there was Miguel, the brother these feds so badly wanted to know about. He was a leader of Los Zetas, a criminal organization raking in hundreds of millions of dollars every year, much of it controlled by Miguel. Because of this vast accumulation of power and wealth—and because of Miguel's unrivaled lust for mass, public, and grotesque violence—he was one of the most wanted drug lords in Mexico.

It had been this way for several years now. So for several years, this was who José was when he showed up at the border: the bricklaying brother of one of Mexico's most wanted men. For all this harassment, José was never any use to the feds. He'd spent three decades as a mason; his callused hands had helped build Dallas's exurban excess and then revive its urban core. No matter how hard the feds tried, they had never been able to connect brick-laying José to brick-smuggling Miguel.

But José was no longer a bricklayer, and that interested the feds. Recently, he had remade himself into a successful racehorse owner. He'd taken the racing business by surprise, quickly maneuvering into its upper ranks by hanging on to the fluttering silks of an undersized colt and partnering with a down-on-its-luck stud farm. Now, after winning a couple of big races, José was buying up some of the most expensive breeding mares in quarter-horse racing, the brand of racing preferred by the cowboys of the American Southwest and Mexico.

José's new career opportunity had come just in time. In thirty years of laying bricks, he had never been able to do much more than keep his family afloat, even as his cartel-affiliated brothers in Mexico amassed cash, property, and power. Now his teenage daughter wanted to be the first in his extended family to finish college, with her three younger siblings hopefully not far behind. A few more breaks on the track and José might be able to pay for it all.

But his success at the track also made these crossings more titillating for the agents who swarmed these borderland interview rooms. Because however mysterious José's little brother was to them, there was one thing they all seemed to know: Miguel *loved* horses.

About ninety minutes after José got pulled in, an agent from Immigration and Customs Enforcement showed up to ask all the usual questions.

I'm not proud of my brother, José said.

My brother has made my life hell, José said.

I don't know where my brother is, José said.

He almost definitely didn't. Few people knew where Miguel was at any given time. The moment people did know, his whereabouts changed.

At about ten-fifteen that morning, two hours after José had been pulled out of line, at least three since he'd stepped into it, the agents handed him back his belongings. There were some clothes, boots, toiletries, and a few coloring books and crayons, which he was bringing back for the youngest of his four kids. They were waiting for him in Dallas, and he was finally on his way.

# CHAPTER ONE

## FOUNDATIONS

You've seen a horse race. Maybe you've leaned over the rail at your local track, hollering at the seven because you bet the seven, for reasons that made sense at the time. Maybe you've donned a floppy hat and gotten hammered off mint juleps, running in from the kitchen to catch the end of—or maybe a replay of?—the Derby. Maybe you've been in a Vegas sportsbook, where not even the immortal gods of American football can muscle the ponies off those little TVs in the corner.

Somewhere, someway, you've seen a horse race. Most likely you saw thoroughbreds, the horses that were loping down the backstretch when you stumbled in from the kitchen. Maybe you watched a steeplechase, for the novelty of seeing these graceful beasts leap through a manicured obstacle course. But it's unlikely that you've ever knowingly watched a quarter-horse race, and, for our purposes, you'll need to see one, if only in your mind's eye or on YouTube.

Be forewarned: There are no mint juleps here. The best we can offer is a lime in your Corona.

The colonists who settled Virginia and the Carolinas invented quarter-horse racing in the 1600s. It was more or less an accident.

They'd brought a handful of Arabians and thoroughbreds with them on the voyage, and between shifts tilling the New World, they started racing through the main streets of their newly settled villages. The races were informal and short, usually about a quarter of a mile, run between two horses down straight streets lined with villagers. But winning them became a point of pride, and over time, the colonists discovered that breeding their horses with those ridden by the natives resulted in even faster racehorses. They called this new breed the quarter-of-a-mile running horse, accurately if not cleverly.

Around this time, a British military captain visited North Carolina and wrote home about his experience. He marveled at the lush tobacco fields, the "shocking barbarities of the Indians," and the horses:

> They are much attached to quarter racing, which is always a match between two horses to run a quarter of a mile, straight out, being merely an exertion of speed. They have a breed that performs it with astonishing velocity. . . . I am confident there is not a horse in England, or perhaps the whole world, that can excel them in rapid speed.

In the 1800s, as settlers moved west, they encountered a racing culture similar to the one established by those original colonists. Three centuries of ranching across Mexico—including in the northern state of Coahuila y Tejas—had propagated a breed of stock horses built for working the farm. They were short, muscular, and placid amid the chaos of a cattle herd. They were "cow ponies," first and foremost. But they could run, too, if only for a few hundred yards, and their serenity with a rider in the saddle made them easy to settle down at the starting line.

The Southwest in the nineteenth century was defined by bloodshed, as Coahuila y Tejas became the Republic of Texas, and then an American state. Throughout it all, though, the white American settlers, Mexican ranchers, and Native Americans challenged each other to quarter-mile races all across the disputed territory. Gamblers would line the track, forming a human rail, with money and property at stake. One race was said to attract such prolific betting that it bankrupted and shuttered an entire Texas town.

The eastern settlers touted their "quarter-of-a-mile running horses." The Texans swore by the speed and smarts of their cow ponies. An imported stallion named Steel Dust quickly extinguished the East-West rivalry. He was already thirteen when he arrived from the East in 1844, but he beat every cow pony they lined him up against. Before long he was being bred with ranch horses from across the new state of Texas, infusing the Spaniards' placid cow-pony breed with a burst of speed and additional weight.

The resulting horses were, as one quarter-horse historian described them, "small, [with] alert ears, a well-developed neck, sloping shoulders, short deep barrel, a great heart girth, heavy muscled in thigh and forearm, legs not too long, and firmly jointed with the knee and pastern close." They were rarely taller than fifteen hands* but could reach twelve hundred pounds. (Thoroughbreds are lither, averaging sixteen hands but just a thousand pounds.) The new breed of horse was even better on the farm and unbeatable in a rodeo ring or on the track, provided the track wasn't longer than a quarter mile. They called him the American Quarter Horse.

By the 1940s, an industry had sprung forth around the breed. In Texas, a group of cowboys founded the American Quarter Horse Association, to manage and regulate breeding and competition. In New Mexico and California, businessmen pushed for pari-mutuel betting, allowing racetracks to collect the bets and manage the payouts. That lured horsemen and gamblers from Texas, Oklahoma, and Mexico for weekends spent drinking and betting on the races, which could now feature six or eight horses instead of two.

---

* One hand is four inches. So fifteen hands would be about five feet tall at the withers.

The quarter-horse meccas built in the 1940s and '50s still anchor the sport today, especially Ruidoso Downs, in the mountains of New Mexico, and Los Alamitos, in the palm-studded suburbs of Orange County, California. They host futurities, for two-year-old racehorses, and derbies, for three-year-olds, with millions on the line. And on any given day, at tracks sprinkled across the Southwest and Mexico, quarter horses as old as five, six, even seven run races with a few grand on the line and a few hundred people in the stands.

The best of these horses are descendants from American Quarter Horse royalty—sired by name-brand stallions like First Down Dash, Corona Cartel, or Mr Jess Perry. They're ridden by jockeys who often learned to ride in unsanctioned match races in the countryside of Texas, Oklahoma, or Mexico. Many of the best are Mexican immigrants.

The races typically cover between 350 and 440 yards. The best feature a little bumping out of the gate and all the way through the finish line. The fastest 440-yard races are run in about 20 seconds, compared to the two minutes it takes the top thoroughbreds to circle Churchill Downs. The short track leaves little time to overcome a stumble. The horses are loaded up, rearing and kicking up dust, and everything goes still. The gates fly and and the race is already almost over. The horse that best taps into its English-Spanish-Mexican-Tejano cow-pony DNA has the advantage, using its hulking haunches and quiet demeanor to go from dead still to full speed in a few strides.

Now maybe you can see it, even if you've never seen it: stocky horses raised by cowboys, racing on short tracks, ridden by jockeys trained in the thick brush of cow country, all a safe distance from the floppy-hatted dignitaries of the Jockey Club. They call thoroughbred racing the sport of kings? This is the sport of cowboys. Muddle your mint elsewhere.

# CHAPTER TWO

## BLOODLINES

POMONA, CALIFORNIA
December 2008

The calculations started as soon as Ramiro's loafers shuffled into the barn, kicking dust particles into the crinkles of the cowboys' boots. As his eyes adjusted to the dark, Ramiro's brain started receiving dispatches about what he was seeing: thick haunches, hinged backs, steep shoulder slopes, and all the other variables that make the difference between racehorse and *runner*. There were some runners in the barns this morning. That was the only takeaway from a stroll through here, some babies that would be blazing down the track by spring.

It was winter in Pomona, one of the dozens of suburbs splayed east of Los Angeles that everyone's heard of but few have visited, a kissing cousin to Covina and Pasadena. Ramiro was born, raised, and still lived in Monterrey, the industrial heartbeat of northeastern Mexico. But he spent a lot of time traversing these suburbs in rental cars. He went to the track in Los Alamitos for the races, the stud farm in Bonsall to buy breedings, private ranches, public auctions, and anywhere else he might find a quarter horse worth studying.

This particular suburb was home to the Barretts auction house, where the final quarter-horse auction of 2008 was about to get started.

It was a small sale, 160 head, compared to 500 or even 1,000 at bigger auctions. Ramiro's particular interests made it feel even smaller. He bought mostly yearlings, one-year-old horses that would hit the tracks as two-year-olds the following year. He also targeted weanlings, which hadn't yet turned one, as well as embryos and foals still in utero, counting on the strength of their genetics alone.

This sale would feature a mix of all kinds of quarter horses, including foals, weanlings, yearlings, stallions, and broodmares. Still, Ramiro had reason to be excited. The Schvaneveldt Winter Mixed Sale, as this auction was called, was run by the family of one of the sport's winningest trainers, Blane Schvaneveldt, and had attracted horses from the best bloodlines in the business. It was also a new venture, so attendance was sparse. That meant less competition on the way to the gavel.

Ramiro moved through the barns, peering through the metal bars of the stall doors. He made small talk in his choppy English with the other horsemen milling about—trainers looking for their next champions, breeders hoping to make a big sale. They were some of the best in the business. Ramiro knew them all.

They knew him, too. They knew him by various nicknames, including "the Horseman" and "Gordo," which they recognized as the Spanish word for "fat." It made sense, given the way his cheeks and midsection curved like birthday balloons, pushing his five-foot-nine frame over 250 pounds. But at thirty-five years old, Ramiro was handsome, too, with eyes that played puppeteer to an electric smile, hair that crashed like a Malibu wave, and polo shirts in every color of Ralph Lauren's rainbow. He was a *fresa*—a "strawberry," a preppy—through and through.

Most of the quarter-horse cowboys knew Gordo by his real name, José Ramiro Villarreal Guajardo. Even if Ramiro didn't exactly fit in—if his loafers seemed impractical, his polos a little bright for this hour, his double-fisted cellphones more than a little obnoxious—Ramiro knew the sellers welcomed the sight of him.

He could be a pain in their asses when it came time to collect, and the old cowboys occasionally had to remind Ramiro just how Ford Tough they were. But Ramiro knew—everyone knew—that when the auctioneer started bellowing his gibberish, Ramiro was welcome here. Especially these days.

The Great Recession was grinding toward its thirteenth month. Home prices were in a free fall. A drought was ravaging Texas and other parts of the West, driving up hay prices. That meant the wealthy ranchers, oilmen, and businessmen who drove the quarterhorse industry were doing what wealthy people did in historic droughts and capital-R recessions: selling their planes and selling their horses. Sale prices were falling. A mixed sale like the Schvaneveldts' averaged ten thousand dollars per horse in a good year; this year might only average six thousand.

That was bad news for the Schvaneveldts but good news for brokers like Ramiro. He was buying not for himself but for horsemen back in Mexico, who trusted him to pick out well-bred babies and haul them back across the border. He never said who his buyers were; they were "Mexican businessmen" and nothing more. He could safely assume that everyone in the barns knew what kind of business those Mexicans were in. But the industry didn't care, so long as Ramiro kept showing up to spend his clients' money.

Ramiro kept coming, and the money kept coming—eventually. Since Ramiro was a reliable big spender, the auction-house managers didn't demand that he settle up before he hauled his horses off to Mexico, as they might with lesser-known buyers. They let him take possession of the horses and then pestered him throughout the year to send the balance. So long as he zeroed out his account before the next auction, he remained a valued customer.

Recently, though, Ramiro's clients had been spending bigger and sending money less reliably. At a small sale in Dallas that summer, he'd spent $112,000 on four yearlings, more money than any other buyer. In two auctions in Oklahoma that fall, he'd spent $370,000 on twenty-eight horses—and then promptly bounced ten checks worth hundreds of thousands of dollars. At one in New Mexico, he'd spent $357,000 on eleven horses. And at another in California, he'd spent

$405,000 on seventeen horses. No other buyer came close to spending that much.

The checks eventually cleared; the wires eventually came through. But Ramiro was falling behind, despite spending hours fielding and making phone calls in an effort to settle his debts. The industry was losing patience. Twice recently, sale managers had pushed Ramiro against auction-house walls, demanding he pay off the balance of his bills.

Yet when Ramiro's hand went up at the next auction, they never told him to lower it. They needed his clients' money. Today especially. The crowd was thin, which meant sellers would be either giving deep discounts or buying back their horses and waiting for a new day. But Ramiro's Mexican clients seemed impervious to economic downturns. They wanted more horses, and the best horses, always.

Walking through the barns, Ramiro could get a sense of a horse's demeanor, its build, its balance, all data points that might influence how high he might be willing to bid. Sometimes he asked one of the handlers to heave open a stall's sliding door and walk the animal around, so he could see how the horse handled itself in space. But the real data was in the catalog he was holding. Each page was covered in size-nothing type detailing a single horse's lineage—sire, dam, their sires and dams, and the career highlights of every horse along the line. Wins in "stakes races" were set in a heavier black font, which allowed seasoned buyers to assess the pedigree with a flip of the page. Their eyes were trained to scan for that coveted black type.

Like all buyers, Ramiro was especially interested in a horse's sire. Like all buyers, he was especially interested if that sire was First Down Dash. A champion racehorse in the 1980s, First Down Dash was the sport's most prolific breeder, responsible for hundreds of winners and millions in earnings.

The auction house offered two positions from which to bid. One was inside, in the small gallery that circled the sales ring. The other was outside, around the artificial-turf walking ring, where the horses were displayed before being led up a faux-brick walkway and inside. Ramiro liked it outside. There was a bid-spotter out there, looking for flying hands, and it was a good place to get one last glimpse of a horse before the bidding started. Ramiro found his post along the rail and struck his usual pose, his belly flung out in front of him and his sales book resting on top of it.

He started slowly. He placed a bid on a "foal in utero," an embryo or fetus still developing in the womb. Buying an unborn horse was sort of a blind wager, with big risks and a big upside. Instead of buying on the strength of a horse's pedigree and conformation—its genetic promise *and* its physical reality—here Ramiro was betting only on the horse's lineage. He did it often. He nabbed that first embryo for $1,500, and several horses later, his hand rose on another. This one had been sired by famous First Down Dash, but it was still a long shot, given that the foal could be born with any number of defects, or could just be slow, or could goddamn die on its way into the world. Still, Ramiro bid $13,500 on it.

Ramiro kept on like that, stocking up on quality breedings for relatively cheap. He paid $30,000 for a horse called Bench Mark Dove, $16,500 for Azeann, $6,700 for Beduinos First Down. By the time the auction reached its final hour, he'd spent a little more than $100,000 on seven horses, including some of the sale's most expensive.

Then the auctioneer called hip number 140, the 140th horse of the auction, its number penned on its hip. A handler walked into the ring beside a sorrel yearling colt. A white racing stripe bisected the horse's face, falling down the steep angle from brow to nose.

"Tempting Dash," the auctioneer bellowed. Ramiro's hand twitched back to life.

The bidding climbed through the low five figures. Ramiro steadily lifted his hand as the other bidders fell away. Maybe it was the horse's May birthday, which meant he'd be one of the younger two-year-olds on the track the following year. Maybe it was his size; he was small, shorter and skinnier than the prime yearlings, which stood somewere around fourteen hands and weighed 850 pounds.

Whatever the reason, Ramiro found himself the last bidder to raise his hand, with the price stuck at $21,500, a meager sum considering Tempting Dash's lineage.

"Sold," the auctioneer said, to the ruddy-cheeked fellow in the bright polo with the phone pressed to his ear. Another bargain for his clients back in Mexico.

# CHAPTER THREE

## FOLLOW KIKO

PIEDRAS NEGRAS, COAHUILA, MEXICO
Summer 2008

I'm here, where are you, are you coming? José was standing outside a gas station one summer evening, talking—and hoping—into his phone. He was in Piedras Negras, a snaking two-hour drive north of Laredo's Bridge One, where he would soon find himself emptying his pocket trash for a rotating cast of badge-wielding Americans. This was a different crossing point on a different day, but José could expect the same riverside indignities whenever he decided to cross back into Texas, probably in a day or two. For now, though, there was a party to attend.

It was a family affair, thrown by his little brother in rural Coahuila, a Mexican border state about a seven-hour drive from José's house outside Dallas. Leaving the United States didn't come with the same harassment, since the Mexican authorities didn't scrutinize José's entries as the American ones did. Still, crossing into Mexico could be treacherous for José and people like him.

It was a travel experience unique to the friends, families, and associates of Mexico's most-wanted criminals. Some American defense lawyers make the trip when they're invited to off-the-radar meetings, traveling to undisclosed locations to update drug lords on the status of various cases against them, their families, and their organizations. The actor Sean Penn took the trip and made it famous with his 2015 visit to El Chapo—the long, blind journey into the remote Mexican countryside, no cellphones allowed.

José made the trip only occasionally, usually for family gatherings or parties like this one. For baptisms, Mother's Day, and other occasions—tonight was a nephew's birthday—his brother Miguel liked to throw the doors open at one of his ranches and invite in people he loved and trusted. He sent out for beer and made sure it was cold, sent out for *cabrito* and made sure it was perfectly smoked. With a busy family life in Dallas, José didn't get there often. This time, he made the trek.

After crossing, José found his way to a gas station near the border, where one of his brother's workers was supposed to pick him up and deliver him to the party. But visiting an extraordinarily wanted criminal is never that simple. José waited there for hours, while his little brother's men surveilled the gas station to ensure that they didn't catch a tail—that a Mexican soldier or cop, with an American agent as backup, wasn't lying in wait, hoping José would lead them to his brother. José kept calling back to the party, calling and calling. I'm here, where are you, are you coming, but they didn't come for hours.

Eventually, after the sun ducked behind Coahuila's scrubby landscape, a pickup pulled up, and his brother's guys drove José down a long road that snaked away from Piedras Negras and into the more remote countryside of Coahuila state, transitioning along the way from pavement to dirt and slipping through thickets of mesquite trees. Even five hundred miles from Dallas, it must have felt like home.

José had every reason to love life out there, in the countryside south of the river, surrounded by rolling hills, towers of hay, and roving bands of livestock. Some of the images he and his brothers clung to from their childhood were of them standing amid horses and cattle and whitetail deer in the open space of Tamaulipas.

There were centuries of tradition in ranching this territory. It was here that, in the 1600s and 1700s, Spanish missionaries established *ranchos* and missions on both sides of the river. When they couldn't find enough Spaniards to staff them, they turned to the Indians they'd managed to convert. This introduction to horsemanship would backfire in later decades, when Mexican and American soldiers encountered more and more Comanches who were lethal on horseback.

It was also here, in the mid-1800s, that Richard King, a United States Army steamboat captain, recruited Mexican *vaqueros*, cowboys, to staff his King Ranch in newly established Texas. A century and a half later, the 825,000-acre Texas ranch is so famous that its name graces a line of Ford pickups. It's also credited with the proliferation of the quarter-horse breed.

And it was here, across those same centuries, that Spanish, Mexican, and even some Anglo ranchers developed the heavily Spanish, Catholic culture, known as Tejano, that would come to define the region long after more aggressive Anglo settlers arrived to dispossess the Mexicans of their land and power.

By the time José Treviño Morales was born, in 1966, these borders were settled. Ranching still ruled. His father worked as a vaquero on ranch land south of Nuevo Laredo, where he taught José and his brothers to care for cattle and the sensible cow ponies that roamed their home state of Tamaulipas. But sometime before José hit high school, his dad left the family. It's unclear whether he abandoned them, migrated in search of work, or disappeared under some other circumstances. Whatever the reason, he was gone, and so was the rancho lifestyle José and his brothers knew. There was nothing for the remaining Treviño clan in the countryside, so they moved into urban Nuevo Laredo and tried to survive.

The economics of that state of Mexico had long been fraught. Cities in the southeast were positioned along the Gulf of Mexico and offered jobs at the ports and in the oil industry. In the West sat Ciudad Victoria, the state capital. But the state's northern tip, where

José grew up, was an economic fault line, always shifting and occasionally rupturing.

During World War II, as the American agriculture industry struggled to find cheap labor, the United States and Mexico developed the Bracero Program, which invited Mexican laborers to cross legally into the United States to work farming jobs left unfilled by soldiers. The program offered a minimum wage, temporary housing, and health benefits, and it drew hundreds of thousands of seasonal workers every year, especially from borderland cities like Nuevo Laredo.

It also upended the culture of migration between the two countries. By the mid-1960s, the United States had issued more than four million work visas to Mexican farmworkers. Then, under pressure from American labor groups, the United States suspended the Bracero Program. But the migratory spigot wasn't so easy to turn off. With Mexican families now accustomed to work-driven migration, and with fifty thousand American farms now accustomed to a steady flow of cheap labor, workers stayed, and workers kept coming—papers or not. Together with new visa limitations and waning Mexican farm jobs, the end of the Bracero Program sparked the influx of undocumented Mexican immigrants to the United States, which helped double the country's Mexican-born population every decade through the 2000s. Instead of a hub for seasonal migrant workers, Nuevo Laredo became a key passageway for undocumented immigrants.

A year after the Bracero Program's demise, the Mexican government launched the Border Industrialization Program, designed to absorb the suddenly idle labor force along the border. The program allowed American and other foreign manufacturers to build maquiladoras, factories, in Mexico and import materials tax-free. Hundreds of new factories created thousands of low-skill, low-wage factory jobs assembling electronics, toys, and other Black Friday grist. But manufacturers, in Mexico and across the globe, targeted women for the jobs, banking that their inexperience in the workforce, combined with old-fashioned sexism, would keep wages low. Eight out of ten maquiladora jobs were filled by young women.

That didn't help the Treviño boys. The Treviño boys—all the Tamaulipas boys—needed jobs. José and his brothers washed cars and worked as gardeners, doing whatever they could to bring in money. But it wasn't enough. If they didn't want to smuggle drugs, the best place to find work was north of the river.

José's big brother Kiko—short for Juan Francisco—went first, in 1978. He had shaggy black hair and a jawline that cast a shadow on his long, muscular neck, which was often exposed by a gaping shirt collar. Kiko was the oldest of the thirteen Treviño children, and he was smooth, able to talk himself up without stumbling into braggadocio. He was savvy, too, not just dreaming of a better way but figuring out a plan. He served as the de facto patriarch after their dad left, and he modeled manhood for his six younger brothers, marrying a local girl and raising a border-zigzagging family in the tradition of Los Dos Laredos.

Kiko's in-laws were bricklayers in Dallas, so Kiko decided to try laying bricks in Dallas. It was a good time, and a good place to start a career in construction. Thanks to an oil boom, Texas's population was growing twice as fast as the country's, as workers and moneymen came to cash in. By 1980, one hundred thousand people were arriving in the Dallas–Fort Worth area every year.

Some of the new Texans were Mexicans and Mexican-Americans like Kiko and his family, but many were middle-class and wealthy white Americans. They needed houses, and schools, and strip malls. They needed Mexicans to build them.

Kiko had never laid a brick, but he learned to do it by watching his in-laws work the trowel. José came a few years later, when he was fifteen, bailing on high school. By the mid-1980s, Kiko had his own company, Treviño Masonry, and a crew of thirty-two fellow Mexicans building three houses at a time. He and José got their work visas, and got their Social Security numbers, and got their tax bills, and paid their tax bills. They banked enough money to buy a few shoebox houses in the working-class neighborhoods southeast of downtown Dallas. After laying bricks all day, they spent their nights remodeling those houses for their families. More work as bricklayers would mean more houses to buy and remodel, and more houses would allow more of their kin to move north. Their sisters had already made their way, and Mom was spending a lot of time in Dallas, too.

By the early 1990s, José was pulling in $43,500 a year, a decent wage for a no-diploma son of Tamaulipas. Kiko was doing well, too. But Kiko craved more, and he saw it in the arrival of the North American Free Trade Agreement (NAFTA).

It was well known that NAFTA would open the floodgates all along the United States' two-thousand-mile southern border, increasing imports from $40 billion to almost $300 billion over the next two decades. Laredo would benefit especially from its place at the southern tip of U.S. Interstate 35, a thumping artery that stretched north from Laredo through San Antonio, Austin, Dallas, Oklahoma City, and beyond. Once NAFTA passed, Interstate 35 would be clogged with thousands of eighteen-wheelers, carrying goods through Texas and into the Midwest.

In 1992, the year before lawmakers passed NAFTA, Kiko bought a 1958 tractor-trailer and returned to the Mexican side of the border. He started moving loads of raw materials from Nuevo Laredo to the maquiladoras of interior Mexico. But he wasn't just preparing for NAFTA's promised impact on U.S.-Mexican trade; he was also betting on the effect both governments refused to acknowledge: the increased flow of drugs across those same borders.

By truck, train, car, and foot, traffic across the border was expected to skyrocket when the law took effect on January 1, 1994. Every vessel that crossed offered an opportunity to satisfy America's unquenchable thirst for illegal narcotics—cocaine, from the wilds of Colombia but shipped through Mexico; heroin, from the poppy fields of Sinaloa; and weed, from whatever patch of land industrious growers could find. Kiko started using his new truck to transport marijuana.

Not much is known about Kiko's previous history as a smuggler, if he had any. But he had come up during a golden age of pot smuggling, after America developed its taste for weed but before its government declared war on it. If you grew up poor in Nuevo Laredo, the business, and the connections, came easily whenever you decided you wanted in.

Kiko wanted in. He bought weed from suppliers in Mexico and smuggled it across the river into Laredo, presumably tucked away in his new tractor-trailer. Then he hired couriers and paid them a few thousand bucks a load to transport it to Dallas.

In previous eras, shipping narcotics north on Interstate 35 was the easy part: keep the speed limit and stay inside the lines and no one would bother you. But in the 1970s, the United States Supreme Court had ruled that Border Patrol agents at checkpoints *within* the country's borders could stop and question motorists regardless of whether they suspected wrongdoing. Now, at checkpoints like the Laredo North station, located thirty miles north of the border on Interstate 35, agents could stop and question any motorist. And they could pull cars and trucks into hard secondary with only the slightest hint of probable cause.

Kiko's drivers moved a few hundred pounds of weed at a time. Usually they concealed it amid construction materials in a trailer. Other times, they used a ranch just off the highway to avoid the checkpoint altogether. They paid a few hundred bucks per trip to enter the ranch on one side of the checkpoint and exit on the other.

Kiko was hardly a kingpin. Other Texas smugglers around that time imported ten times what he did. But he made enough to expand his trucking company. He moved back to Nuevo Laredo, sleeping in a small living space behind his office while his wife and kids stayed back in Dallas. He had nine employees, including a bookkeeper, messengers, and drivers who delivered paper, aluminum, and other raw materials to factories across Mexico.

Between legitimate shipping and marijuana smuggling, Kiko was making enough to keep expanding the Treviño clan's nest in Dallas. He bought new trucks for his shipping business, a new pickup for himself, and a motorcycle for his son.

José, now in his mid-twenties, stuck to bricklaying. He met a woman named Zulema, an American citizen eight years his junior. She had dark-chocolate eyes and wavy black hair, and her round cheeks gave shape to a determined face. She shared José's Mexican heritage, privilege-free upbringing, and bottomless work ethic. She was just seventeen when they married, around the time Kiko pivoted into smuggling. She gave birth to their first child, Alexandra, a couple of months later.

José became a naturalized citizen and kept working the trowel for whatever contractor would take him. He rose before the sun and put in long days, building homes and schools and stores in and around Dallas. He wanted nothing to do with smuggling. If he lived with some festering indignation over his family's economic abandonment—by his father, by his fatherland, by his adopted homeland—he never expressed it to the people around him. Instead, he was building a life the way he stacked bricks in the morning shade: slowly and dutifully, actively rejecting the smuggling heritage of his hometown.

But occasionally, big brother Kiko called in a favor.

José likely longed to say no. But he was lugging that word of rejection uphill. He possessed a deep sense of what social scientists call "familism," a commitment to family over self. Social scientists routinely pin that quality on immigrants, especially Mexican ones, citing a cocktail of factors: religion, large family size, and economic necessity. And maybe immigrants do rely more heavily on family, as a tool against marginalization, using flexibility and fluidity as antidotes to systematically limited opportunity. But also, it's just what some families do: They stick the hell together. They say yes.

The Treviño brothers' early years in Dallas would have tantalized those familism-obsessed social scientists. The siblings found each other work, built each other homes, shared cars, and cared for each other's kids. This unflagging devotion to family may or may not dissipate in future generations, but José's generation was the first. If big brother asked, José said yes.

Whenever Kiko's drug couriers arrived in Dallas with the weed, they would hole up at the La Quinta, the Travelers, or some other access-road dump, waiting for one of Kiko's workers to pick up the delivery. Before they returned to Laredo, they wanted their few-thousand-dollar delivery fee. A few times, they beeped José to collect it. He got the cash from Kiko and delivered it to the motels.

Kiko's enterprise didn't last long. Late in 1993, before NAFTA even took effect, Kiko's couriers tried to pass through the Laredo North checkpoint at three-thirty in the morning. A drug-sniffing dog named Wondo perked up, leapt onto the tires, sniffed, leapt back down, and sat up straight. The agents knew what that meant, so they opened the trailer, and the dog started jumping like, *Let me in.* He was an old dog, so for him to be jumping, that meant something.

The agents waved the truck into secondary. The trailer was stuffed with Saltillo tile, destined for the kitchen of some Spanish-style McMansion. The agents hoisted themselves in and clinked their way to the back, following Wondo. That's where they found the duffel bags, stuffed with 280 pounds of cellophane-wrapped marijuana.

Kiko went to trial in 1995. José wasn't indicted, but his name did come up a couple of times. That probably explained why José wasn't in the courtroom to see Kiko sentenced to twenty years—two decades in a Colorado federal prison for moving a drug that, by the time he got out, would be legal in the state where he served his time.


With Kiko in prison, the Treviños kept grinding. Zulema earned a high-school diploma online and slogged through the best work she could find. She made $6 an hour working food service at a middle school; $6.50 as a McDonald's crew member; and, now, $500 a week working full-time for a temp agency.

José found a steady masonry gig with a residential contractor in the suburbs, and he stuck it out there for six long years. In 2007, he landed a full-time job with a contractor who did brickwork on some of the city's most prestigious projects: the new basketball arena at Southern Methodist University; the new campus of Booker T. Washington High School, one of the country's best performing-arts schools; and the new Cowboys Stadium, a monument to American excess fans dubbed "the Death Star."

José surely knew he worked harder than his paychecks suggested. The incomes of immigrants were systematically stubborn, especially in Texas, where so-called right-to-work laws suppressed union organizing and wages. Texas bricklayers made less than those in most every other state, and 50 or 60 percent less than those in Illinois, California, and New York.

José did manage the occasional pay bump, and he was up to $20 an hour by 2009, from $16.50 when he'd started his previous job. He could load up on hours, too. He'd clocked 240 hours of overtime in his first full year at his new job, including 28 overtime hours one week when the average temperature was 104 degrees.

Still, it was hard to do any more than survive. That's why they were stuck on their stubby street in Balch Springs, one of the inner-ring suburbs southeast of Dallas. Seventy-five percent of the suburb was black or Hispanic. Almost a quarter were immigrants. Half of the people there spoke something other than English at home. A quarter lived in poverty. The rest lived where the Treviños did, just above it, with the city's median household income barely scraping forty grand.

If this was the American Dream, it was a sweaty, stressful version of it, land of the free but also of the overdraft fee. The Treviños kept a savings account, but it had never held more than $100. Their checking account had topped out in recent years at $8,692, and that was after a $4,900 tax refund. Most months it hovered around a couple grand. It wasn't much, but it was enough to take the kids back-to-school shopping at American Eagle and Limited Too; to dine on whatever they could afford at Carnival, the Latin-food grocery chain; to load up at Walmart; to make small donations to the March of Dimes; and to pay for Alex's braces. And, soon, to help Alex pay for college.

She was their biggest investment, really, the asset they nurtured in hopes that it would pay off for future Treviños. In this and other ways, José and his brothers seemed rooted by the same qualities. They were strivers, willing to bust their butts for what they felt they deserved, and willing to take risks to accelerate their return on investment, which was sluggish by design and decree. They just assessed that risk differently. Kiko had tried to complement his legal shipping business with illegal shipping. His other brothers, the ones José was visiting at the ranch, had written off their own futures in pursuit of riches that paid out sooner and bigger.

José was playing a longer game. If he stayed the course, his American Dream would be deferred to his daughter and her siblings. José may never experience the payoff, but perhaps one day he could see it in her round, beaming face. He made sure to pay the orthodontia bill.

Despite the relentlessness of this life, and despite the travel ordeal, José managed to get to Piedras Negras for the party at Miguel's ranch. There were four or five structures on the property, including stables for the horses and a sprawling house, and outside a cook grilled meat and veggies. José found his way under the *palapa* and sipped from his beer.

A man named Poncho approached. Poncho was one of Miguel's guys, known for his skills as a logistics manager, overseeing the exportation of vast quantities of cocaine into the United States, and the importation of millions of dollars back into Mexico.

José told Poncho about his life. How he'd grown up like this, in the country, among the animals. How he worked as a bricklayer—"like a regular person" were the words that would stick with Poncho. They sat there for hours, drinking and talking.

From the palapa, José could surely see that his brother had managed to remake their old life on this ranch. A couple of calls and Poncho could cut José into all this, no sweat. But José told Poncho no, that he "didn't want to have anything to do with what was crooked." The code of familism seemed to have found its limit. So they just sat and drank beers while the sun set on the ranch of the man they called "Cuarenta."

# CHAPTER FOUR
## CUARENTA

Miguel Treviño Morales was born in 1973, seven years after José. Like José, he was just a kid when Kiko led the family expedition north for Dallas. Like José, he idolized trailblazing Kiko. Like José, he dropped out of school after eighth grade and came to Dallas as a teen, staying with his mom in one of the small brick houses bought by Kiko.

Miguel learned English and worked odd jobs, cutting lawns and sweeping chimneys, taxing work for a scrawny teenager whose family called him "Miguelito." As he approached manhood in the early nineties, though, Miguel could hardly be described as the baby brother. He was still a raily five foot eight, and his black mustache worked hard to announce itself, but he carried himself with an edge. He could throw back his head and squint his eyes to send a vague but unmistakable message: *Don't fuck with this*. Even at the baptism of José's baby daughter, Alexandra, eighteen-year-old Miguel's glare overpowered the pastels in his shirt and the chubbiness of his niece's cheeks.

Miguel talked openly about wanting to lift his family out of poverty, finishing the job Kiko started. In 1992, when Miguel was nineteen, a door creaked open in that pursuit. He married a young American woman named Ana, in a ceremony in Laredo, and they had a baby. They moved in together, into one of the houses Kiko had bought in Dallas, and Miguel's wife filed a "Petition for Alien Relative," the first hurdle on the way to securing Miguel a green card.

Along with that petition, the government required Miguel to submit to a medical and psychological examination, which found him to be in relatively good health. He tested positive for marijuana, which he admitted to smoking occasionally, and he said he'd been drinking since he was seventeen, though never heavily. He'd never been violent, and though the doctor found that he exhibited some antisocial behavior, he showed no signs of being harmful to other people or himself. His wife's petition was approved, putting him on the path to citizenship.

Then Kiko got indicted. It's unknown what, if any, role Miguel played in his big brother's smuggling racket, though it's likely he played some small one, especially in the absence of more legitimate work opportunities. Around the same time, the cops tried to pull Miguel over in an unregistered Cadillac. Police records don't say whose car it was or where he was going, and Miguel apparently didn't want to discuss it. He blew a stop sign and ignored the wailing pleas of their sirens for a few blocks before turning down a dead end and surrendering. He pleaded guilty to evading arrest, and they cut him free. Not long after, as Kiko's trial approached, Miguel crossed back into Mexico, basically for good.

He loved his native Mexico enough to get the words *Hecho en Mexico*—"Made in Mexico"—tattooed onto his back. But he also saw his homeland as a country that rewarded only the powerful and left poor and broken families like his for dead. He saw the United States as the country that stood by and did nothing about it.

In Mexico, he returned to the barrios of Nuevo Laredo, where the job market offered opportunities that didn't require the backbreaking servitude demanded by his homeland or his brothers' new home across the border. He found work as a gofer for Los Tejas, a gang of local smugglers.

Los Tejas was part of a tradition that went back generations: smuggling illicit product over the Rio Grande. During prohibition, smugglers loaded boats with cases of whiskey and tequila and floated them across under moonlit skies. In the 1960s, American demand for Acapulco Gold was so high, and regulation so lax, that Mexicans were throwing it across the river to hankering buyers. Cocaine and meth and heroin have floated across. And people— wading, boating, swimming, and trudging, hundreds of thousands of Mexican migrants were making the trip every year as Miguel was coming of age in the 1990s, when the United States' Mexican-born population grew from about four million to about nine million.

As business boomed for Los Tejas, its bosses accumulated cars that needed washing and cash that needed retrieving or delivering. As a gofer, Miguel performed these sorts of tasks well enough that he graduated to driver and bodyguard, making sure the boss got where he needed to go safely. No doubt he could see himself in the boss's seat one day. He just needed a chance to take it.

Back then, most Mexican border towns were controlled by the so-called drug cartels. The term was birthed by Pablo Escobar's famous Colombian cocaine mafia, the Medellín Cartel. It wasn't precisely what an economist would label a "cartel," since it wasn't collusion that kept cocaine prices so high but the toxic mix of American demand and American prohibition. But the name "cartel" stuck and became synonymous with the gangs that ruled Mexico's underworld.

The cartel label wasn't the only thing Colombia's cocaine producers shared with Mexico's smugglers. Throughout the 1980s and '90s, Escobar and company had come to rely on Mexican traffickers to ferry their cocaine into the United States. For the Colombians, it meant slightly less in profits, since they'd have to pay the Mexicans a *piso,* or a tax, for smuggling the cocaine into the States. But it also meant less risk. For Mexican traffickers, it meant an inroad into a new market. Cocoa plants require tropical conditions, which limited Mexican growers to cultivating marijuana and heroin. Partnering with the Colombians offered a way into the lucrative cocaine and crack-cocaine business.

The arrangement became known as the "Mexican Trampoline." By the 1990s, the Colombians were moving billions of dollars' worth of cocaine through Mexico every year—more than 90 percent of all the coke snorted, shot, and smoked in the States. The two thousand miles of border between Mexico and the United States were becoming more valuable to Mexican criminals every year.

Each region had its dominant player in the cocaine market. Two hundred miles southeast of Nuevo Laredo, the Gulf Cartel leveraged its geography to import and export Colombian cocaine by air, land, and sea. To the northwest of Nuevo Laredo, where Ciudad Juárez bled into El Paso, Texas, the Juárez Cartel ruled. Farther west, the Arellano-Félix Organization moved product from Tijuana into San Diego and up California's own narcotics superhighway, Interstate 5.

Looming over all of them was the Sinaloa cartel, the richest and most powerful gang in Mexico. Based in the poppy-draped hills of Sinaloa state and nestled against the Gulf of California, the Sinaloa cartel was helmed by Joaquín Guzmán Loera, better known as "El Chapo." His main operational advantage was experience. Sinaloans had been cultivating their lush native soil for opiates for decades, and exporting those opiates across the U.S. border since Chinese immigrants pioneered the trade in the early 1900s. His innovation was to turn the old trade into an empire, effectively controlling the smaller cartels in Mexico's western half. El Chapo was also believed to have the support of the Mexican government, all the way to the halls of Los Pinos, the presidential palace.

As Miguel Treviño rose through the ranks, no cartel controlled his hometown. Instead, a series of small, family-run gangs, including Los Tejas, moved drugs across the river. They'd done it this way for decades, dividing up Nuevo Laredo's streets under the guidance of an independent drug lord nicknamed "El Chacho." Each group paid El Chacho sixty grand or so a month. In exchange, El Chacho kept the peace among the groups and with the neighboring cartels.

As Kiko had intuited, though, NAFTA changed all that. Between 1995 and 2000, the number of trucks crossing north through Los Dos Laredos nearly doubled, from about 68,000 a month to 133,000, each offering an opportunity for traffickers to conceal drugs flowing north. As a result, the city became more porous, more lucrative, and more attractive to every cartel. It was only a matter of time before they came for Nuevo Laredo.

The Gulf Cartel was the city's most natural suitor. It already controlled Matamoros, another major port of entry from Tamaulipas to Texas. And it had a new boss who longed to control Miguel's hometown.

His name was Osiel Cárdenas Guillén. He'd risen to the Gulf's helm after arranging the murder of his co-leader. The killing earned Cárdenas a nickname, "El Mata Amigos," or "the Friend Killer." It also earned him control of a business that was believed to be clearing a billion dollars a year, if not more.

Before Cárdenas advanced on Nuevo Laredo, he approached his bodyguard and confidant, a former elite soldier who'd deserted the Mexican military to serve as his personal protector. Cárdenas wanted more soldiers like him.

"I want the best men," Cárdenas said. "The best armed men that there are."

"They are only in the army," his mercenary said.

"I want them."

They started recruiting. It wasn't hard. Mexico's Grupo Aeromóvil de Fuerzas Especiales del Alto Mando was a special-ops unit trained in guerrilla tactics: sniping, breaching, mountain climbing, survival. Some of its men had been trained by American Special Forces at Fort Bragg, in North Carolina, and at the controversial School for the Americas, where the United States Army trained Latin American soldiers in counterinsurgency tactics. Cárdenas worked them slowly. First he brokered peace by sending food, women, and cash. Then he offered them jobs, including pay raises, better working conditions, and a chance to win for once. They defected by the dozens.

Under Cárdenas's command, the defectors created an elite unit of mercenaries whose job was to protect and expand the Gulf's interests. They imported strict military principles and practices, preached discipline and loyalty, and vowed never to leave a compatriot on the battlefield, dead or alive. They even honored their military roots in their name. Colloquially, they became known across Mexico as La Compañía, or "the Company." Officially, they needed something slicker. In the federal police, Cárdenas's bodyguard had used the radio call sign Z-1. Since he was a "Z," they would all be "Z"s. They called themselves Los Zetas.

One of the Zetas' first orders of business was to take over Nuevo Laredo. Cárdenas sent his most trusted men, including Heriberto Lazcano Lazcano, or "the Executioner," and a gangster they called "El Winnie Pooh." They showed up in convoys and informed Los Tejas and the town's other incumbent smugglers that they would work for the Gulf or be vanquished from the city.

As it turned out, Los Tejas' leaders weren't interested in subcontracting for the Gulf and the Zetas. But Miguel was. He helped the Zetas track down and kill his Tejas boss. He worked for the Zetas now.

Miguel teamed up with another freelance smuggler from his neighborhood—Iván Velázquez Caballero, nicknamed "El Talibán"—to make sure Nuevo Laredo fell under the command of the Zetas. They dressed in fatigues and roamed their hometown in caravans, recruiting young men who could help the Zetas eradicate the remaining holdouts and discourage other cartels' aspirations.

Now in his late twenties, Miguel no longer drank or did drugs. He preferred to be outdoors. His brother Fito was a hunting guide on the outskirts of Nuevo Laredo, and Miguel spent many mornings hunting whitetail deer. But he was always working. On one hunting trip, he befriended a visitor from Dallas, offering him shoot-ing tips and inviting him out to meals. Soon Miguel was plying the young man with thirty-five kilos of Gulf Cartel coke a week, to be smuggled into Texas.

They found other recruits in the clubs clustered near the border. Señor Frog's was the more tourist-friendly chain bar, with a dress code management said kept the "riffraff" away. The gangsters pre-ferred a club called 57th Street, which blasted hip-hop and was con-sidered a safer place to conduct business. And there was always Boys Town, the walled-off strip of cantinas and brothels where young prostitutes offered cheap fucks on creaky mattresses.

These were the places frequented by the boys Miguel and Tali-bán hoped to recruit. Boys like them—young Mexicans and Tejanos who might *exist* on both sides of the border but didn't feel wanted or needed on either. Teenagers who'd dropped out or been kicked out of school. Guys who needed jobs and weren't troubled when the job description included a possible prison sentence or death.

Miguel and Talibán also made sure the local cops and journalists fell in line. They made the traditional offer, *¿Plata o plomo?* ("Silver or lead?"): You take the bribe or you take the bullet. The prices across Tamaulipas ranged from a few hundred bucks a week for a street cop or reporter to a couple grand for a local police chief.

Many took the bribe, but the town didn't fall easily to Miguel and Los Zetas. Not all of Nuevo Laredo's independent smugglers were on board with the hostile takeover; nor did every cop, civic leader, and businessman accept their bribes. A turf war broke out, and violence rocked Nuevo Laredo. Bodies were discovered buried in backyards and on ranches. A state police commander and his lieu-tenant were gunned down in broad daylight.

Mexico fought back, too. In 2000, the Institutional Revolution-ary Party (PRI) was vanquished from the presidency after seventy years of rule. The election of Vicente Fox, a Coca-Cola executive and member of the conservative National Action Party (PAN), led Mexico into a new era. It also undercut the government's existing relationship with the cartels, with whom they could occasionally forge compromises and understandings. Without one-party rule, cooperation fizzled. Fox flooded the disputed territories with troops, aiming to take down top drug bosses.

In 2003, troops swooped into Gulf Cartel territory and captured the Zetas' founder, Osiel Cárdenas, leaving Nuevo Laredo up for grabs. To the west and east, every other key city—the "plazas," as the cartels called their crucial smuggling outposts—was controlled by Mexico's most powerful criminal gangs. Now those gangs saw a chance to take Nuevo Laredo. None more so than El Chapo's Sinaloa gang.

In the weeks after Cárdenas was captured, El Chapo called a summit with a loose network of gangsters who controlled smuggling from Juárez to Tijuana. These were generational smugglers playing under the old rules, which respected history and geography and traditional power. They divided up territories, leaving the Juárez natives to control Juárez, the Baja families to run Tijuana, and so on. They honored whoever was next in line, paid off whoever needed paying off, and killed only when necessary, though "necessary" was loosely defined.

To take on the Zetas, El Chapo dispatched his own native of Los Dos Laredos, a former Texas high-school football player named Edgar Valdez Villarreal. His nickname, "La Barbie," had been coined by a Texas football coach enamored of his light-blue eyes and pale skin. But La Barbie had fallen into Laredo's street gangs and fled across the river when American law enforcement caught on, and he'd been a faithful drug warrior ever since. He'd earned his stripes as a cartel assassin, and now he was expected to build an army of *sicarios* to take on the Zetas.

A war broke out. Miguel and La Barbie were its colonels, two formerly impoverished street kids fighting for control of their hometowns. La Barbie recruited gang members from El Salvador's powerful criminal gang, MS-13, and showed up in Nuevo Laredo with a message for the Zetas: Retreat or face the wrath of Los Negros, which is what Barbie had dubbed his own mercenary unit. The name translated to "the Black Ones."

As the Zetas battled Los Negros, Miguel revealed himself to be a charismatic leader but also happy—desperate even—to mix it up in firefights. The specific roots of Miguel's bloodlust are hard to pinpoint. People who have fought and done business alongside him take it for granted now, as if his thirst for violence is among his immutable traits, like his chocolate skin or night-sky hair. But there was no known violence in his childhood; his de facto patriarch, Kiko, wasn't believed to spill any blood during his short-lived criminal career.

It appeared that Miguel was driven by a combustible combination of resentment, ambition, and cynicism, a man seizing at power that was once, and would soon be, laughably out of grasp. He didn't expect to live into his forties, and he behaved that way as he and the Zetas seized Nuevo Laredo. He and the Zetas murdered four cops associated with El Chacho, then killed El Chacho, dumping his body in the town square clad in women's underwear. Later, he ordered the Nuevo Laredo police, whom the Zetas now basically controlled, to round up any smuggler who had resisted the Gulf's takeover. There were thirty-four such holdouts crammed into the house by the time Miguel arrived dressed in black fatigue pants and black boots, a makeshift uniform designed to evoke the power of a Special Forces unit. He picked one out and brought him forward, then asked the assembled men whether anyone knew the location of the heart. No one answered, so Miguel offered a visual anatomy lesson, plunging his knife into the man's chest and watching him die.

As the battle for Nuevo Laredo raged, the Zetas continued recruiting ex-soldiers, growing in power as the arm of the Gulf Cartel. Each was assigned a call number based on seniority: the first to defect was Z-1; the second, Z-2; and so on. Technically, only soldiers could be Zetas. But Miguel exhibited such savagery that he was bequeathed a call number, despite never having served a day in the military. By then he was the fortieth so-called Zeta, Z-40, but everyone just called him Cuarenta. "Forty."

Throughout the 2000s, Forty accumulated enough power within the Zetas, and enough enemies outside of it, that he could have gotten away with hiding out on his ranches all day while his killers fought his war. But he remained a grunt. He dressed modestly and ready for battle, in fatigues and T-shirts, with knives, assault rifles, and grenades on his hips. He was still among the first out of the truck when the bullets started flying.

He continued roaming the streets of Nuevo Laredo, enticing poor teenagers to join up. But there was a problem: they couldn't fight. Though the Zetas now included hundreds of members, most had no military training at all. So Forty improvised.

He traveled to Guatemala to recruit former Special Forces, known as Kaibiles, to train his young recruits. He shipped them to a camp in the mountains near Ciudad Victoria, the state capital, where they slept side by side on cots. In grueling training sessions, former Special Forces from Mexico and the Kaibiles taught them to wage war. They crawled and breached and ran, stripped guns and shot all manner of weapons. They learned the art of urban warfare, practicing bursting through doors and clearing houses.

Forty himself taught them to kill. He tied up some enemy he'd captured and offered his recruit the choice of a sledgehammer or a machete. The ones who didn't start swinging were relegated to duty as *halcones*—"hawks," or lookouts. The ones who did became Forty's sicarios, and they helped the Zetas grow their brand, which was defined by headline-grabbing violence. From decapitations to swinging corpses to bodies burned in oil drums, Zeta-style killings would come to define Mexico's drug war.

It was a blood binge fueled by several factors, starting with the Zetas' background as paramilitary soldiers. Smuggling had long been a family business in Mexico, governed by unwritten rules like the ones that governed the American mob wars. But the Zetas weren't a party to that social contract. They were mercenaries, with all the training of an elite killing squad but none of the duty to protect.

There were other factors at play, too. Scholars believe the Zetas' penchant for beheadings was influenced by the Kaibiles, who favored the practice. It's believed the Zetas' desire to videotape the beheadings, and to use social media to disseminate them, was inspired by Al-Qaeda.

There may have been religious influences, too. Though Forty and most other traffickers practiced Catholicism, some Zetas worshipped at the feet of *Santa Muerte,* or Saint Death, a folkloric goddess whose graces are sought by some impoverished Mexicans. Shrines to her stand tall in stash houses and prison cells across Mexico. Some other Zetas practiced Santería, an Afro-Caribbean faith that borrows from Catholicism. One early Zeta named Mamito considered himself a *brujo* of this faith, someone to whom the burden of violence fell directly from the hands of God.

Or maybe the extreme violence was a simple business calculation. Forty and the Zetas were disrupters, a small upstart seeking power in a system tightly guarded by dynastic, politically influential families. They'd come to fuck things up.

If fighting off La Barbie and the Mexican government wasn't enough, the Zetas soon discovered a new enemy: its *patrones* at the Gulf Cartel. In 2007, four years after he was captured, Osiel Cárdenas, the Zetas' founder, was extradited to Texas, where he faced charges that would land most drug dealers in prison for life. But Cárdenas agreed to plead guilty and forfeit fifty million dollars in assets. In exchange, the inventor of an elite killing squad would spend just twenty-five years in prison.

Though his agreement was shrouded in secrecy, it was easy for the Zetas to deduce how Cárdenas had landed such a sweet deal. He'd agreed to snitch. Feeling betrayed, Forty and the Zetas started to splinter off from the Gulf Cartel, a division that would alter the criminal landscape and increase bloodshed across Mexico.

It was the rise of the paramilitaries. As the Zetas helped the Gulf expand, and Barbie's Los Negros fought for Sinaloa, rival cartels responded the way rival businesses do: they chased the trend. The Juárez Cartel recruited former police officers for its enforcement wing, La Linea. Artistas Asesinos, a Juárez street gang, went to work there as enforcers for the Sinaloa cartel.

These new groups weren't generational smugglers, inheriting traditions from their poppy-farming fathers and grandfathers. They were embittered warriors who had opted out of Mexico's rule of law. Human smuggling, gun-running, oil thievery—all crime was now on the table. All violence in its pursuit was an acceptable cost of doing business. Paramilitary tactics became the norm.

Local politicians and business owners, once in contract with community-oriented, moblike smuggling enterprises, decried the new tactics, putting even more pressure on the Mexican government to respond. It did. Capos kept falling. Leadership shifted. New factions and alliances formed. The paramilitary groups, the best equipped to seize power, seized it. The Zetas seized the most.

Vicente Fox's strategy—using military force to aggressively target cartel leaders—was clearly hopeless. Yet in 2006, his successor, Felipe Calderón, doubled down, declaring "war" on the cartels. He found a willing partner in the Bush administration, which agreed to send billions of dollars in aid, to be spent on training, military helicopters, and surveillance planes.

In accepting the Americans' aid, Calderón was accepting the American strategy of attacking the source of supply (the farmers in Colombia, the traffickers in Mexico, the dealers in the States) rather than the source of demand (American users and drug prohibition laws). It was plainly Sisyphean, if Sisyphus had lugged his boulder by Black Hawk. Economists far and wide argued that spending money on treatment and education in the United States would have a greater impact on the flow of drugs. Even more impactful would be decriminalization. Reducing the risk involved in making and selling drugs would, economists believed, reduce prices, decrease the value of the shipping channels, and decrease the blood spilled defending them.

But the economists' notion is hopelessly rooted in basic respect for black and brown bodies. The Nixon campaign, searching for answers in 1968, had figured out that the nation's fascination with getting high was not an addressable issue but a political opportunity. Demonize weed, demonize the hippie; criminalize heroin, criminalize black people.

The politicians contrived evil. Capitalism took it from there. Industries sprang forth from a racist campaign strategy, including militarized counternarcotics forces and a profiteering private prison system. Across the United States and Latin America, curtains fell on new theaters of war, with a bonus for the white warmongers in the directors' chairs: most of the bodies piling up were black and brown.

Things would change one day. White people would fall victim to heroin addiction, and white politicians would discover how much money there was in weed. Until then, send in the choppers. In the years after Calderón's declaration of war, the murder rate across Mexico doubled. Forty ordered hundreds of those murders, and committed scores himself. He told the people around him he had trouble sleeping if a day passed without someone dying by his hands.

In his early years with the Zetas, Forty occasionally snuck up to Dallas, where his brother José and other family still lived. He laid no bricks. He was a different dude than the thin-mustached Miguelito who used to live there, joyriding in Cadillacs and looking up to his weed-slinging brother. He was thicker now and prone to wearing tight black shirts that showed off his huskier build. *He* was the patriarch now, a boss in every way.

He frequented the city's grittier strip clubs and a Latin hip-hop joint called DMX Club, apparently in search of workers for the Zetas' fulfillment operation in Dallas. How much time, if any, Miguel and José spent together during those trips is unknown. They weren't known to be the closest of brothers. Miguel was tight with his younger brothers back in Mexico. José was close to Rodolfo, his fellow stateside construction worker, who, like José, had tried to shun the smuggling business.

As Forty rose in the ranks, he couldn't get to Dallas anymore. He was under indictment in Mexico and Texas for drug trafficking, and federal agents across the American Southwest were beginning to obsess about his whereabouts. They perked up every time an inter-cepted phone call included mention of a "Miguel," "Mike," or "MT," and they had snitches lined up to tip them off if he sneaked into the States. If the brothers were going to see each other, José would have to come to Miguel.

# CHAPTER FIVE

# EL HUESOS

NUEVO LAREDO, TAMAULIPAS
April 2009

The crowd formed early for the Futurity Nuevo Laredo, the town's big annual race for promising two-year-old quarter horses. The race typically drew about two thousand people, but there was an early buzz and a swelling crowd at this year's event, which marked a new era: it was the first big race at the town's new track.

Fans settled into the shiny bleachers that flanked the track, shaded by sweeping steel overhangs. Others found tables inside the air-conditioned restaurant that was perched at the top of the grand-stand, protected from the elements by tinted glass. When all those seats filled up, people stacked themselves four or five deep near the sturdy new rail, relying on their collective canopy of wide-brimmed cowboy hats for shade.

The trainers on the backside had no such worries, prepping their horses in covered stalls built from brick and painted a pristine white. And all across the track, from the shit shovelers in the stalls to the cops roaming the concourse, people whispered gratitude for the track's benefactor and foreman, Forty. He loved horse racing so much that he'd built his hometown a new track, using farm equipment bought with drug proceeds in the United States and shipped back across the border. Pretty soon his most prized colt would burst from the track's new starting gate.

Like José, Forty talked longingly about the family's upbringing on the ranches of Tamaulipas, and about his family's collective passion for days spent under the beating sun, among roaming cattle and sensible horses. If their father's departure had cost the Treviños a romantic countryside life, Forty seemed hell-bent on re-creating it.

And he'd found a man who could help him do it. His name was Mario "Poncho" Cuellar. An experienced trafficker in his forties, Poncho had been on hiatus from the cocaine-smuggling business for a few years, trying to make a go of selling and junking old cars along the border between Piedras Negras and Eagle Pass. He was also spending more of his time racing horses. A few years back, Poncho had started buying racehorses in the United States and shipping them to Mexico to race against his friends. To get the best horses he used the best broker, Ramiro Villarreal.

Then, in 2007, Forty and the Zetas showed up in Piedras Negras. Their relationship with the Gulf Cartel on the rocks, the Zetas were branching out from mere enforcement, starting to buy, smuggle, and sell their own cocaine. The Zetas asked Poncho to go to work for them. He wanted to say no, but the way they asked—stripping him to his underwear, binding his hands and feet, killing his friends who'd tried to refuse—made him think otherwise.

They delivered five hundred kilos of cocaine to Poncho. He went to work, smuggling it through Eagle Pass. Business got good fast for the Zetas in Piedras Negras, and Forty started spending more time there. He bought multiple ranches, sometimes by force. (*Plata o plomo* is a versatile ultimatum.) Then, with Poncho's help, he started stocking his new ranches full of high-end quarter horses and hosting regular races. More than ever, racing became a fixture in Zeta culture.

Traffickers have a hard time articulating their passion for horse racing, which is hardly a staple of Mexico's modern sporting culture. Soccer dominates the landscape, especially in cities. In the country, *charrería*, a more artistic cousin to American rodeo, rules. But in their rural hideaways, traffickers, especially those from the Gulf and Zeta cartels, have embraced match racing as one of their go-to pastimes.

There is a romance to it, a link to Mexico's past. If they knew their homeland's history, they could picture Hernán Cortés's army arriving at Veracruz in the early sixteenth century, overwhelming the natives with his lance-wielding soldiers, who blazed across the battlefield on hulking creatures the natives had never seen. Actual racing, too, could be traced back to Cortés's first days on Mexican soil, when he ordered his soldiers to race in pairs across the sand in an effort to impress the natives.

Early Spanish colonizers of Mexico organized races not unlike the ones being run in Virginia and the Carolinas: You bring your fastest horse, I'll bring mine, and we'll put some property on the line. In the mid-nineteenth century, horse owners joined forces and created clubs that could compete against each other in occasional meets, but they were still informal—parties, basically, with two runners and lots of side bets as the entertainment.

Later in the 1800s, as Mexico's ruling class thrived under military dictatorship, Mexico City's elite appropriated the sport. They formed a Jockey Club and organized regular races attended by buttoned-up generals and elegantly dressed women. But the sport has always thrived in Mexico when it has embraced its ranching roots, pitting one horse, one ranch, one town against another with as much pride as money on the line.

All of this is romanticized in countless *corridos*, the traditional, poetic folk songs that chronicle working-class Mexican history and culture. The most traditional corridos tell epic tales from the *revolución*; today, so many songs are devoted to drug criminals that they've given birth to a new subgenre, *narcocorridos*. But horses and match racing have always played key roles in corridos, reminding working-class Mexicans of the animals that helped their countrymen win wars, land, money, and pride.

The traffickers are also drawn to the controlled violence of quarter-horse racing, an adrenaline-pumping competition that rarely ends with anyone dead. Gambling helps fuel the intensity, like dice, cards, and sports betting for other gangsters. There is a soothing escapism to horse racing, too. When you're as deeply entrenched in the drug trade as Forty and his compadres, there is hardly a person in your life untouched by its pistol-whipping reach, or one whose loyalty can't be questioned. The horses just nuzzle and run.

By the time Forty arrived in Piedras Negras, Zetas and other narcos all across Mexico and South America were obsessed with weekend match races. As Forty bought up horses and land in and around Piedras Negras, he began holding regular private races there. Bring your best runners, Forty would say to Poncho and other associates, and they would race all afternoon. Sometimes it would be just the bosses and their inner circle, plus the armed guards clustered in armored SUVs that formed a perimeter around the property. Other times they invited people from the nearby towns and villages, to create goodwill and build their network of potential lookouts. There was always beer in the cooler and some cocaine in case a boss wanted a taste.

They bet big, $100,000 or more for each race. Forty usually took it home. Sometimes he had the best horse. Sometimes the winner was reluctant to collect. Sometimes Forty's opponents told their jockeys to take it slow to avoid disrespecting the boss. It was around this time that Forty ordered his sicarios to take out a man nicknamed "El Gato" at a track in Saltillo. The conventional wisdom was that Forty had ordered El Gato killed because he was a rival trafficker, which he was. But Forty's beef wasn't work related; he told friends he killed El Gato because El Gato's horses had been outrunning Forty's. After the murder, Forty ordered his associates to keep racing, and bragged when his horses took home the money.

Horses consumed Forty, and he was amassing some truly fast ones with the help of Poncho and Poncho's favored broker, Ramiro. None was faster than an undersized yearling that had arrived in Piedras Negras late in 2008. His name was Tempting Dash.

———

At the auction in California, Ramiro had actually intended to purchase Tempting Dash for a gangster named Jesús Enrique Rejón Aguilar, nickname "Mamito." He was Z-7, the seventh Special Forces defector to join the Zetas. But after Ramiro had hauled Tempting Dash to Poncho's ranch, Forty had decided to keep the colt for himself. He'd ordered Tempting Dash shipped to Monterrey to be worked into shape by one of the best trainers in Mexico.

There's a cutoff for racehorses just as there's a cutoff for kindergartners, and breeders, like overattached parents, work hard to be on the right side of it. For racing purposes, all horses born in a given year are considered one-year-olds the following January 1. Breeders, then, naturally prefer foals to be born as close to January 1 as possible, but never before, so their one-year-olds become two-year-olds with the earliest possible birthdays.

Tempting Dash was born in May. So when he arrived in Monterrey, he was young and skinny, still growing into the frame bestowed on him by his famous sire. The grooms in the stables started calling him "El Huesos." "The Bones." It stuck, becoming the name Tempting Dash raced under in Mexico.

Early that spring, before El Huesos even turned two by the calendar, Forty put his new colt to the test. He entered him in a qualifier for the annual Futurity Nuevo Laredo, one of the first futurities on the Mexican quarter-horse calendar. El Huesos stumbled in the trials, failing to qualify for the main event. But he did earn a spot in a consolation match race the day of the big futurity, and Forty's trainer made sure the colt was ready.

It's unclear whether Forty was there that day. He would make appearances at that track and others over the years, but his fugitive status made his presence hard to guarantee. If he was there, he was probably hanging near his fleet of pickups, surrounded by watchful bodyguards and left alone by whatever local cop might see him.

El Huesos versus El Caramelo was the eighth race of the day. For Forty and his fellow Zetas, things weren't going as planned. They'd entered horses in most of the races that day, but the big futurity and the bulk of its quarter-million-dollar purse had been won by a horse owned by Los Piojos, a small, rival drug gang whose dominance on the quarter-horse tracks was driving Forty mad.

El Huesos was Forty's last chance to show his hometown what was up. At just 250 yards and with a five-figure purse, the race was mostly designed to test the young colts' speed in competition. But a race was a race, so the crowd stuck around, huddling in the shade of the bleachers.

The gates flung open. The jockey riding El Huesos pulled the horse hard left, toward his opponent, then in front of him, then away, leaving him in a literal cloud of dust. No one was quite sure how hard the opposing jockey was trying, given that El Huesos was rumored to be owned by Forty, but official heats like this were generally run fair and square. Either way, everyone agreed: El Huesos could fly.

After that, Forty decided he wanted to race El Huesos in the United States. Zetas had run horses in the States before, usually under Ramiro's name or some other front. As usual, Forty didn't find his predecessors' strategy aggressive enough.

Now in his mid-thirties, Forty had existed in this underworld for more than a decade. He had managed to stay alive, but two of his brothers had been killed in Mexico: Jesús, reportedly gunned down by fellow Zetas for ignoring company rules, and Fito, the hunting guide, murdered by Forty's rivals despite apparently staying out of the smuggling business. Forty knew his time would come, too, and the heat was cranking. In the summer of 2009, after El Huesos went blazing across Forty's new hometown track, the United States Department of Justice unsealed indictments in New York and Washington, D.C., naming Miguel and his brother Omar as principal leaders of the Zetas. The government was offering a $5 million reward for information leading to Forty's capture. He knew what that meant: the snitches were lining up at the feds' door.

So, Forty decided it was time to secure some assets for his family. If El Huesos ran well in the States, he would win his money not under Ramiro's name but under José's.

Like all of Forty's schemes, this one was fraught with risk but filled with upside. If it failed, he might needlessly drag José, José's family, Ramiro, and others onto the feds' radar. If it succeeded, whatever money he could earn in the horse business would forever stay in the Treviño family, untouchable by the whims of the drug war.

His associates were skeptical. They worried that it would draw too much attention from the Americans. But Forty was done playing by the old rules, the ones that said that Mexican traffickers couldn't operate in the United States without American law crashing down on them. Fuck the Americans, he seemed to be saying: They snort our drugs, they use our beaches, they buy their cheap shit made by our poor workers. The least they can do is lose to our horses.

Whether Forty ever discussed this plan directly with José remains unknown. Talking on the phone was impractical, given the likelihood the feds would be listening, and it was hard to meet in person. Forty going to Dallas was out of the question, and José didn't often come to Mexico. But it was around this time that José found his way across the border, to the gas station, onto the ranch, and under that palapa, to sip beers and talk with Poncho Cuellar—about loving the country life but not wanting anything to do with drugs.

Forty had a different plan for José, and he'd told Poncho to put it in motion. Poncho knew the horses, knew the Horseman, and had connections on both sides of the border. He was the perfect guy to kick off what they called Operativo Huesos.

# CHAPTER SIX

# THE LAUNDRY

Say you're at a party. You didn't want to come, because you've been running in the mornings, trying to form a habit as the self-help book you've been skimming suggests. Being at this party is not going help you keep your streak. But you came! You're here! You've also been trying to say yes more, to form a habit of being *open* to things, like that other self-help book recommends, so you turned on music and drank a Modelo in the shower and made a thing of it. You got here and you're here and—

Wait, what? Your friends still fuck with drugs? Your friends still fuck with drugs, as evidenced by the fact that you're in a bedroom, pushing aside a pile of coats and sitting on the edge of a low-slung IKEA bed. Katy is pulling a bag from her pocket, and it's been so long that you honestly don't know what she's going to dump from it. You hope it's not weed, because you could have smoked that at home, and you hope it's not Molly, because people in their thirties should not be doing drugs with cute nicknames, and you hope it's not heroin, because you read the news. You sort of hope it's not cocaine. But you also hope it is.

It is. Katy angles the baggie and taps her finger to shake the coke loose. It falls in a line, forming a little ski run on the metal serving tray she's hunched over, a few moguls but nothing you can't navigate. She starts smoothing it out, and you, being an educated, *Narcos*-binging citizen of the world, start thinking about the journey that cocaine made—from the jungles of Colombia; to the safe houses of Mexico; to the border; over the border or maybe under it, if you prefer *Weeds;* to Katy's dealer; to Katy; to here, in the bedroom with the cheap bed and the coats.

You're thinking about it wrong. The cocaine's journey is interesting, but the more epic odyssey is the one that will be taken by the twenty in your wallet, which you're planning on leaving on the tray for Katy after using it to snort that line, and which Katy is planning on using to buy more cocaine.

Here's what happens to that twenty. Say it's 2009, and say you live in Dallas. In these days, in these parts, most of the rolled-up cocaine twenties wind up in the possession of a Dallas-based kingpin named Junior. Though only in his late twenties, Junior is one of the largest regional cocaine distributors in the United States, responsible for moving one thousand kilograms of cocaine *every month*. That means he's responsible for sending around $20 million a month in cash *back* to his supplier in Piedras Negras, Mexico, who is a Los Zetas operative named Poncho.

To help him pull this off, Junior owns, under various names, at least a half-dozen stash houses spread across Dallas, some for drugs and some for money. He also keeps a fleet of "trap cars" to move the money south. He owns tractor-trailers that he packs with millions of dollars, stuffing stacks of cash into the recesses of Whirlpool washers and LG ovens. He owns a minivan, too; a 2003 Toyota Sienna. Junior paid some guys in Guadalajara $18,000 to get it retrofitted with a secret compartment that can be accessed only by starting the car, engaging the parking brake, putting the car in reverse, turning on the defrost system, and selecting a specific fan combination—in that order. It's some real MacGyver shit, but it fools the dogs every time.

Sometimes, if Junior's drivers aren't satisfied with their trap-car options, they improvise, like the time one bought a horse hauler, hollowed out the bottom, stuffed it with cash, piled hay on top of it, and then bought a cheap, old horse to complete the effect. No one's sure what happened to the horse, but the money made it across, no problem.

Above all, Junior prefers to use pickups, with the cash vacuum-sealed and floating in the gas tanks. He hires drivers to haul anywhere from $300,000 to $800,000 back to Mexico at a time. They usually cross in Eagle Pass without issue.

Once they get the money across, the drivers find their way to one of the Zetas' stash houses in Piedras Negras, and Poncho and his team go to work "cleaning up" the bills. They start by removing anything smaller than a twenty, as well as anything that's been ripped or written on. They use these small and damaged bills to pay off drivers, lookouts, and other workers who help the drugs and money flow smoothly. They package up the remaining money—the big, clean bills—and deliver it to a man named Cuno.

Cuno is the Zetas' accountant in Piedras Negras. He keeps meticulous records, using both a paper ledger and laptop to track every shipment of cocaine that comes in or goes out, every American dollar that accumulates, every buyer, and every supplier. Thanks in part to Junior's steady shipments, there is always $30 million, $40 million, $50 million stacked high in Cuno's stash house. Much of it will be counted, packaged, and shipped back to Colombia. But much of it will be distributed to the cartel leadership, including Forty. And Cuno's money house is just one of several where the Zetas have millions piled.

All told, as Katy texts her dealer and you roll up a second twenty, the Zetas are clearing $350 million, most of it in U.S. dollars. It is a fraction of the American drug market, estimated to be tens of billions of dollars, but still far too much to leave piled in Cuno's stash house.

Forty and the others can spend some of this money freely in Mexico. They can buy cars, homes, horses, and sex, all with "dirty" American cash. Some of the Zeta bosses even buy exotic animals. According to narco lore, Forty and the Zetas' leader, Lazcano, liked to feed their lions and tigers with the corpses of Zeta rivals.

But Forty knows that eventually his run will end and he will disappear—into the ground, into a prison cell, or into hiding. He knows that for his money to last beyond his time as a kingpin, and for his family to make use of it beyond the underworld, he has to somehow turn your tainted twenty into a crisp one pulled from the ATM. He has to launder it.

The first step to laundering drug money is called "placement"— getting it out of the safe house and into a legitimate financial system. The easiest places for criminals to start the laundering process are banks, which, despite increased regulation, accept and move trillions of dollars of drug proceeds. As the Zetas rose to power in the 2000s, the Mexican branches of HSBC, a British bank, accepted large cash deposits so willingly that cartel operatives started making them in boxes designed specifically to fit through teller windows. Around the same time, a Zeta operative opened an account with Banamex USA, a division of Citigroup that operated along the Mexican border. In his application, the operative described himself as a small-time cattle breeder who would deposit only hundreds of dollars a year. Then he deposited $60 million in drug proceeds without raising a single red flag at the bank—not even *after* he was indicted on money-laundering charges.

Eventually, the banks, like the operatives using them, get caught. The only difference is what happens next. For "cleaning" just $550,000 of drug proceeds, launderers caught in the United States can face up to twenty years in federal prison, and the feds can seize every dime they can find. When investigators discovered that HSBC allowed Mexican and Colombian traffickers to launder $900 million through its U.S. bank, among other violations, the Justice Department called it too risky to the international financial system to indict any bank officials. Instead, they reached a settlement with the bank, which would forfeit about a billion dollars, plus pay a $700 million fine. With $2.7 trillion in assets, HSBC managed to survive.

Once in bank accounts, drug money can easily be "layered"— moved from account to account in an effort to distance it from the initial deposit and confuse investigators. It can be whisked across borders, into businesses and investments. Eventually it can land in the hands of family members living cleanly in Mexico, the United States, or elsewhere. By then, it's harder for the feds to trace or seize.

The Zetas bosses flow a good chunk of money through small businesses. They use your rolled-up twenties to open nightclubs, restaurants, car washes, and other businesses in Los Dos Laredos and across northern Mexico. The other cartels do the same. One Gulf Cartel money launderer famously laundered drug proceeds through a soccer club called Los Mapaches, or the Raccoons. The team wasn't any good and didn't have much apparent revenue, but they pulled new uniforms out of the box for every game.

In Mexico, the top drug lords, like El Chapo and Forty, have the assets, power, and connections to pour their money into larger-scale ventures. They use their illicit cash to invest in real estate developments, oil-field companies, and other big-money enterprises, creating assets that they or their families can cash out of down the line, often with the help of well-paid lawyers.

In the United States, washing cash through bigger business is often too difficult: too much red tape, too much paperwork, too much regulation, and too much talking. It can be done, though. The Sinaloa cartel did it for years through the Los Angeles garment and textile industry, paying a fee to flow hundreds of millions of drug proceeds into the middle of international textile transactions. And around the time your twenty makes it from your wallet to Katy to Junior, from the stash house to the gas tank to Cuno's stacks, Forty will have decided to pump some money into the American horse business.

# CHAPTER SEVEN

## WILDCAT

ELGIN, TEXAS
November 2007

You can only spread the shit so thick. That's the headache, Tyler Graham was saying, getting the shit spread
evenly across every acre, so the regulators who test the
soil don't accuse you of overshitting it. Spread too little and you end
up with excess shit, which is a problem when you shovel fifty tons a
week. Spread too much and something will set the regulators off—
if not the nitrates, then the potassium; if not the potassium, then
the sulfur. It's always something with "the environmental people."

Tyler was talking a lot about shit. He was doing an interview
with a food journal called *Southern Foodways Alliance* about his
grandfather's cattle-feed yard, one of a handful of livestock businesses his family owned in the rolling hills east of Austin, Texas.
The feed yard was an hour south in Gonzales, but luckily Tyler and
his interviewer were on his family's thirteen-hundred-acre horse
farm in Tyler's hometown of Elgin. Even with their heyday reced-
ing in the rearview, these stables remained the jewel in the Graham
dynasty's crown. They smelled better, too.

There wasn't much to Elgin. The area had been settled in the 1800s by members of Stephen F. Austin's "Little Colony," who received land grants from the Mexican government to help make something of the Coahuila y Tejas state. The settlers escaped Comanche raids and survived the Texas Revolution, and in 1871, after a flood forced the Texas Central Railroad to alter its route, their colony became one of the few rail stops between Houston and Austin. Elgin, named for the area's land commissioner, was born.

The population boom in trendy Austin, twenty-five miles to the west, eventually spilled into town some, finally giving the big-box stores reason to open out here. But even by Tyler's day, downtown Elgin still consisted of just a couple of blocks of red-brick storefronts, including the train depot–turned–history museum and the musty offices of the town newspaper. The rest of Elgin was mostly covered with small, simple homes, some strip malls, and a lot of gnawed-on grassland.

Tyler seemed to love his hometown, and why not? He was a star here. His last name got that ball rolling.

Tyler's paternal grandfather, Dr. Charles Graham, founded the Elgin Veterinary Hospital in the 1960s, catering to the cattle and horses that grazed central Texas. From there, Doc Graham built a livestock empire. Down in Gonzales, those thirty thousand cattle Tyler was talking about were fattened up on a mix of brewer's grain and steamed flake corn, then sent off to slaughter. There was also a cattle-trucking company, a cattle-auction house, and a horse-auction house in Oklahoma.

But it was this ranch, Southwest Stallion Station, that really made the Graham name ring in the ears of central Texans. Doc Graham had started it back in the 1960s, and over the years his horses had been responsible, as runners or breeders, for $65 million in racetrack winnings.

The Texas ranching business wasn't always kind. After cattle prices soared in the late 1980s, an oversupply of beef sent them plummeting, forcing ranchers across the country to thin or liquidate their herds. At the same time, peso devaluations in Mexico forced ranchers there to sell their beef for cheap, further flooding the American beef supply. The cattle industry limped through the 1990s; when Doc's company applied for a $7 million credit line, the bank expressed concern about the business's negative working capital. But things always rebounded. And Doc himself was well positioned to pass his wealth to future generations of Grahams. By the time his grandson, Tyler, went off to college in 2002, Doc Graham could list more than $30 million in assets on a personal financial statement.

In turn, Doc Graham always made sure to reinvest his money in the institutions that supported his interests. He donated hundreds of thousands of dollars to political candidates from both parties in Texas. After watching New Mexico and California become quarter-horse racing meccas, he successfully pressured reluctant Texas lawmakers to approve racetrack gambling. He also pledged enough money to his alma mater, Texas A&M, to get a campus street named after him. He was a member of the Texas Horse Racing Hall of Fame and the American Quarter Horse Hall of Fame, and soon he would be inducted into the Texas Cowboy Hall of Fame, alongside Nolan Ryan, Tommy Lee Jones, and George Strait.

Like a lot of successful cowboys, Doc Graham was feared, too, and always game for a fight. He'd sued a neighbor over a road that their properties shared, and he'd sued two business partners. Just recently, he'd sued his own bankers, over some seemingly private and vaguely derogatory comments they'd made about his cattle operation. (The parties agreed to dismiss the case.)

Doc's intensity even appeared to affect his prizes stud farm. During the 1980s, Southwest Stallion Station had been the dominant quarter-horse breeding farm in Texas, a page-after-page presence in sales books and industry publications. As Doc bragged to clients, its success was in no small part owed to the farm manager at the time, David Graham, who was Doc's son and Tyler's father. David was a workhorse, springing into action whenever a potential stud showed itself on the track. But by the 1990s, David Graham had left Southwest Stallion, a split he attributed to the difficulties of working for Doc. He now ran a small feed-and-supply shop in Elgin. According to David, he and Doc rarely spoke.

"Being a Graham ain't easy," Tyler's daddy liked to say, but for better or worse the Graham name went some distance in paving the way for Tyler. To his credit, though, Tyler didn't just live in the shadow of Doc Graham's big white hat or David Graham's commanding personality. From a young age, he formed his own shadow, in the best place a central Texas kid could: under a flood of Friday-night lights.

Tyler went to Elgin High, the same school where his dad had played quarterback and been a champion roper. Tyler had a thick neck, and he could muster a stern, don't-fuck-with-this glare on picture day. He played receiver and cornerback, the positions dictated by his six-foot-tall, 165-pound frame.

After high school, Tyler moved on to Texas A&M, just like his granddaddy, and studied animal science. He graduated and came back to Elgin. With Tyler's dad out of the family business, the Graham empire was Tyler's to inherit if he wanted it. Now, at twenty-four, he had become the manager of all of Doc's businesses. It was a big enough job that he'd been asked to give this interview to *Southern Foodways*. "We're double-stacking cattle," he was saying now. "We're building pens as fast as we can build them, buying land—every piece of land we can pretty much put our hands on."

Along with managing the cattle business, Tyler longed to return Southwest Stallion Station to its former glory. But it had been four decades since Doc Graham founded his stallion business, and things had changed. Breeding had modernized. Without Doc's son, David, to keep up with the technology—to keep up with the times—Southwest Stallion Station had fallen behind.

Every stud farm needs a stud to hang its name on. In California, First Down Dash anchored a famous ranch called Vessels Stallion Farm. In Oklahoma, Lazy E was the dominant breeder, thanks to a topflight stud called Corona Cartel. In Texas, Mr Jess Perry had helped turned the Four Sixes (6666) Ranch into the state's new top dog.

Southwest Stallion Station, meanwhile, had next to nothing.

And for Tyler, the simple reality was that as much fun as it would be to run a major stud farm, it was fattening up those thirty thousand cattle that paid the bills. Feed 'em, shovel their shit, and on to the next. "This is where I started and that's where I'm at," Tyler told his interviewer.

At least until a good stud came along.

# CHAPTER EIGHT

# ONE FAST BOOGER

ELGIN, TEXAS
October 2009

One day, David Graham, Tyler's daddy, was behind the counter of his Elgin feed store. This was typical. David had bought the store two decades before, after his falling-out with Doc, and he'd hardly changed a thing, from the wood-paneled walls to the black-and-white letter-board menu hanging behind him. There was a wood-paneled office in the back, adorned with mementos to both his own high-school glory and his son's. There was a table out on the floor where he could bullshit with friends or customers. And there was a coffee machine to which he made frequent visits, refilling the same Elgin High mug, stained as it was beyond recognition. But most often he was there, behind the red countertop, holding court about better days, his elaborate storytelling punctuated by the occasional plunk of Skoal spit landing in the trash.

This day, though, was not typical. Not after Chevo walked in.

"Chevo" was the nickname of Eusevio Huitron, a successful

Austin horse trainer who owned a ranch nearby and occasionally came in to stock up. He was built like a bowling pin, five foot five with a formidable paunch. He stalked the aisles with his typical fervor, looking for vitamins and going on in broken English about a new colt he had in his stables. David listened up.

Despite his falling-out with ol' Doc Graham, David shared his son's desire to see Southwest Stallion Station returned to prominence. Tyler was still working to catch Southwest Stallion up with the industry, stocking up on equipment that didn't exist when the ranch was last relevant. He'd taken some flyers on cheap racehorses that might become decent studs, and he'd found some mare owners who were willing to do business. Chevo was one of those mare owners.

But Chevo was best known as a trainer, and he apparently had a new runner in his stables. The horse's name was Tempting Dash. He'd run fast in Mexico, Chevo said, and in a couple of days the colt would run his first race in the United States, at the track up in Dallas. If he ran well, he would qualify for a big-money race later in the month.

David Graham listened from behind the counter. On the one hand, he knew that winning in Mexico didn't mean much. As big as the unregulated match-racing scene was in Mexico, its sanctioned races didn't draw the same level of competition as the circuit in the American Southwest. Nor was Graham particularly moved by Chevo's boasting. Chevo loved to boast.

On the other hand, Graham knew that plenty of fast, well-bred horses had been coming north from Mexico lately. He also knew that Chevo had been working closely with Ramiro Villarreal, "the Horseman," who seemed to have a bead on all the best young runners.

Most important, David Graham, after a lifetime in and around the breeding business, knew this: if his son, Tyler, was ever going to lure a real stud to Southwest Stallion Station, it was going to require a shit-barrel full of luck. If Chevo's colt was indeed a topflight racehorse, then Chevo's colt might one day be a topflight breeder. And the Grahams might be first in line to breed him.

"You got a chance?" Graham asked Chevo from behind the counter.

"Oh yes," Chevo said, roaming the aisles. "*Fast* sonofabitch."

"Really?" Graham asked.

"Oh yes," Chevo said. "I'm gonna win it. I'm gonna win it."

▪ ▪ ▪

SAN ANTONIO, TEXAS
October 2009

"*Hablas medio rapida,*" Ramiro was telling his client, trying to get a handle on this latest development. "You talk kinda fast."

It had been about ten months since Ramiro snapped up Tempting Dash at that SoCal auction. Now Ramiro was back in Texas, getting ready for one of the horse's first big races in the States. He'd just landed in San Antonio when the voice of one of his top clients—maybe his boss?—called out through his Nextel push-to-talk.

Traditional cellphones were considered too traceable, so the Zetas relied on a two-pronged communication strategy. For instant messaging, they used BlackBerry's encrypted system, which required knowing a user's unique PIN. For conversation, the military-bred Zetas had pioneered a communication system that relied on radios like Nextel's push-to-talk phones, which they believed were harder for the feds to intercept. To expand the network in Mexico, they installed antennae on buildings, trees, radio towers, and, in one case, the roof of a local police station. Until recently, they even had an in-house communications pro, nicknamed "Tecnico." He worked out of a storefront radio-equipment shop in the Texas borderlands. But he'd been arrested, so the Zetas had resorted to kidnapping Nextel technicians and putting them to work.

One day they'd all be texting over allegedly encrypted smart-phone apps. But today, it was still Nextel for Ramiro, and this incoming "callout" was an important one. It was Forty's younger brother Omar, Z-42.

Forty-Two was in his mid-thirties, the third-youngest of the Treviño kids. He was five foot seven, shorter and thicker than Forty, and his black hair was streaked with gray. He liked to wear his shirt spread open to reveal a tan, smooth chest covered in tattoos, including a hulking bird of prey.

Like Forty, Forty-Two had never served in the military, making his place among the high-ranking Zetas a curiosity to the group's ex-soldiers. But like Forty, he'd shown a willingness to protect the Gulf Cartel's interests with unrepentant force, earning the trust of the Gulf bosses.

Forty-Two didn't care much about horses, but he knew how much his brother did. And a few weeks before, Forty's best horse, Tempting Dash, had qualified for the Dash for Cash Futurity in Dallas, a Grade 1 stakes race with a $445,000 purse. There was a lot to talk about. But given the news Ramiro had just received, it seemed like a strange time for Forty-Two to check in on Tempting Dash.

"Forty told me you just had a shoot-out," Ramiro said, in Spanish.

"Yes, quite a while," Forty-Two said. "Like an hour."

"And Miguel was there?"

"Yeah, he was," Forty-Two said. "He was there in the truck with me talking to a man, and I was on the passenger side, then I jumped to the seat, and it was off."

"Man, take really good care of yourself," Ramiro said. "Fuck."

"Once again we took care of them," Forty-Two said.

"But you are all right?" Ramiro asked.

"It's bleeding," Forty-Two said.

"It's coming out?"

"It's bleeding, it's bleeding," Forty-Two said, letting the drama build.

"Where'd you get hit?" Ramiro asked.

"On the tip of my dick!" Forty-Two told him.

Then he started laughing.

"No way, man, don't scare me!" Ramiro said.

Ramiro laid down his own laughter over Forty-Two's. In truth, he was out of his depth. Ramiro was no aspiring trafficker or Special-Forces wannabe. His dad was a bookkeeper; his mom was a teacher.

He'd grown up in Monterrey, Nuevo León, a cosmopolitan city long known as a haven from the violence of Mexico's drug war. There were American companies there, Pepsi and Caterpillar and others. When Ramiro was a child, it was one of the few places everyone seemed to agree should stay quiet.

Ramiro's obsession with horse racing seemed born from native talent. As a teenager in Monterrey, he'd cobbled money from friends and relatives to buy cheap horses at auction and race them at the small tracks that dotted the Mexican countryside. His horses always outperformed their purchase price, which got the attention of other horse owners. Ramiro started making a living by picking and buying promising young quarter horses for ranchers and other wealthy businessmen.

Eventually Ramiro's keen eye got the attention of the drug criminals, including the original Zeta they called "Mamito," a play on Mamita, the common term of endearment for Latina women. Mamito's plate was full. He paid bribes to state policemen and soldiers, and he collected pisos from traffickers who wanted to move drugs through the Gulf's territory. If they didn't pay those pisos, he was usually ordered to kidnap them, torture them, and, if the piso was offered too late or not at all, kill them.

Like many of the high-ranking Zetas, Mamito found time for racing horses. He'd become interested in 2004, and he'd noticed Ramiro's talent for picking fast horses. He asked Ramiro to pick him some winners at the auctions in the United States and bring them back to Mexico to race.

Throughout his twenties, Ramiro had built a sustainable income as a broker, but Mamito's business offered more revenue. The more expensive the horse, the higher Ramiro's commission, and Mamito wanted some of the priciest horses. Ramiro started showing up at the big auctions in Oklahoma City, Dallas, and southern California, bidding on horses from Mamito's favored bloodlines—First Down Dash, Corona Cartel, and others.

Usually Mamito found a legitimate Mexican businessman to pay off Ramiro's debts at the auction houses, instructing them to send a check or a wire and promising to repay them from his stash of drug money. But in 2008, Ramiro smoothed out the process by enlisting a Monterrey currency-exchange house to launder the money.

Here's how it worked: The Zetas took cash from one of their stash houses and delivered it to Ramiro. It always took too long for Ramiro to collect, because the drug lords moved around so much and dropped their phones so often. But he eventually got the money and brought it to the *casa de cambio* in Monterrey, anywhere from a few thousand to several hundred thousand. Sometimes he showed up himself, parking his silver BMW 750 in front and lugging the cash in an envelope. Sometimes he sent his secretary, a woman who organized his affairs. Sometimes he sent a courier he used to run errands like these, although that didn't always work out. The courier had a gambling problem and once gambled away $600,000 of drug money. Somehow he and Ramiro survived.

The owner of the exchange house didn't know where the money came from, and didn't ask. He simply exchanged it for pesos, then back to dollars, in keeping with the normal course of his business. Then he fired wires all over the American Southwest in smaller amounts, to whichever American auction houses and breeding farms Ramiro currently owed money.

Once the horses were paid off, Ramiro could either keep them in his name or transfer them into the name of a friend or associate— someone who didn't care or didn't even know that he owned a narco's racehorse. No matter whose name it was in, it was actually owned by Mamito or whichever gangster had instructed Ramiro to buy it. Ramiro collected a fee, anywhere from a thousand dollars to five thousand dollars, depending on the quality of the horse.

Ramiro operated like this throughout most of the 2000s, well into his thirties. Though he was buying for narcos, he had managed to remain independent, a safe distance from their business and their culture. But around the time he bought Tempting Dash in 2008, some guys approached and told him that a Zeta named Forty wanted to do business together.

Ramiro politely declined, saying he preferred to stick with his freelance horse brokerage. But the guys came back and said, This isn't optional, Horseman.

Soon after, Ramiro showed up at a track in Monterrey. Two armed men found him and escorted him to a cluster of SUVs and pickups parked near the track. A man stepped forward and extended his hand.

So you're the famous Horseman, Forty said.

How can I help you? Ramiro asked.

I want you to buy horses for me, Forty said.

I'm too busy.

Think about it, Forty said. He left Ramiro alone to watch the horses run. Later, he returned.

I really need you to buy horses for me, Forty said.

I'm sorry, Ramiro said. He insisted he didn't have time.

Forty's bodyguards stiffened. Their boss pulled back his shirt to reveal a pistol. Forty asked, Do you have time to save your family?

What do you mean? Ramiro asked.

If you don't buy my fucking horses, Forty said, you won't have a family.

So now, Ramiro bought for Forty.


The machismo of Mexico's narco culture didn't suit Ramiro, but he tried his best. He could *talk* like a narco at least, prattling on about associates who could "fuck off" and occasionally feigning a violent streak. He was prone to elaborate descriptions of his friends' flatulence, and he talked constantly to friends about women. Sometimes he actually talked *with* women, sex past and future crackling through the phone calls.

Mostly he spoke with one woman, an apparent girlfriend in Mexico. They spoke several times some days, about the innocuous things that make up the closest relationships, including a skin cream she'd bought for him. He liked it, but he wasn't using it daily as directed.

"My skin is already beautiful," he told her.

"Do you miss me?" she asked.

"All day long," he said.

Ramiro spoke with friends about wanting to move in with her, but they rarely saw each other. She lived in Guadalajara, a territory controlled by the Zetas' rivals in the Sinaloa cartel. Ramiro wasn't going there. And she couldn't come to Monterrey. Not now. The turf battle between the Gulf and the Zetas was in the process of shattering the city's relative placidity, as hooded gunmen bombed police stations, traffickers jacked cars to use for transportation, and the American consulate sent anxious cables back to Washington: "It is now clear that the ongoing war between the Gulf and Zeta drug trafficking organizations (DTOs) has reached Monterrey."

The increasing violence had Ramiro spooked. When friends back home told Ramiro of the bloodshed, he responded by saying he would remain in the States for a while. He stayed in San Antonio a lot, though he preferred California. He talked about moving there someday.

Spooked or not, Ramiro at least appeared to have a luxurious life under Forty and the Zetas. As he traversed Mexico and the American Southwest, he racked up $300 bills at steakhouses and found time to jaunt to Las Vegas. And, damn, could he shop. He preferred the colorful short-sleevers at Lacoste, where those little gator logos could make $240 or $360 of Ramiro's money disappear in an afternoon. But he also made trips to Louis Vuitton, Nordstrom, Neiman Marcus, and other high-end stores. His voracious spending kept his checking account from ever climbing, but there was always enough to spend. If seventeen grand went out one month, twenty grand came in.

There was no sign of business slowing down. With every passing year, the Zetas' zeal for horses seemed to increase. The group's leader, Lazcano, was prone to throwing private parties anchored by match races, including one where he injected his horse with so much cocaine that it died on the track. But it was second-in-command Forty who really changed Ramiro's business. Forty didn't want Ramiro just to *buy* horses in the United States; he wanted Ramiro to run them there. And he wanted them to win.

For Ramiro, even getting the horses into the country required some ingenuity. A highly contagious tick-borne disease called equine piroplasmosis had broken out in Mexico. Then it started to show up in horses in South Texas, after an outbreak at the famous King Ranch. Health regulators were panicking. The Texas Animal Health Commission had once crossed into Mexico to test horses before they could be imported, but the violence made that too dangerous. Instead, they set up bays at border checkpoints to quarantine and test horses. Since some of the horses the Zetas wanted to race in Mexico likely carried piroplasmosis, there was no hope of legally trucking them across the river. Even if they weren't infected, there was a waiting list and paperwork and other bureaucratic hurdles that Forty and the Zetas had no time for.

So Ramiro smuggled them across. There was a tradition of informal movement of horses across the border, just as there was with smuggling drugs and humans. Mexicans, Tejanos, and Americans, both native and imperialist, had ridden horses across the river in battle and in search of new land to ranch. But by 2009, the folks on the American side of the river were actively policing the border for rogue horse crossings. The United States government had even employed cowboys to roam the borderlands in search of livestock that had either strayed or been smuggled across the border. They caught and captured hundreds every year.

They didn't catch Ramiro's horses. He hired associates from the racetracks to ride the horses across the river at night, at the same low-flowing sections where the Zetas crossed some of their cocaine. Once they were across, he made sure they got wherever they needed to go.

After Tempting Dash won his heat in Nuevo Laredo, Ramiro had smuggled him across to run in the States. Once the horse was safely in the States, Ramiro knew just where to take him: Chevo's place.

Chevo and Ramiro had met at the track years before, and they'd struck up a partnership. It was easy enough to understand what Ramiro saw in Chevo. Since around 2006, he had become a fixture in the stables at some of the sport's biggest tracks—Sam Houston

Race Park in Houston, Retama Park in San Antonio, Lone Star Park in Dallas, and Remington Park in Oklahoma City. He worked his horses hard, and more and more they were finding their way into the money.

Ramiro also may have appreciated Chevo's willingness to test the limits of his horses, and the limits of his sport's feeble doping regulations. Horse racing had for years been known as a place where performance-enhancing drugs were abused with too little oversight or punishment. Even in higher-profile thoroughbred racing, trainers were known to use any substance they could to gain an advantage. Steroids helped horses recover more quickly from workouts. Painkillers helped mask injuries, allowing horses to pass prerace medical exams. Stimulants made them run faster.

Like other sports, thoroughbred racing had promised to crack down but lagged behind industrious cheaters, who always found a drug their horse wouldn't be tested for. Cancer drugs were popular. Viagra, too. It would take an especially attentive lab worker in Denver to identify one of the stranger painkillers trainers were using: a natural opioid squeezed from the back of an exotic South American frog.

Quarter-horse racing had been even slower to change. Needles remained rampant and testing limited. Even when a doper was caught, the punishment was often laughably light.

Two years earlier, five of Chevo's horses had tested positive for elevated levels of banned substances, including phenylbutazone, an anti-inflammatory drug that's legal in training but banned on race days. Too much "bute" can cause ulcers and other issues in horses, but if the sport was taking it seriously, it wasn't reflected by its discipline schedule. Those five bad tests cost Chevo only about twelve hundred dollars in fine money, and no track time was taken away.

Later that year, another of Chevo's horses tested positive for too much nicotinamide, a form of vitamin B3. That earned Chevo a six-month suspension from the track in Houston, but those six months basically covered when the quarter-horse season was dark. He was back at Sam Houston the next summer, racking up small-time fines for entering ineligible horses into races. He was also at Texas's other tracks, like Austin's Manor Downs, where he was suspended for three months after a horse tested positive for an unnamed substance, and Dallas's Lone Star Park, where he was fined $250 for having two hypodermic needles in his truck. Later, his horses would test positive for elevated levels of clenbuterol, a respiratory drug that mimics a steroid and helps horses build muscle.

Whatever Ramiro saw in Chevo, they made formidable partners. The summer Tempting Dash arrived in the States, they teamed up on a few winning horses. Chevo finished the season as Sam Houston's second-winningest trainer, taking down $75,000 in earnings. Ramiro finished as one of the track's top "owners," though his horses all actually belonged to Forty or other narcos.

So, Ramiro told Chevo, let's keep it going. He hauled Tempting Dash down the gravel road that led to Chevo's falling-down training center southeast of Austin. Chevo and his brother had built it a few years back, after Chevo, who'd learned to train in Mexico, started winning races. They'd constructed crude stables from sheet metal and plywood, poured dirt for a quarter-mile track, and trucked in a used starting gate. The plywood was rotting now; the white fence posts that formed the track's rail were rusted. Trash piled up outside the two-story house the brothers had built on-site for the grooms and assistant trainers who came on staff to help. Even by the standards of quarter-horse racing, a sport proud of its comparative humility, the place was a dump. For Chevo, it was an American Dream fulfilled.

Ramiro had gone out there to watch Tempting Dash run the day before Forty-Two called him. The horse was a bit of a diva; whenever no one was tending to him, he huffed and kicked dust onto the rotting plywood that formed his stall. They took him out and walked him on the red-and-white hot walker, the sort of equine merry-go-round trainers use to cool down a hot horse or warm up a cold one. They hosed him down in the bathing pen, its red paint chipping a little more with every spray. They led him through the deep training pool Chevo's crew had constructed, and Tempting Dash, head held high, clung to the bit with his teeth, as the white racing stripe that bisected his face peeked out of the murky water.

Eventually, they took the horse out to the track on the edge of the property. He liked company in the stall, but he hated it out there. He basically refused to run if there was another horse on the track. So Chevo cleared the other horses and put Dash in the gates alone.

He flew.


On the phone with Forty-Two, Ramiro, still reeling from the phantom dick-shooting, steered the conversation back to the horses. He said Tempting Dash was looking good.

"What's up with Chevo?" Forty-Two asked. "How's the forecast? How's he?"

Chevo was ready, Ramiro said. But that was hardly enough for the Zetas. They were under assault from so many angles—from the Gulf, from the Sinaloa, from Calderón, from the Americans. The idea of losing something as simple as a horse race seemed unfathomable to them, and they took every step to avoid it.

Along with doping their horses, they loved to fix races, especially the unregulated ones in Mexico. Sometimes they bribed the "starters," who manage the gates, and their assistants, who load the horses into the gates, paying them to hold on to their opponents' horses for a millisecond. Other times the Zetas paid off the groundskeeper to drag one lane of the track until the dirt was packed tight, letting the briber's horse fly across the harder surface. Often they slipped their jockeys a little battery-charged device that sent a shock wave into the horse, reminding him to pick up the pace. All of these cheats were methods favored over the years by American cowboys, but the Zetas were especially zealous in their application of them.

Ramiro told Forty-Two about the deal he'd cut with the gate crew at Lone Star Park: five hundred dollars each, plus four thousand for the head starter and an extra thousand for the one who made sure Tempting Dash got out clean. Operativo Huesos was in motion. But there was a second phase, which was what Forty-Two wanted to talk about now.

"Hope he wants to run, because once the jolts are applied, it doesn't matter," Forty-Two said, referring to the electric-shock mechanism he wanted Ramiro to slip the jockey.

The jockey they'd tapped to ride Tempting Dash was Julian Cantu. He'd grown up navigating the bush tracks of rural Mexico, unregulated, poorly groomed courses carved out of the trees or desert, with fans forming the rails. Julian was known as a smart jockey who raced with an edge—sometimes too much of an edge. He'd been fined recently for bumping his horse into another. Julian was on board, Ramiro assured his boss. (Cantu was never formally accused of being a buzzer, and no evidence was ever found that he did. This may only have been bravado on the part of Ramiro.)

Forty-Two would soon hang up abruptly, as he often did. But not before making his prediction.

"You will win, Gordo," Forty-Two said. "We're going to win."

■ ■ ■

DALLAS, TEXAS
October 2009

Ramiro hardly had time to reflect on what it might mean to win the Dash for Cash Futurity. His days barreled past. Trainers called to ask when shipments of medicine would arrive. Vets called to talk about horses they'd treated. Auction managers called to ask Ramiro whether he planned to pay up before the next sale. His secretary called to out-line options for whatever flight or hotel or rental-car reservation he wanted to change at the last minute. He moved perpetually and im-petuously among Dallas, Oklahoma City, Los Angeles, Houston, San Antonio, and Monterrey, not to mention the ranches dropped into the barren stretches in between. He never wanted to pay the change fee. He always paid the change fee. Everyone pays the change fee.

The morning of the Dash for Cash, Ramiro flew to Dallas from Oklahoma City, where he'd just spent $113,000 on nine horses. He drove to the track in a rental Nissan. It was finally cool in Dallas, that brief window of fall that graces north Texas around Hallow-een. He called his parents, who were flying in from Monterrey for the race. Ramiro's dad reminded him to bring a jacket.

Ramiro arrived early at Lone Star Park, a prefab oasis of stucco and glass rising from the suburbs west of Dallas. The track was built in 1997, and after twelve years, it felt only gently used. Many nights, it was. Racetrack attendance was in decline across the country, as the sport faded in the shadow of more popular pastimes. The tracks in Texas were falling prey to the sport's most deadly predator, casino gambling, which flourished across each of Texas's American borders. At Lone Star, and at tracks around the country, the betting window looked ever more like something that belonged in a sports museum.

Only big-money quarter-horse races brought crowds of more than a couple thousand people, and the Dash for Cash Futurity was one of them. It was the first stakes race of the track's quarter-horse meet. Lone Star wasn't the highest-dollar track in quarter-horse racing; only New Mexico's Ruidoso Downs and California's Los Alamitos could reasonably make that claim. But since Lone Star's meet took place late in the season, it offered one of the last chances of the year for owners to squeeze another quarter-mile from their best colts and fillies. That, along with the purse, lured some decent horses and a decent crowd.

Ramiro found a table with his parents, and they fixed their eyes on Tempting Dash. He moved fluidly, which was lucky. He was the youngest horse in the field. He had also chipped a bone in his knee during one of the races in Mexico, so Ramiro had taken him to a Texas vet to get the knee cleaned up. Technically, he was running on a surgically repaired leg, and he'd run hard on it just a couple of weeks earlier, in the qualifier for this futurity.

That'd been quite a sight: Tempting Dash, the horse no one had heard of, crashing hard toward the rail and cutting off half the field on his way to a two-length win. Chevo and Ramiro figured that his hard move toward the infield was just his way of shielding his young eyes from the track's harsh lights, since he'd never before run at night. But it had looked like an act of aggression.

That was just a qualifier, though. This was the race Ramiro cared about, because this was the race Forty cared about.

The starters herded the horses into the gates one by one. Their cow-pony genes kept them calm, but even in that regard, Tempting Dash stood out. The vet from the Texas Racing Commission, who'd examined all the horses before the race, couldn't help noticing how placid Tempting Dash was as the race approached. A two-year-old? With this kind of crowd on this kind of night? As chill as the doc had ever seen.

All went quiet. The gates flung open. If Ramiro really had paid off the gate crew, they didn't hold up their end of the bargain. Another well-bred horse, one of the favorites, burst into an early lead. Who knew if a chipped-knee horse, once so skinny they called him—

El Huesos! About six seconds in, Tempting Dash sped past the lead horse and shaded toward the rail, away from those lights again. Just like that, he was ahead. His lead grew, and suddenly Ramiro could feel his family's eyes turning away from the track and toward him. When he checked the scoreboard, it confirmed that Tempting Dash had not just won the $445,000 race—$178,000 to the winning owner—but that he'd covered the 400 yards in just 19.379 seconds. It was a track record.

Ramiro pushed through the crowd and down to the winner's circle. His Nextel rang out with calls of congratulations, and he called friends to tell them the news. He made plans to celebrate that night, and he secured some kick-ass tickets for the next day's Dallas Cowboys game, from a friend who happened to play in a Grammy-winning norteño band called Intocable. "Untouchable."

As Ramiro pulled out of the parking lot, another call came through. It was El Flaco, a Zetas boss in Monterrey. Ramiro could hear Forty in the background.

"His horse won, right?" El Flaco asked in Spanish. They rarely called Forty by his name on the phone, worried the Americans might be listening in. He was referred to only in vague terms like "the boss" or "that guy."

"Yes, his horse won," Ramiro said. "It's a track record."

"Again?" El Flaco asked him. "I didn't get that last part."

"Tell him it is a track record," Ramiro repeated. "A track record."

"Got it, sir," El Flaco said. "Got it."

"We have to celebrate!" Ramiro told him.

"I know. That's how he is also," El Flaco said. "My boss will respond later, sir. When you—"

The phone went dead.

■ ■ ■

DALE, TEXAS
October 2009

One prolific stallion—a horse like First Down Dash or Corona Cartel—can turn a stud farm's luck around. He can come out of nowhere, too, taking his genetic gifts and somehow multiplying them, changing the course of his lineage. That's part of the allure of breeding, in horses as in all animals: the potential to make something better of the next generation, and the next.

Knowing all that, Tyler Graham paid close attention when Chevo bragged about Tempting Dash. "I'm gonna win it!" Chevo had said, and he had won it, not once but twice under the lights at Lone Star Park. If he kept winning, Tyler's relationship with Chevo might one day put him in position to lure Tempting Dash to Southwest Stallion Station to breed.

Tyler was a big college football fan, his Aggies specifically. When he talked about running a stud farm, he sounded like a college coach. First came the scouting. After Tempting Dash's big win, Tyler and his dad drove down to Chevo's training center. It would be a while before Tempting Dash would retire and start breeding. He had more races as a two-year-old and likely a three-year-old season, which could be almost as lucrative as this one. But Tyler knew he needed to get in line early if he wanted the horse to eventually stand at Southwest Stallion Station.

They arrived at Chevo's place to find a party in progress. Smoke, scented with the flesh of pig and goat, rose over the property. Mexican men leaned over the rusty rails, waving five-dollar bills as yearlings clambered past with kids on their backs. The Grahams found a ranch hand and asked if they could see Tempting Dash. He walked them into the stables. They peered inside a dark, rotting stall.

"No," Tyler's dad said, looking at the short, thin colt. He hadn't seen the horse up close at the race, but he was pretty sure this wasn't him. "We want to see the horse that won the futurity last night."

"That's him."

They walked into the stall.

"This is the horse that set the track record?"

"Yeah."

They'd gone looking for Godzilla and found a horse built more like an insurance-shilling gecko. He couldn't weigh a thousand pounds. They asked the guy to pull Tempting Dash out of the stall and walk him around. He did, and they started drawing invisible lines across his body, this way and that, doing their horseman geometry. That's when they saw it. His short back created a tight, fast hinge. His deep heart girth gave him great lung capacity. The slope of his shoulders, the proportions of his legs. It all added up to "one fast booger," as Tyler's old man put it.

Tyler already knew Ramiro "the Horseman" Villarreal— everyone in the business did—but Chevo had made it clear that Ramiro was the owner in name only. It wasn't clear who the real owner was, but Tyler knew how to find out: by getting to the race-track in Dallas.

# CHAPTER NINE

## THE WINNER'S CIRCLE

DALLAS, TEXAS
November 2009

Night fell on Lone Star Park, a winter night in name if not forecast, and the horses clicked beneath the grandstand and through a parting sea of horse-racing fans, who themselves were swarming from the track to the ornate saddling paddock. This ritual had repeated itself before each of the night's ten races: the grooms paraded the horses from the track, beneath the grandstand, through the crowd, around an ornately landscaped walking ring, and into the saddling paddock, where the horses were prepped by their trainers, loved by their owners, mounted by their jockeys, and led *back* through the crowd, toward the starting gate, to wait for the gates to fly.

At other tracks, this ritual took place on the inside of the track and felt like something private for the horse's connections. At Lone Star, it happened *behind* the grandstand. A crowd formed. Bettors squinted and looked for signs of a winner. Kids marveled from high on their daddies' shoulders.

The crowd grew especially large before the Texas Classic, the biggest race of the night. Outside the paddock, the onlookers studied the horses, which snorted and neighed as their trainers jostled to get riding saddles and blinkers in place. The crowd strained to find the favorite and found him in the seventh paddock. If the horse was small, he didn't look it next to his squat, mustachioed trainer, Chevo, or the man who was now listed as the owner, José Treviño.

After Tempting Dash's record-breaking win in the Dash for Cash, Operativo Huesos had been put into motion. Forty tasked Poncho, the Piedras Negras trafficker, with making sure Tempting Dash was legally transferred into José's name from Ramiro's. That way, any money the horse won could be kept in the Treviño family. José, Ramiro, and Poncho met in Mexico to finalize the deal. Thirty years after leaving Tamaulipas, José was back in northern Mexico, taking on the challenge and responsibility of owning an animal, and he seemed thrilled. Thrilled, and yet insistent that the deal come with a clear paper trail. He and Ramiro signed a sales agreement. Poncho asked his wife, a notary, to authenticate it after the fact.

José would never say publicly what he knew of Forty's plan. He had a chance to buy Tempting Dash for cheap, he'd say, and he took it. The stated sale price was twenty-five thousand dollars, a bargain given that the horse had already won a half-million-dollar race. So they backdated the agreement to September, *before* Tempting Dash's first big win. Later, if anyone wondered why Ramiro would sell a winning horse so cheap, the paper trail would show that he sold it before Tempting Dash ever won a thing.

It's also unclear exactly how much money changed hands between the two of them, although José did later send a check to Ramiro for fifteen grand. It's possible he paid the rest some other way, a fact he'd cling to for years to come.

Forty paid Ramiro a fifty-thousand-dollar bonus for finding Tempting Dash. Still, none of it had gone over well with the Horseman. He was upset the horse went to Forty instead of Mamito, who was pissed and jealous that Forty had wound up with that horse. For low-level cartel operatives, this was one of many hells to navigate: pleasing the many masters. Mamito was Z-7, one of the earliest Zetas, so he had more seniority than Forty, and he seemed to resent the rise of nondefectors like Forty and Forty-Two. But Forty was higher on the org chart. He was the guy Ramiro needed to keep happy.

More than that, Ramiro worried that selling the horse to José— "the clean brother," as Ramiro called him—would create a needless paper trail between him and the Treviño family.

"Oh Lord, hopefully there won't be a problem," he told a friend on the phone around that time. "Hopefully there will never be a problem."

"It's all good," his friend said, trying to reassure him.

"Yeah, the shit will land on the one whose name it's on," Ramiro said, trying to reassure himself. "Plus," he said, "his brother has nothing. He's clean. He's just an ordinary guy. All the fuckin' way."

"That calms some of your fears, right?" Ramiro's friend asked.

"It's true!" Ramiro said.

The night of the race, José walked into the paddock, his first public act as the owner of Tempting Dash. He wore blue jeans over shiny tan boots, a light coat over a blue button-down, and a ball cap that made him look less like a winning horse owner and more like a career mason. In fact, he'd worked his final day as a bricklayer a few weeks before, leaving the best-paying job he'd had in years. His last weekly check had come to a little more than five hundred dollars for thirty-two hours of bricklaying. If his horse won, he'd make $445,000. Still, it was a risk. After fifteen years of steering clear of the feds' radar, he was at least skirting it now, taking ownership of Tempting Dash in the middle of the horse's hot streak.

The paddock was packed with owners and trainers and horses from serious pedigrees—elite cowboys who planned on keeping José from seeing that cash. If he did win, they'd surely try to leverage his naïveté to take advantage of him. José might have grown up around horses, but this was his first foray into the *business* of American horse racing. And while his fellow Mexicans grew more influential in the business every year—particularly in the saddle and the training barns—the industry was still controlled by savvy old white guys. Right there in the saddling paddock, one of them walked up to José and asked to buy Tempting Dash.

He's not for sale, José said. He was off to a good start.

Chevo led Tempting Dash out of his stall. José followed. Julian, their trusty jockey, hoisted himself up and trotted the horse back through the grandstand and onto the track.

As Tempting Dash sauntered toward the gates, the crowd herded itself onto the concrete patio that sloped down toward the track. On big quarter-horse nights, this patio was a party, flanked by bartenders in low-cut tank tops. Mexican and Mexican-American families filled every table and the spaces between, sloshing beers and waving betting tickets. It lacked the casual raucousness of a Mexican match race, where the Tecate is pulled from personal coolers, the tacos cost less than five dollars, and instead of betting tickets, the spectators wave the cash they bet among each other. But for Ramiro and José and Chevo and Julian, it had to feel less like the infiltration of an American world than the importation of a Mexican one.

Or maybe neither. Even four hundred miles from Bridge One in Laredo, this patio felt like an extension of the borderlands—as if the border were not a river or a wall or an invisible line but a rubber band that stretched no matter how far north or south you wandered. You could try to escape it, and people on both sides of the border did, entrenching themselves in communities that ignored or rejected the cultural influences of the other side. But not José, who, unlike Forty, seemed to relish both his assimilation and his identity as a Mexican—speaking Spanish and English, shopping at American Eagle and Carnival, laying bricks but dreaming about something more. Not Chevo or Julian, either. Not most of the people here. They were stretching the rubber band to its limits. They knew it would probably snap and send them all tumbling one day, but they were here anyway.

José and his family moved upstairs, to the cushioned box seats they'd secured behind the sloping glass. His mom was there. His wife, Zulema, was there. Their daughter Alex was there, too. She had flowing, jet-black hair and round cheeks that lifted high when she smiled, which was often. She'd been a gifted student at their local public school and was now in college. Her boyfriend, a high-school sweetheart, wanted to be a cop.

Whether Alex recognized it or not, the horse sauntering toward the gate meant as much to her as it did to her dad. For José, stepping into this world offered a connection to his past and potential stability in the present. For Alex, Tempting Dash was a potential foothold in the future. If he ran well, that future might start several rungs above where her parents' did.

The Treviños watched as the horses loaded up. All the pressure builds in the gate. Horses get claustrophobic; they buck, they revolt, they rear. Performance-enhancing drugs can exacerbate this behavior or mitigate it, depending on the drug. But for whatever reason, Tempting Dash was cool, as if he knew he was a 1-to-2 favorite. The closest competitor was 6 to 1.

The gates flew open, and Tempting Dash was almost immediately halfway down the track, as if by teleportation. Julian, the jockey, squeezed his glutes and lifted his ass off the saddle, tucking his face behind the mess of Tempting Dash's mane. Then Julian just sat there, still as dawn, and let the horse's physiology lead them.

Tempting Dash's hind legs propelled them together, horse and jockey, and stretched out in front of his hocks like contrails, nearly parallel to the ground. They easily slipped past the number six horse, past the five, in front of the four, and in a matter of seconds the announcer was basically calling the race. The end of the race came down not to "if" but "by how much." In the end, Tempting Dash won by three lengths. He'd covered 400 yards in 19.205 seconds, replacing his own month-old track record with one that would stand for years.

José and his family hugged and cheered and made their way downstairs. They pushed through the crowd and into the winner's circle, the seas parting, and they graciously shook hands with the people there with the horse. The race's million-dollar purse must have been top of mind. José had never known a sum like this. His brothers probably had, but look where that landed them: Kiko, still in prison; Miguel and Omar, hunted on both sides of the border; Jesús and Fito, in the ground. He was a little like them now, in the way that large sums of money had improved their lives while putting them at great risk.

At risk but full of rewards. Alex joined him in the winner's circle, her smile as wide as her dangling hoop earrings.

Chevo's family and jockey Julian's family were in the circle, too. And there was another family there: the father-and-son duo Chevo had invited from the feed store. The Graham family. They wanted to meet José.

Tyler worked it slowly, as good recruiters do, especially when time is on their side. He didn't mention that he wanted to one day bring Tempting Dash to his stud farm. He just congratulated José and told him to call if he needed help marketing the horse. The industry vote for Colt of the Year was coming up, and Tempting Dash had the résumé. But he was nowhere on the power brokers' radars. He would need a push to get in front of voters. Tyler gave his business card to José and left it at that.

José had been a player in the business for about ten minutes now, but he could see the angle the Grahams were playing. He could also figure that the investment they were suggesting was one worth making. If some ads in *Track Magazine* helped Tempting Dash become Colt of the Year, that would forever live on the horse's résumé, making him more valuable in a sale or as a breeding stud. It would live on José's résumé, too.

It was also an investment José could suddenly afford. Two weeks after the race, he deposited his winnings into his Bank of America account—$441,855, about $435,000 more than that account had ever held.

■ ■ ■

BALCH SPRINGS, TEXAS
December 2009

They should have been in bed. Luis had school the next morning; Alex had to get up early to help get her little siblings out the door. After that she had to trek across town to take a book back to her college campus. The clock was hurtling toward midnight. But this was a young couple seemingly high off the glow of an instant-message screen. They kept chatting.

Alex had met Luis at West Mesquite High in the spring of 2009, the last semester of her senior year, somehow finding him among the sprawling inner-ring public school's eighteen hundred kids. He was younger, a junior, but cute—closely shaved head, thick lips, teenage muscles stretching snug T-shirts.

Alex could talk to anyone and did. She took honors classes and took them seriously, and she was always quick with her opinion in class. She spent a lot of time with her fellow orchestra geeks, but she also liked to make videos of her and her friends that alternated between mature and not so much. She dubbed her nascent production outfit Asswipe Studios.

After she graduated, she enrolled at the University of Texas at Arlington, a twenty-five-minute drive from her brick house in Dallas's working-class suburbs. But she stuck with Luis, who existed on her instant-message screen as "The love of my life!" They'd made it all the way into those final days of the first semester, when kids were driving to school in the dark, snug in yanked-tight hoodies.

They were making plans for the weekend, but Alex wanted to tell Luis about her family's changing luck. To seek his counsel, too. He was younger but felt older somehow, with a maturity aided by his hyperconfidence and his plans to become a cop or maybe even a soldier someday.

*alexandra*

*we got it made if this business goes good. my dad finally got a company going and made his will leaving us as the first ones to get everything and put me in charge of handling finances and something else. . . . because he said i have a good head on my shoulders and he trusts me . . . idk he told me not to go to school the other day . . . its weird . . . but i just wanted to put that out there. . . . idk how you feel about all this*

The company did make it more legit. After the races at Lone Star, José had gone to a storefront accountant near his house and asked her to set up an LLC. He'd called it Tremor Enterprises, borrowing from his family's paternal and maternal surnames, Treviño Morales. He promptly planted the winnings from Tempting Dash in the new company's new bank account.

*alexandra*

*oh AND we got land!! lol my dad said hes going to build each one of his kids a house just in case*

José didn't have the land quite yet, but he had his eye on a place down near Austin. A vision was emerging, of José and his immediate family taking the winnings from Tempting Dash and parlaying them into a thriving quarter-horse business. Never mind who people believed *really* owned Tempting Dash. The horse was in his name, the money was in his account, and racing was just the beginning. José's new friend, Tyler, estimated that Tempting Dash could one day be worth eight million dollars as a stud horse. If José could turn his luck into a sustainable business, his life might one day look like a more successful version of his own father's, only in the safety, economic and physical, of the United States.

*The love of my life!*
*And wtf r u gonna do if you dont go to school*

*alexandra*
*im not gonna quit!*

*The love of my life!*
*And the horse will die pretty soon*

*alexandra*
*ummmmm the horse is 2 years old lol*

*The love of my life!*
*It could break a leg then its done!!*

*alexandra*
*it already broke a leg and they are going to make baby tempting dashes mix it with a winning lady horse*

Luis was on board. He had a job already, and planned on enlisting after high school; he was hardly allergic to work. Alex had a job, too, working the register at a store in Mesquite, to go with her crosstown commute to college and taking care of her little brothers and sister.

*alexandra*
*idk i think they chose the right family to give this business to. i know my family isnt perfect but we are hard workers*

It was almost one in the morning now, five hours before Alex needed to be up to help get her little brother out the door for school.

*alexandra*
*goodnight baby*

**The love of my life!**
love you!

**alexandra**
i love you too!

# CHAPTER TEN

## NEW PLAYERS

OKLAHOMA CITY, OKLAHOMA

January 2010

Long before America's quarter-horse men arrived at the annual Winter Mixed Sale, the Winter Mixed Sale came to them. It was one of the little joys of professional horsemanship: the arrival, in a reinforced envelope or even a cardboard box, of the auction catalog.

To lay eyes, an auction catalog is hundreds of pages of hieroglyphics. To experienced horsemen, it is a world full of promise, carefully indexed, perfectly bound, and on their doorsteps just in time.

Every horseman has his own way of handling his sales book. Some keep theirs pristine, marking their favorite horses with small, color-coded tabs and wrapping the books in personalized leather cases. Others love theirs harder, scrawling their names across the thick fore edges with Sharpies. Their books are creased and bent and crawling with inscrutable notes to themselves.

However they preferred to handle their books, the cowboys attending the Winter Mixed Sale were sure to lug them to Oklahoma

City that weekend in January 2010, six weeks after the races at Lone
Star. It was the first big quarter-horse event of the year, and it would
take place at one of the sport's meccas.

The Heritage Place auction house was built in the 1970s by a collection of moneyed horsemen, including Tyler Graham's grandfather. Doc Graham and the other wealthy cowboys had decided that
Oklahoma needed an auction house as regal as Fasig-Tipton, the
century-old thoroughbred auction house in Lexington, Kentucky.
So they built Heritage Place, and three or four times a year they invited the industry's top horsemen to descend on its grounds.

Many made the drive the night before or that morning from
Texas, Oklahoma, and New Mexico. Other horsemen flew in for the
weekend, from as close as Dallas and as far as southern Mexico and
Ontario, Canada. It was no king's-sport excursion to Kentucky;
there were no bourbon tours and no Saudi royalty. Even with its
white-steepled rooftop and columned entrance, the auction house
was as humble as its hometown—a square patch of dirt a few miles
from the Will Rogers World Airport, tucked between a mobile-
home park and a wholesale-tire company.

Early on the first morning, catalogs in hand, the cowboys began
passing through the auction house's heavy double doors. Once inside, the first thing they saw was the sunken sales ring, lined with
fresh-cut flowers and a row of spacious, private boxes overlooking
it. The eight-hundred-seat arena offered mostly general admission
seating and was rarely full, but the top row was lined with boxes
reserved for the sport's biggest players. No one had a better view
than Tyler Graham and his family, which made sense: Tyler's
grandpa owned a 25 percent stake in the auction house. Tyler served
on the board.

Past the arena was the café, with its blend of odors, two parts
fried food and one part horsehair. Beyond that arena was a hangar
the size of a football field. That's where the action was.

Corridors shot off in every direction, each lined with hundreds
of stalls. The serious buyers hit these sale barns early in the morning, working methodically through their dog-eared catalogs. Their
eyes shifted from book to horse, book to horse, as showmen and

showgirls led the horses from their stalls and walked them up and down the aisles. The cowboys studied the horses' conformations, their structures, running their hands through their gleaming coats like a car buyer fondling a leather steering wheel.

Occasionally, one of the sport's top trainers strolled through. One was Blane Wood, a handsome West Texas horseman who stalked the aisles in his typical uniform: a big black cowboy hat and a pressed button-down tucked behind a gleaming belt buckle. The *best* trainer in the sport was Wood's rival, Paul Jones, out of Los Alamitos Race Course in California. He had a thick chest and belly and a thin mustache. He didn't dress the cowboy part, favoring sneakers and golf shirts over boots and button-downs, a look that should have made him stand out. But somehow he managed to slink around the stalls without drawing much attention. He preferred it that way. Like Wood and the other top trainers, Jones was often approached by wealthy buyers and offered carte blanche to bid on the best horses, on the condition that he train them. If competing buyers like Ramiro saw Jones studying a horse, they knew that horse was probably worth bidding on.

As the auction started, everyone moved on to the concrete concourse at the heart of the auction house. They leaned over the four-foot-high brick wall and stared into a square walking ring, where the horses were paraded before they headed to the sale ring. This was where potential buyers could get a last look at a horse's gait or size, being careful not to be fooled by the optical illusion of a tall or short showman clutching the horse's halter. They might notice a horse's demeanor, though the good buyers knew to forgive any rambunctiousness. You'd rear back and kick, too, if you'd been cooped up in a stall all morning.

The square concourse, like the sales arena, was lined with booths representing the sport's best breeders. They offered comfortable chairs for anyone who wanted to stop by and bullshit about a particular bloodline, along with plenty of literature about the studs they had back at their farms or yearlings they had for sale. The smart breeders offered coffee and candy. The lucky ones offered proximity to the well-stocked bars that anchored each side of the concourse.

Tyler Graham's family had prime real estate out here, too, a well-branded booth on a busy corner of the concourse. But they didn't have much to advertise. A few years after Tyler had returned home to run his granddad's businesses, Southwest Stallion Station still wasn't in possession of any of the top stallions, and they weren't selling any horses at this auction. Outside of Doc Graham's stake in the auction house itself, everyone expected them to be spectators.

The night before the auction, Tyler had begun the work of puncturing that image—of him on the sidelines on one of the biggest weekends of the year. Every January, the American Quarter Horse Association invited the previous season's top horsemen to Heritage Place to celebrate and hand out awards. Among the most coveted honors was a two-year-old Colt of the Year. The twelve finalists from 2009 included horses owned and trained by some of the sport's most familiar names, cowboys from across the Southwest. But with Tyler's encouragement, José Treviño had pushed to make sure voters knew about his upstart colt's record-breaking season. It worked.

"And the winner," the emcee had said at the ceremony, "unknown before October and a sensation two months later: Tempting Dash."

José stepped onto the stage to accept, having ditched his baseball cap for the white cowboy hat that would become his trademark. Chevo took the stage with him. So did Tyler.

"I got lucky buying that horse," José said. "It was cheap. I think that was the reason they sold that horse, because he got chips. It was small. I know you guys noticed that horse was small. But he's real fast, too."

The cowboys in the audience enjoyed José's humility, which paired nicely with the way he'd seemed to luck his way into the winner's circle that winter. They were dubious, too—dubious of just how fast that horse had run. Dubious of how he'd been sold in midseason. Dubious of the horse's association with Ramiro Villarreal. And dubious, or at least curious, about what the hell Doc Graham's grandson was doing up there celebrating with José.

Now, as the auction itself kicked off, Tyler and José were to-gether again. Tyler walked into a concrete corridor that bridged the regal arena and the noisy concourse. There was a spotter sitting high in a chair out here, allowing potential buyers to place bids without putting out their cigs or putting down their drinks. A lot of the serious buyers hovered out here. Ramiro had been posted up here much of the weekend.

Tyler had never been considered a serious buyer, but earlier that morning he had successfully bid $250,000 on a mare. Now he was back, raising his hand on the auction's biggest prize: a champion mare named Dashin Follies.

She was chocolate brown with the slow gait to be expected of a horse of her age, eleven. She'd won a grand total of $475 in her brief racing career. She came from good stock, though, so years back a breeder had taken a flyer on pairing her with one of the sport's premier studs, Corona Cartel. The word "cartel" had been used for decades in racehorse names, projecting a dominant eco-nomic force. But once Corona Cartel started breeding in the nine-ties, it became a signal that his genes were in the mix. And once Dashin Follies started breeding to Corona Cartel, she became a broodmare in demand. The first foal the pair produced won almost a million dollars at the track.

Everyone expected Dashin Follies to be the sale topper, the high-est selling of the thousand horses to be sold that weekend. She might well sell for half a million dollars, twice as much as the mare Tyler had just signed for. Tyler already knew he was going to be the highest bidder.

He'd been working José, and José seemed to appreciate the help and attention. After they met at the track, Tyler had invited José to go hunting. José rose in the dark, climbed into a truck with his teen-age son, and drove down to a ranch in South Texas. He and Tyler spent the next few days stalking the land with hunting guides, peer-ing through the mesquite for movement, and—*pop-pop*—dropping whitetail bucks and squatting next to their carcasses for photo ops, gripping the sprawling antlers like motorcycle handlebars. The whole trip cost thousands of dollars. Tyler's ranch picked up the tab.

After that, José had approached Tyler about partnering up at this Winter Mixed Sale. Coming off Tempting Dash's big win, José told Tyler, he was looking to buy some high-priced mares. He didn't say whether he was buying for himself or for someone back in Mexico, or where the money would come from, since Tempting Dash's winnings wouldn't cover what he was planning to spend. Tyler didn't ask; he wanted the man's business.

Sellers were known to surreptitiously bid up their own horses when new, wealthy Mexicans started bidding, figuring that if the money came from where they thought it did, the Mexicans would keep coming over the top. (Regulars like Ramiro were more respected.) But José guessed that if Tyler, who basically *owned* the auction house, was the one doing the bidding, maybe no one would drive the price up on him. He asked Tyler to act as the so-called agent—basically a straw buyer—on his deals that day.

Tyler didn't know who José or his brothers were, but all the insiders assumed José's money came from the drug trade. Most didn't care, figuring it wasn't their business. Tyler had never been faced with the choice of so publicly stepping into the industry's muck. Telling José no might keep his hands clean. But if he wanted to lure Tempting Dash, the 2009 Colt of the Year, to his struggling stud farm, saying no wasn't an option. He agreed.

"Ready to go, somebody oughta get two hundred, get 'er the money," the auctioneer shrieked after they announced Dashin Follies. Soon the air was being pierced by the *whoop* of bid-spotters hollering after every raised hand or wipe of the nose. Some buyers make a show of bidding, wanting the world to know that they've got scratch to spend. Others, including top trainers like Paul Jones, prefer to do it quietly. They either work out a signal with the spotter or simply dispatch someone to bid in their stead. Why let the competition know that a horse caught Paul Jones's eye?

Tyler raised his hand.

"Three hundred!" the auctioneer boomed, and then, in his auctioneer tongue, "threeandamunathreeanda—

"Fifty! Threefiftyandthree, three and a moment ago, fifty!"

Tyler's hand, flying.

"Fourhundredwhatareyougonnadosomebodygiveme . . .

"Five!

"Five hundred fifty!

"Six!"

Tyler, Tyler, Tyler.

"Six-fifty!

"Six-seventy-five!"

On and on Tyler pushed. It wasn't his money, so the higher the price the better for the Grahams, since the auction house they owned took a 5 percent cut of every sale. José was right in the alley with Tyler. Buy the horse no matter what, he told Tyler as the bidding escalated.

One of José's brothers, Rodolfo, was there, too. Like José, Rodolfo, a former truck mechanic, had so far steered clear of Mexico's underworld. Now he was shouting into a Nextel phone, nodding at Tyler to keep bidding.

"Seven-seventy!

"Eight hundred!

"You're lookin' at eight-twenty-five, eight-and-a-quarter!

"Half!"

Whoever was on the other end of Rodolfo's phone didn't seem to care how high it went, because Rodolfo kept nodding at Tyler, and Tyler kept raising his hand. Eventually the emcee suggested they just "go ahead and get a million dollars for this mare."

They didn't quite get there. The bidding ended. A ticket runner, dispatched by the auction house, hustled into the crowd and identified Tyler as the winning bidder. Tyler signed the ticket, testifying that he'd just won the bidding and promising that the horse would be paid for. The official sales price was $875,000, the most anyone had paid for a broodmare in the history of public quarter-horse auctions. The official buyer, according to the form Tyler signed, was an "undisclosed Mexican buyer."

# CHAPTER ELEVEN

## TOO TEMPTING

RUIDOSO, NEW MEXICO
September 2010

From the east, the climb into New Mexico's Sierra Blanca mountain range sneaks up on you, starting impercepti-bly before the peaks come into focus through the insect killing ground that is your front windshield. Before long you're climbing so fast the highway's switchbacking, and if you're smart, you kill the AC, crack your windows, and bid the Texas summer farewell.

If you're a quarter-horse man, you make this trek multiple times every summer, and always on Labor Day weekend. Texas and Mex-ico may claim the sport's roots, and Oklahoma may be home to its best breeders, and southern California may be its high-class respite from cowboy country, but Ruidoso Downs is its Everest: the peak, literal and figurative, you must ascend to be considered the sport's best.

In 2010, the sport's biggest weekend would climax, as it always does, with the two-million-dollar All American Futurity on Labor Day afternoon. It was the most prestigious and one of the richest races in the sport, with the owner of the fastest two-year-old taking home one million dollars.

Officially, the weekend would kick off the Friday night before, with the Ruidoso Select Yearling Sale. Featuring five hundred horses sold over the course of three nights, the Ruidoso sale is the premier auction of one-year-old racehorses in the business—a beer-fueled celebration of the industry that begins in the afternoon, bleeds into late night, and spills from the barns to the dimly lit dive bars in town.

But for the competitive quarter-horse men who climbed into Ruidoso that weekend, the work started when all work starts for cowboys, in the soft light of morning. In the Sierra Blanca mountains, in late summer, this was welcome morning work, especially for those who had trekked from Texas or Mexico or Oklahoma, where summer was still dug in like a tick. Here, the coffee steamed.

Early that Friday morning, the cowboys found their way to the sale barns, which were nestled between scrubby foothills and the backside of the racetrack. All the top breeders were there—mostly white men, middle-aged or older, who'd trucked in horses from Texas and Oklahoma and California. They brought with them a mix of Mexican immigrants and peppy 4-H kids to care for and show off the horses.

The potential buyers who stalked the barns were a multicultural bunch—a mix of Anglo and Hispanic businessmen, breeders, trainers, and other equine obsessives. A lot of them knew each other. They'd been coming to these things for years, seeing the same faces and watching them age, buying and selling and breeding each other's horses. That Friday morning, though, there was a pair of guys in the barns who were relatively new to the business, and they weren't wading in cautiously. They were pulling out the most expensive horses and scribbling with purpose in their catalogs and notebooks, a cloud of cologne following them through the barns. They would be much better known by the weekend's end, mostly by their first names and often one after the other: Carlitos and Fernando.

Carlitos and Fernando.

For the hours and days and years to come, Carlitos and Fernando.

When Carlitos and Fernando were interested in a horse, it was going to be a good day.


Carlos "Carlitos" Nayen Borbolla was twenty-four, and he appeared coded for maximal coolness. He had hair the color of deep space, and while it was hardly short, swooping like a roller coaster, it always looked freshly cut. He seemed especially fond of gravity's pull. He was always leaning, lounging, draping an arm, whatever he had to do to avoid supporting the entirety of his body weight, which was perfectly proportioned to his five-foot-eight frame. He spoke with his hands, conducting each syllable with his invisible baton. When he listened—he preferred talking, but it happened—he often tucked his hands into his armpits and left his thumbs sticking out, pointing up toward his head, like, *Eyes right here, people.*

He was born in the city of Veracruz, where a bustling port serves as the chief import-export channel for Mexico's growing auto industry. As a baby, Carlitos was abandoned by his parents, who felt they couldn't properly care for him, and raised by his grandmother. But his father was a well-known restaurant owner in Veracruz, and an avid horse racer, which meant Carlitos always knew where to find Dad if he needed to.

By the time Carlitos was a teenager, he was spending every weekend at one of the many unsanctioned racetracks that dotted the state of Veracruz, watching the quarter horses run. One day, Carlitos was strutting around the track when he came across a man lying in the grass. The man introduced himself as a businessman from Monterrey, and he asked Carlitos about a quarter-horse ranch his family owned in rural Villarín. The sprawling property included a two-story house, horse stables, and, half a mile down the road, a quarter-horse bush track, perfect for match racing. But his dad had let them fall into disrepair, Carlitos explained.

The man seemed interested. He invited Carlitos to have breakfast the next morning. Carlitos agreed.

After his chance encounter with the businessman, Carlitos's friends asked him: Do you know who that was?

"No," Carlitos said.

"He's the boss of Veracruz!" they told him.

That was true. His name was Efraín Teodoro Torres, Z-14. He was a former soldier in the Mexican Army, and he was among the most powerful Zetas, claiming control over the entire state of Veracruz as well as prime Texas borderland. He was responsible for one of the Zetas' many prison breaks, which happened with such frequency that Mexican prison guards were known to jokingly ask the inmates who would be staying for dinner.

The next morning, Carlitos and Fourteen had breakfast and drove to the abandoned ranch. Fourteen asked what kind of resources Carlitos would need to make the place suitable for the horses of a "plaza boss," the title the cartels give to regional drug capos like Fourteen. Money, Carlitos said, and guys to run it. Fourteen sent both.

Carlitos graduated from high school soon after that, but he had no need for college. Fourteen found him work managing a stolen-credit-card ring, one of the Zeta boss's side businesses. Carlitos did that during the week and spent the weekends at the races. He made sure Fourteen's best horses made it to the track in shape, ready to run against the horses of whichever trafficker he was betting against that day.

It went on like that for a few years. With every race, Carlitos fit more comfortably into the inner circle of the Veracruz gangsters, even though he'd never moved a shipment or pulled a shift protecting a boss. He strutted around the tracks shirtless and traded ballbustings with the highest-ranking Zetas. And each Christmas he found himself at the annual *narco posada,* an elaborate party organized by cartel brass to celebrate the year gone by and ring in the one to come. The Zetas' fêtes were infamous for their abundant buffets of vices—booze, weed, coke, heroin, prostitutes, and gambling. They invited the top norteño and *banda* musicians to perform and gave away cars and jewelry to top-performing employees. The Company bosses also managed to sneak in some business, using the gatherings to assign managers to new plazas and promote loyal workers up the ranks. It was uncommon for outsiders to be invited, but year after year Carlitos was there, the official horseman of the Zetas' Veracruz plaza.

Eventually that role would send Carlitos to roam the stalls at Ruidoso, but to rule them he needed his second half: Fernando. They found each other in Veracruz, at the tracks, bonding over their similarly backdoor paths into the Mexican underworld.

Fernando Garcia Solis was born in Nuevo León, the state in northeastern Mexico anchored by cosmopolitan Monterrey. He moved to Texas when he was three. His dad raised cattle and horses in Mission, Texas, a rural border town, and by age ten Fernando was obsessed with the horses. There was something special about the way the quarter horses moved beneath him, cutting, starting, and stopping like shifty midfielders, driven by native guile.

As a kid, Fernando worked gathering cattle for his dad and taught himself to inject a needle into a horse's jugular vein, a key skill for drawing blood or administering an IV. But his true love was match racing. In grade school, he crossed the border to watch bush races in rural Mexico. In high school, a cousin gave Fernando a horse as a present, and he trained the horse to a victory in its first race. After high school, in 2004, Fernando enrolled in the University of Arizona's racetrack industry program, a course of study devoted entirely to the business of racing horses.

He and his classmates, most of them white, spent their free time at the local tracks. But Fernando introduced them to *real* horse racing the day he invited them to some match races down in Nogales. Nogales, Arizona, is that state's version of Laredo: a humming inland port that, in tandem with its sister city across the border, moves billions of dollars' worth of product, industrial and narcotic, into the United States every year. What Fernando didn't mention was that the races weren't in Arizona. They were in Mexico's Nogales, just across the border. By the time his friends realized they were leaving the United States, it was too late to turn back. "You lied!" one friend shrieked. "You're taking us to Mexico!" Fernando smiled and kept driving.

Fernando and his friends found real estate along the dirt drag strip, bought cold Tecates from a roving vendor, and watched horses named La Burrita and El Zani Saint kick dust down a narrow track, a roving mariachi ensemble filling the quiet between races. With no pari-mutuel window to be found, they slipped Fernando ten bucks to bet with some guys in the crowd. They won more than they lost.

The Mexican match races were Fernando's practicum, where he learned to see and hear and feel things his professors could never teach. They were also how he came to know a valued mentor who went by the name Caine. Caine's real name was Gerardo Ochoa, but when he was a kid, he sold meat on the streets of Veracruz, a job that required shouting to anyone within earshot, *"Carne! Carne!"* He pronounced *carne* as *"cai-ne,"* and the nickname stuck. By the time Fernando met him, around 2005, Caine had traded street meat for large quantities of cocaine, which he trafficked for the Zetas. He offered Fernando work buying horses in the United States and shipping them to Veracruz for the match races.

Soon, Fernando was buying up to thirty yearlings a year for Caine, pulling down five grand a month. He decided to quit school, swapping Arizona's racetrack industry program for Mexico's match-race industry. As he earned Caine's trust, he spent more time at the tracks in Veracruz.

That was Fernando's new classroom. That was where he grew from the skinny, horse-obsessed kid to a bulkier horseman, with broad shoulders and a little perma-smile that portrayed a deep knowledge of the world he'd finally penetrated. That was where he met some real badass Zetas, like Fourteen and Mamito. Soon Fernando was buying horses for Mamito, too.

The tracks of Veracruz were also where Fernando met cool Carlitos, another early-twenty-something horseman on the rise. And it was there that, one afternoon in 2007, everything changed for Carlitos, Fernando, and the balance of power in Los Zetas.

It was springtime. Carlitos and Fernando were out at the races like always, this time at the ranch that Fourteen and Carlitos had refurbished in Villarín. It was six in the evening. The fading sunlight was filled with smoke from a grill. The races were over, but Carlitos was lingering near the track, clutching a bag Fourteen had asked him to hold. The bag was filled with grenades and a pistol. Fourteen was off collecting a bet somewhere nearby, flanked by a dozen bodyguards. Fernando was standing down the track.

As the sun fell, Carlitos and Fernando saw a man they didn't recognize walking straight down the middle of the track toward Fourteen. "You won't outlive this one," the man yelled. He started shooting.

Bullets flew. Fernando ran from the track and hid at a nearby elementary school, before fleeing back to the States. Carlitos hit the deck and then bailed. It didn't take long for the news to trickle out: Fourteen, the plaza boss of Veracruz and Carlitos's mentor and protector, was dead.

After the shooting, Carlitos hid out at the ranch of a wealthy Veracruz businessman he'd met at the tracks. His name was Francisco Colorado Cessa, and he, too, would become an important presence in the Ruidoso sale barns. But for the moment, he was just Carlitos's compadre, another older, successful man who had helped fill the void left by Carlitos's dad.

One day, a maroon diesel truck pulled up to Colorado's ranch, and out stepped Forty. Carlitos had met Forty once, at the races in Tuxpan, and had left under the impression that Forty was not a fan. Carlitos had been wandering around the track shirtless that day. Forty demanded that Carlitos put on a shirt. Forty asked, Are you a man or a clown? Carlitos put his shirt on.

Back then, Carlitos needn't worry. Fourteen, an original Zeta and the boss of Veracruz, could protect him. But now Fourteen was dead. And word around Veracruz was that Forty had dispatched the sicario who killed him.

A rift had developed within the Zetas. On one side were the original Zs, defected soldiers like Mamito and Fourteen who favored a more traditional business model and military practices. On the other side were Forty and Forty-Two, who wanted to split from the Gulf Cartel and preferred a more diverse portfolio of crimes, especially extortion and human smuggling. Forty had been lusting after Veracruz, and Fourteen had even caught Forty stalking around there a couple of times and told him to leave.

Now Fourteen was dead. There was one less traditionalist in Forty's way. And he had Veracruz all to himself.

At the ranch, Forty introduced himself as the new plaza boss. Carlitos and Colorado knew that Forty had already killed at least one of Fourteen's associates, apparently as a way of letting the traffickers in town know what would happen if they questioned the transfer of power under way. So they pledged fealty to the new boss, leading him around the ranch, showing him the cattle, stopping to feed the fat catfish that gulped at the surface of the ponds.

Just like that, Carlitos worked for Forty. Now he was traveling to races all across northern Mexico, helping manage Forty's horses when they ran against gangsters in Saltillo or Nuevo Laredo or Monclova. He also started attending races in the United States, including Tempting Dash's half-million-dollar win, where he introduced himself to Forty's brother José. José didn't know Carlitos and started asking around about the slick youngster in the winner's circle. But whether José knew it or not, Carlitos was about to become a key player in Forty's horse business.

By Labor Day 2010, Forty had become skeptical of Ramiro, whom he found disorganized, and whom he feared could be cooperating with law enforcement. So before the Ruidoso auction, Forty called Carlitos and Ramiro to a meeting in Mexico, where he ordered Ramiro to turn over ownership records for many of his horses.

Ramiro was out; the only question was what Forty would do

with him. Carlitos was in. He offered Fernando five grand a month, plus track earnings and other bonuses, to serve as his deputy and translator. Fernando didn't hesitate; he was in, too.

So here they were, Carlitos and Fernando, in the mountains of New Mexico, striding up and down dim rows of stalls, peering through the bars at some of the most promising—and most expensive—young quarter horses in existence. In a way, it was just another weekend with the horses, which is how they'd spent nearly every weekend of their young lives. In other ways, it was their biggest weekend ever, because Forty was their biggest client ever.

Forty's brother José would join them at the auction that night, which sucked. If there was a meeting between José and Forty discussing his new role, Carlitos and Fernando never knew of it. All they knew was that "the clean brother" they'd heard so much about had quit bricklaying to pursue life as a horseman full-time. Great for him, they thought, but shitty for them. When José wasn't around, they could move through the auction house freer of suspicion, just as Ramiro had done for years. Yes, they were making money off their relationship with one of Mexico's most feared criminals, but so was everyone else in the auction house, from the poor Mexican sweeping shit from the stalls to every rich old white dude on the grounds. *Laundering* Forty's money? They were *taking* Forty's money, in exchange for services rendered.

The presence of José complicated that equation. They knew how badly the feds wanted Forty, and they figured the feds might use José to get to him. So *with* José around, Carlitos and Fernando weren't just another pair of Mexicans with access to big Mexican money. They were José's guys, which made them Forty's guys, which was a riskier distinction.

They tried not to stress about it, resigning themselves to the fact that people knew whom they bought for and that law enforcement might one day come knocking. *"No puedes tapar el sol con un dedo,"* they often said. "You can't cover the sun with a finger." But José seemed to wear his concern like a bad cologne. He was paranoid,

Carlitos and Fernando noticed, straining to act as if they weren't all working together. It put them on edge. Carlitos did his best to be polite to the boss's brother, but when José wasn't around he bemoaned the intrusions of that *viejo mierda,* that "shitty old man."

José wasn't with them now, so Carlitos and Fernando floated easily through the main barn, an open-air sanctuary that doubled as a pop-up community center for these morning gatherings. Old cowboys and their sons, and *their* sons, reclined in cushioned patio chairs in the barn's open center, shooting the shit. The patio sets were strategically positioned so they faced the center of the barn, where the cowgirls paraded the horses that Carlitos and Fernando asked to see. They cared mostly about the horses' pedigrees, about the black type under their names in the sales book. But they studied the horses' conformations, too, sketching their invisible lines. They watched the horses' feet, to make sure they fell in line, and watched their heads, to see if they kept their eyes ahead as they walked. They noted the size of their haunches, which they knew acted as the motor of a worthy quarter horse.

Though Fernando was no longer in college, he remained studious. He carried a black spiral notebook in which he scribbled observations about the horses—"bad wheels," "short, short neck," "left toes in," and "right toes out." In the back, he jotted down bits of wisdom he'd found in old magazines and books on horsemanship. "Price does not indicate potential performance," he scribbled at the top. Farther down, he wrote, "Perfect conformation does not make a racehorse." And finally, "Ensure you are inspecting horses that have the genetic ability to run."

There were plenty of those at this sale, and they'd be going for a lot of money—many of them $50,000, some of them $100,000, and one or two that might top $250,000. Not one was out of range for Carlitos and Fernando.

The auction started that night. Like other auction houses, the Ruidoso sale was anchored by two rings where horses preened and people watched them. The one inside, where the seats were cushioned and the auctioneer sat on high, was quiet and studious. The one outside was a party.

It was a series of concentric circles, each rowdier than the next. At the center was the dirt walking ring. Around the outside, people leaned over the railing and reclined in red plastic chairs, studying the horse on deck. Outside *that,* cowboys and cowgirls slugged cans of Coors Light and paid only half attention, bullshitting instead about the Aggies' home opener and the headaches of owning horses. Kids slalomed through the crowds and slept in strollers.

Many of them—perhaps more than ever—were Mexican or Mexican American. Like the states where it was so popular, the sport of cowboys had become increasingly Hispanic over the years. There'd always been Mexicans and Mexican-Americans at sales like this one, but they used to be in the stalls shoveling manure or leading the horses into the ring. Now, more frequently, they were buyers and they were sellers and they were part of the crowd.

Every year, more and more young Mexicans and Mexican-Americans formed that exterior, Coors-chugging ring. Some dressed in traditional norteño cowboy garb, with wide hats and tight jeans and shiny belt buckles the size of pancakes. Others dressed with Carlitos's and Ramiro's more "Narco Polo" flare, in dark jeans and polo shirts; or tight, graphic tees; or button-downs splayed open at the top. They wore no hats—nothing on their heads but enough gel to keep things in place—and they didn't give two shits about the Aggies.

Everyone assumed they were narcos. Even some of the Mexicans assumed the *other* Mexicans were narcos. Partly because some of them *were* narcos. Or at least, like Carlitos and Fernando, they had narcos for clients and confidants.

Because of the region's rich history of ranching and horsemanship, livestock has always been a popular investment vehicle for drug criminals on both sides of the border. In the early 1980s, a powerful Texas rancher was caught bankrolling a weed-smuggling crew nicknamed the "Cowboy Mafia"; he used phantom cattle sales to cover his tracks. In the late 1980s, the federal government hired Tyler Graham's dad to manage a dispersal sale after seizing hundreds of horses from a Mexican drug trafficker. In the mid-2000s, the Treasury Department used the federal Kingpin Act to freeze the assets of multiple Mexican cattle businesses connected to El Chapo's Sinaloa cartel. That same weekend, as Carlitos and Fernando stalked the barns, a New Mexico–based Sinaloa cell was preparing to funnel drug proceeds into quarter horses. And Los Piojos, the gang whose horses had raced past Forty's in Nuevo Laredo, was known to send buyers to the big American auction houses.

In this setting, José, a middle-aged Hispanic man, could reasonably expect to blend in as he took his seat outside, dressed in a work-blue button-down and his trademark white cowboy hat. Still, he tried to keep his distance from his brother's young emissaries, Carlitos and Fernando. He was still new to all this—to letting anything besides his name connect him to his brother. Bricklaying, for all its drudgery, never kept him up nights, never forced him into feints. He was what he was. Now he was someone, something, different.

Carlitos was also just sloppy, at least by José's standards. With Forty's new spending habits, it was hard for Carlitos and Fernando to find businessmen to wire money the way Ramiro had. Carlitos had resorted to smuggling cash into the United States to pay off Forty's bills. To pay off Dashin Follies, the $875,000 mare Tyler and José bid on, Carlitos delivered the final $100,000 in cash to Tyler's ranch.

Tyler would deliver the cash to the auction house. IRS forms would be filled out, suspicions raised. Though the horse wasn't in José's name, José worried it would draw attention to them all. He told Carlitos to open a bank account, so he could deposit the cash there before wiring it to the auction house, or Tyler's ranch, or wherever he owed money.

Along with Carlitos's sloppiness was his swagger. While José tried to stay low-key, favoring muted dress shirts and a quiet disposition, Carlitos kept being Carlitos. He was constantly on his phone and dressed more for Vegas nightclubs than Ruidoso barns, in dark jeans, shiny dress shoes, and a pink button-down splayed open to reveal the necklace that dangled across his chest. As the auction kicked off, José fell back into that familiar role, trying to put space between himself and his brother. The distance was harder than ever to find.

José was a horseman now; he hadn't laid a brick in nine months. He'd spent the spring and summer driving around Texas and Oklahoma, attending auctions, watching races, and checking on his prized colt, Tempting Dash. He also made trips to Mexico, for some mix of business and pleasure. And every time he crossed the river, his association with his brother—and his brother's favorite pastime—followed him.

Late one night in May, as he tried to cross into Eagle Pass from Piedras Negras, the feds had stopped the truck he was riding in with the respected Mexican veterinarian who was caring for Tempting Dash at the time. The agents pulled them into secondary, patted them down, rifled through their pocket trash, and sent them on their way in short order. But six weeks later, José wasn't so lucky. This time, he tried to cross into Laredo on foot. They kept him there for two hours, pestering him with questions about Forty before cutting him loose. At least they let him take his kids' coloring books.

Could he have stopped then? He'd made some money from Tempting Dash's big win, more than he'd made in *years* as a bricklayer. Could he have left Bridge One, walked into downtown Laredo, bought some stationery, scribbled Ramiro and Forty a thank-you note, sold the horse, and lived off the six-figure avalanche in his long-empty bank account? What would Forty—what would the feds—have said to that?

It didn't matter. José didn't stop. After Tempting Dash won, he devoted his life to Tempting Dash. He directed his accountant to keep detailed books, tracking every dollar that flowed in and out of his new LLC. He deposited his $445,000 in winnings, then immediately wrote a check to his brother Rodolfo, who had helped him with Tempting Dash. He paid Chevo, Tempting Dash's trainer, his

$50,000 commission. He paid a $100,000 premium for an insurance policy for Tempting Dash. Finally, José wrote himself and Zulema a check for $100,000, a previously unrivaled hit to their personal wealth.

He hoped to race Tempting Dash, his reigning Colt of the Year, as a three-year-old during this 2010 season. The derbies, for three-year-olds, were less prestigious and generally less lucrative than the futurities. But the big ones still paid out in the seven figures, which could have created some much-needed revenue for José's company, Tremor Enterprises. To increase his chances, he moved Tempting Dash from Chevo's falling-down barns to a larger training center he rented near Austin, and brought in a new trainer from Mexico.

If Forty's plan was to keep pumping tainted drug money into the horse business, José didn't need to win races to stay in the black; the money would just show up one day, floating in a gas tank or obscured in a stackable washer. But there appeared to be some hope, on José's part if not Forty's, that José could keep his new business separate the way he'd always kept his life—connected by blood but with a river between them.

There was a story he could tell himself, similar to the one he'd told his daughter Alex and the one he'd told onstage in Oklahoma: "I got lucky buying that horse." For whatever reason, his brother had directed Ramiro to sell him Tempting Dash for cheap. Tempting Dash won, allowing José to send money to Ramiro, and invest in Tempting Dash's future. If the horse won again—and even if he didn't—Tempting Dash would one day stand as a breeding stallion, potentially throwing off millions of dollars in revenue. And that "clean" revenue would be for *José's* family, not for the Zetas. He wouldn't send it *back* to the cartel so it could further invest in its wars with the government and the Gulf and El Chapo. He'd use it to buy groceries and pay Alex's tuition bill.

Maybe Tempting Dash would one day breed with Forty's horses, including the high-end broodmares Tyler had helped buy at the auction. But that would make Forty José's client, not his co-conspirator. And maybe Tempting Dash's success would lead to José buying more horses to raise, race, and breed himself. But maybe it didn't have to? Maybe once "the babies start popping," as Alex put it, one good stud would be enough.

As the 2010 racing season approached, José asked Tyler to send the vet from Southwest Stallion Station to run the requisite annual tests Tempting Dash would need to race in California that year. Most of the tests had been in place for years. But after the outbreak of piroplasmosis—the tick-borne disease that forced Mexicans to smuggle their horses across the border—health regulators were requiring a piro test. Tyler sent his vet right over, part of his continuing effort to recruit Tempting Dash to Southwest Stallion Station.

Tyler and José didn't talk on the phone much. José was never comfortable on the phone, maybe because of his strong but still accented English, or maybe because phones were untrustworthy. But here was Tyler, calling late on a Friday night. José picked up.

It's Tempting Dash, Tyler said.

The horse had piro.

José, Carlitos, and Fernando drove to Tyler's ranch the next morning. They discussed what would happen next. Tempting Dash would be moved from the nearby ranch where he had been training to a quarantine facility run by the Texas Animal Health Commission. The disease didn't affect every horse it infected, but the most severe cases could lead to chronic fever, swelling, even death. And health officials knew so little about it that they didn't know how risky it would be to put Tempting Dash in a barn, in a saddling paddock, in a starting gate with other valuable horses.

But what about breeding? That's where the real money was anyway, in the years of stud fees stacked against minimal costs and minimal risk of injury. That was where José could create steady income for his new LLC. Now that dream was quarantined as José scrambled to figure out whether health officials would let him even breed Tempting Dash.

In the meantime, racing season had trudged on, without their star colt, who was banned from the track, and without any new revenue. So here was José, in Ruidoso, to watch the auction and watch the races. He couldn't know exactly what kind of business Forty planned to throw his way, since Carlitos and Fernando were in charge of the buying. But once the hands started flying, it started to become obvious: Operativo Huesos was just the beginning.


The emcee introduced each horse slowly, clearly, announcing the hip number, the pedigree, and finally the name. Then, like a SWAT team after a polite knock, the auctioneer stepped in, laying his soothing gibberish between the bids he hoped to attract.

José never raised a hand. Neither did Carlitos or Fernando. It's possible Carlitos had gotten word of what happened at a previous auction, when a bid-spotter, noticing how quickly Carlitos was bit-ing, started playing him against nonexistent bidders to drive up the price. To avoid that and to keep a low profile, Carlitos had hired young Mexican men to bid for him. The only way anyone would know they were the buyers was if they noticed Carlitos snapping photos of the results board after every big purchase, then texting the photos to Forty. José looked on from nearby as Carlitos's guys snapped up horse after horse.

Dreamgirl Jess, sold, $140,000.

Better Part of Valor, bidigun bidigun sold, $100,000.

Too Tempting—

Now here was a horse they would need to get. A full brother to the 2009 Colt of the Year, Tempting Dash. Another breeding from First Down Dash and A Tempting Chick, the California pairing that had resulted in Tempting Dash.

bidigun bidigun ahundredthousand

bidigun bidigun howbout twohundred

bidigun bidigun—

The gavel clapped. They'd just bought Tempting Dash's brother for $300,000. It was the second-highest sale of the weekend. Now they needed to pay for it.


The auction managers had always been lax with Ramiro, who spent big but kept a lower profile. Now Ramiro had mysteriously stopped showing up in the sale barns, and stopped buying big when he did.

Wherever Ramiro was, his replacements were different animals. Carlitos and Fernando were spending even bigger than Ramiro, announcing before the auction that they planned to spend millions on behalf of their Mexican clients. José was friendlier and low-key like Ramiro, but he had been winning the sport's biggest races and accepting industry awards, injuring the cowboys' pride in a way Ramiro never had. José also had a last name that, when typed into Google, took all the guesswork out of which criminal this crew was buying for. In the upper echelons of the quarter-horse industry, where most gringos spoke a little Spanish, Miguel "Z-40" Treviño and Los Zetas were becoming household names. And the auction managers were starting to worry.

For the most part, theirs wasn't some moral anxiety over the source of the money or the blood spilled in its collection. They weren't even especially scared about getting mixed up with violent drug criminals, figuring they were insulated by the drug war's rules of engagement. It was all business: with every debt that mounted, every penny owed by Ramiro or Carlitos or Fernando or José, the auction managers worried that the real buyers would be arrested or killed, or simply become disinterested in horse racing and abandon their unpaid debts.

Before the Ruidoso sale, the industry had considered adopting new rules specifically for Carlitos and Fernando, including charging them interest on unpaid debts. In the end, they told the group they wouldn't allow them to remove any horses from the property until all of the horses were paid off—a change in protocol from the more lenient Ramiro days.

Forty had plenty of money to spend, but it was stacked in Cuno's stash houses; as flexible as the auction house was, it would not accept payment in the form of vacuum-sealed cash dumped from the gas tank of a Toyota Tundra. Nor could Forty get the money from José's new company, whose coffers had dwindled to about thirty-five thousand dollars.

With Ramiro out of the picture, they no longer had access to the Monterrey exchange house that had reliably wired money after so many auctions. They'd used another Mexican businessman for a while, a small-time customs broker who wired money from his accounts, apparently in exchange for cash delivered in Mexico. But he'd gotten spooked and ducked out.

They needed a new business partner. So Carlitos came up with a plan. He enlisted Francisco Colorado, his millionaire compadre from Veracruz, to front the money. Theoretically, Colorado could later be repaid with drug money, which he could mix into the cash flow of his oil business, although whether or how he was actually repaid would remain a mystery. Either way, Colorado's money was "clean," and Carlitos planned on spending a lot of it.

He dispatched two young Mexican workers to the auction house to ensure that their bids would be honored when the auction started. Carlitos has taken on Ramiro's Mexican clients, they said, and like Ramiro, Carlitos was good for the money. The auction-house manager, knowing the group would spend big, had no choice but to let them bid, but he tried to set some boundaries. You can spend a million dollars, he told them, but after that, we'll need some form of payment before you keep bidding. Fine, they said, but then Carlitos blew past a million so fast that the auction manager called his guys back into the office and demanded proof that they could pay. They called his bluff. They told the guy they had the money locked in their truck, and the auction house relented. Carlitos and Fernando kept bidding.

By the end of the auction, the group had bought twenty-three horses. That included fifteen for more than $50,000 and $300,000 for Too Tempting. For the second auction in a row, they also bought the sale topper: $340,000 for a Corona Cartel colt named Mi Flash.

If they did have cash in the truck, they didn't get to break it out. Colorado showed up at the auction house to deliver a check the next morning. He made it out for $2.3 million.

They'd spent almost five times as much as the next-biggest buyer—such a spending spree that it forced the auction house to revive a dying tradition. In the past, whoever spent the most money got a trophy—a small bronze horse mounted by a bronze jockey. Over the years, as the industry became more sophisticated, breeders were partnering up, buying shares of each other's horses, or using straw buyers like Ramiro. It wasn't always easy to tell exactly who'd spent the most. The auction house hadn't given out a trophy in years.

But they still had a few lying around. They gave one to Colorado, watched him sign his check, and sent him on his way.

# CHAPTER TWELVE
## MOUNTAIN GODS

RUIDOSO, NEW MEXICO
September 2010

The sun rose over the mountains and perched itself high above the track. Down below, maintenance workers swept up popcorn remnants and discarded betting tickets from the day before. It was quiet for now, the morning silence disturbed only occasionally by the chatter of exercise riders, their horses bouncing through the fine dunes of red dirt. As the morning progressed, the quiet was occasionally disrupted by something less innocent, the sound of a freight train or a gathering storm. A horse barreling past at full clip. A jockey scrunched low in jeans and a sweatshirt.

It was Labor Day, the biggest day on the quarter-horse-racing calendar. The 2010 All American Futurity would be run that afternoon, with two million dollars up for grabs, including a million for the winning owner. All weekend long, Carlitos, Fernando, and José, no matter how far they sat from each other, had basically told the industry: We're in charge now. They didn't plan on stopping anytime soon.

After replacing Ramiro, Carlitos and Fernando weren't only charged with buying Forty's horses in the States. They were also responsible for training and racing the ones he already owned.

Early in 2010, they'd taken inventory. Several of Forty's horses were stabled at a training center in Arizona. Carlitos and Fernando drove there before the season to take stock. They found an unpaid bill and a stable full of neglected horses—skinny, mangy, with dinged-up and weary legs that hadn't been properly iced and wrapped after running. Fernando and Carlitos cut the trainer a check for thirteen grand and hauled the horses to Tularosa, New Mexico, an impoverished village down the hill from Ruidoso that offered cheap housing for track workers and ample space for trainers to exercise their horses. They rented some space at a training center and went to work.

They started by changing the horses' names. That was another thing Forty did that was a departure from his more low-key predecessors: changing horses' names to make them more personal. It was a bizarre strategy. The naming conventions in horse racing are designed to capitalize on pedigree, paying homage to the sire, the dam, or both. Tempting Dash, for instance, was a cross between sire First Down Dash and dam A Tempting Chick.

Forty had no interest in convention. So one day that spring, Carlitos, Fernando, and José had climbed into José's blue Silverado and driven from Tularosa to Amarillo, Texas, to the offices of the American Quarter Horse Association, to set about changing some horse names. José, at least, was easier to be around in the privacy of a road trip, where he couldn't pretend not to know them. Carlitos and he managed to get along, and over lunch at Red Lobster, José even opened up a little about his brother. He recalled a young Forty pointing to a corner drug pusher and bragging that one day, the corner boy would work for him. José also told Carlitos and Fernando how Forty, an avid hunter since youth, had always been a great shot.

In Amarillo, they got down to business. Fernando had brought along a three-ring binder filled with the original registration papers for each horse in training in New Mexico. They filed into an office, where an AQHA staffer would type the new names into the database, and Carlitos started rattling off new names. He named horses after sports cars or girlfriends or trivia relevant only to them. Sometimes the new names even tipped off who the real owners were, pedigrees be damned. A well-bred horse named One Famous Patriot became Tamaulipas Boy, a tribute to the Treviño family's home state. One Proud Feature became Forty Force. Racing Down a Dream became Number One Cartel.

Eventually they got to a promising colt named Maverick Perry. Ramiro had paid eighty-one thousand dollars for the horse as a yearling the previous fall, part of an eighteen-horse buying spree that cost Forty almost half a million dollars. The horse's name was a tribute to his high-dollar sire, Mr Jess Perry, and they had high hopes that he could become the group's next Tempting Dash—the next horse to win big on the tracks and maybe in the stud barn.

Carlitos was out of cool names, so Fernando blurted out, "Mr Piloto"—taking the "Mr" from Mr Jess Perry and "Piloto," the Spanish word for "pilot," from his dam, Ms Pilot Point. It didn't have the same ring as "Number One Cartel," but Carlitos agreed. Mr Piloto it was.

Back in Tularosa, Carlitos tried to train Mr Piloto himself for a few months, but all spring, the horse failed to qualify for any of the big-money races at Ruidoso. The rest of the horses struggled, too, at tracks all across the country. Then, as the summer plodded toward fall, Carlitos, whose visa had expired, went back to Mexico to spend time with Forty. By then, Carlitos had graduated from merely a capable manager of the horse business to a trusted confidant of Forty's. They still mostly bonded over horses, but Forty also enlisted Carlitos in tasks related to his core business, dispatching him to Brazil to procure a new warehouse and to Veracruz for new ranches. He promised to pay Carlitos in bricks of cocaine, which would put him on the path to his own trafficking revenue.

With Carlitos in Mexico, Fernando took charge in New Mexico. As a teenager, Fernando had visited Ruidoso and vowed to win the

All American one day. Now here he was, a college dropout in charge of his own New Mexico stables. He looked at the two dozen horses, bred from some of the best bloodlines in the business, owned by one of the biggest drug lords in Mexico, and he thought, *This is my chance.*

He went to work on Mr Piloto. He ramped up the colt's regimen and slowly improved his time enough to enter him into the trials of the All American. Then something unexpected happened: Mr Piloto qualified. He was the slowest qualifier, and he was the long shot at 22 to 1. Still, his place in the sport's richest race gave Forty another opportunity to win.

It also gave him a chance to officially expand José's involvement beyond Tempting Dash. Although José had been helping out—attending auctions, changing horse names, ensuring that Carlitos didn't make an ass of himself—so far, José's company, Tremor Enterprises, owned only one horse: Tempting Dash. Most of the horses Forty and his operatives had amassed were technically owned by small front companies started by smaller fish like Carlitos, Fernando, and other trusted associates. The less activity that occurred in the Treviño name, the better—until that activity could rake in some money.

Mr Piloto was technically owned by Fernando, and he was proud of that, unsavory connections be damned. But before the big race, Carlitos instructed Fernando to transfer the horse into the name of José's company, and to backdate the transfer so it looked as if José had bought the horse *before* he qualified. Then, to keep things quiet, they asked Fernando to take a backseat to a "program trainer"—a well-known and respected trainer who could wave to the cameras on race day.

Fernando was pissed. He worried that the transaction between his company and José's would raise red flags. And he wanted credit for the horse's success. But what could he do? He was pulling down five grand a month, straight cash, training and managing the Company's horses, which happened to be the best horses in the business. José also cut him a check for one hundred thousand dollars, in exchange for giving up the horse he'd trained into relevance. Fernando said OK, transferred the horse, and deposited the money whenever, and however, it came.


The day of the All American, José arrived at the track early, well before Mr Piloto's race, to catch the handful of lesser, lower-stakes races. He knew to get there early because on All American day, the place filled up, a rising tide of cowboys until the two-million-dollar futurity that afternoon, when the track would be standing room only.

The track was divided neatly by class. The casino, ringing with slots and flickering with horse races from around the world, was down near the starting gate, offering its hunched denizens no view of the track. Next, in the middle of the track, came the free bleachers, their sticky concrete baking in the sun. Closest to the finish line was the Jockey Club, a members-only loge that offered the best seats in the house, if you could put up with the white tablecloths and the whiff of thoroughbred exclusivity. Many of the real cowboys couldn't.

For them, the best real estate was the Turf Club. That's where José spent a lot of his time at Ruidoso. Overlooking the home stretch, the Turf Club required a twenty-dollar ticket and offered reserved seating. But it also offered old leather chairs and a humming bar and waitresses who, before the crowd showed up, rolled silverware and gave each other shit in an even mix of Spanish and English.

The sport of bullshittin'—that might be a more accurate name for quarter-horse racing, at least when viewed from inside the Turf Club on a big race weekend. There were ten races that afternoon, but most were cheap-claiming races, and each took only twelve or twenty or forty seconds, spread fifteen minutes apart. That left a lot of time for bullshittin'. The old-timers studied their race books, looking for the jockey that had been running well, the good-ol'-boy trainer, the pedigrees they recognized. They alternately expressed confidence and bewilderment before moseying to one of the several betting windows, where they rattled off their bets —*Five-dollar box with 3-7-6 plus ten on the 3 to win and . . .* —as fast as the clerk behind the pari-mutuel machine could plug them in.

José wasn't much of a bullshitter, but he was becoming more comfortable in environments like this. He dressed the part, in his crisp blue shirt and his trusty white cowboy hat, and schmoozed with other owners and breeders—asking about their families, telling them about his.

The day of the All American, he fled the Turf Club's chaos early. He walked downstairs and through the dark, cold tunnel that led under the track and into the infield, crossing beneath the invisible border that separated the outsiders from the insiders. He hung on the rail for a while, chatting with Tyler and watching the early races. Then, as the big race neared, he found his way to the saddling paddock, the half-circle of empty stalls where trainers would do their final preparations before the race.

He was alone this time, without his wife or kids. Zulema's new job might have had something to do with that. After several years at the temp agency, she had finally landed a steadier job. She'd started in the late spring, as Tempting Dash's prospects as a racehorse and breeder were dimming. She was now a customer support coordinator at Ernst & Young, the $20 billion tax consultancy. She made $29,000 a year.

In the saddling paddock, everything went quiet. A small crowd gathered on a grassy knoll that formed an organic grandstand looking down on the stalls. They were the connections—the friends and family of each horse's owner, trainer, and breeder—and they knew what was at stake.

For the owners, it was one of the season's last chances at life-changing, business-sustaining victory—a million-dollar check, a bold-faced win on the résumé, future earnings as a breeder, and all the bragging rights the sport had to offer.

For the trainers, winning the All American would mean all the same bragging rights, 10 percent of the winnings, and a deluge of job offers from the sport's best owners. It was a career maker, the win after which all the best trainers lusted most. The race's best storyline was whether the sport's top trainer, Paul Jones, would win his fourth All American, or whether his rival, Blane Wood, could finally capture his first.

The realities of the sport were also setting in, as trainers slipped bright-colored blinker hoods over their horses' faces, stroking and assuring. Horses go down, horses break down, especially here in the thin mountain air. All across horse racing, animals were breaking down at such alarming rates that Congress had recently pressured the industry to take steps to make it safer. That included cracking down on doping, which experts believed was masking small injuries, forcing horses to run hurt, and leading the horses to snap limbs and otherwise fall apart.

The sport talked a lot about change, but at almost seven thousand feet, Ruidoso on race day could feel like the waiting room of a vet hospital—a bunch of people hoping for the best, fearing the worst, and too often witnessing a horse dying on the track. Roughly a thousand horses died on racetracks every year, and no track had more serious incidents than Ruidoso. The season before, kids hanging on the rail had witnessed multiple horses go down, including one they watched be euthanized on the track. Not today, the trainers seemed to be saying as they patted haunches.

The jockeys flung themselves aboard, which sucked even more chatter out of the place. The jockeys trotting the horses toward the track were the sport's very best. They were gritty, wispy riders, a mix of southwestern cowboys and Mexican immigrants whose heritage reflected the sport's roots. Finally, they stood to make some real cash. So many afternoons, they punished their bony bodies for fifty or eighty dollars guaranteed. Even if they managed to *win,* the majority of races were small-time claiming races, the low-rent races that keep the tracks open and busy. In a claiming race, the owners agree to offer their horses for sale for the same amount as the purse. In quarter-horse racing, that's often just a few thousand dollars, meaning the horses are untested and slow. The payout for the winning jockey is often just a few hundred bucks.

In almost every race, the reward simply doesn't warrant the risk.

Like horses, jockeys frequently go down, especially on the accident-prone tracks of New Mexico. Their horses crumple beneath them and the jockeys hit the deck, breaking their thinly protected bones, or worse. Earlier that year, at a different track in New Mexico, a jockey had been crushed beneath his horse and suffered a deadly head injury. Another jockey, in southern New Mexico, had suffered a broken back and a ruptured aorta, barely—miraculously, his family thought—surviving. Two weeks later, at the same track, another jockey broke her back and woke up from surgery with two rods, four hooks, and eight screws holding her spine together. She was back racing three months later, for purses so small it was difficult to make a living without winning one of a handful of big races.

Mr Piloto's jockey was a vet named Esgar Ramirez, who grew up on both sides of the border between El Paso, Texas, and Juárez, Mexico. He was a fixture at the New Mexico tracks, as was his brother, Raul, who worked on the backside. They were pros, and Raul at least had experience appeasing these kinds of owners; over the years he'd trained horses for a group of narcos from El Chapo's Sinaloa cartel. Now he and his brother had a new owner and a chance to win the All American. José watched as Esgar bounced Mr Piloto toward the starting gate.

As the horses loaded up, José found his spot against the rail. Carlitos was close by, his black suit jacket baking in the sun, and Fernando wasn't far away. Tyler Graham joined them, too. With several of the group's horses now residing in his stables, he seemed like a shoe-in to stand Tempting Dash as a stallion. But recruiters know to never leave their prospects alone with other suitors. Plus, with Mr Piloto in the All American finals, there was another potential stud on Tyler's radar. Being there was Tyler's job.

■ ■ ■

NAVA, COAHUILA, MEXICO
September 2010

That afternoon, Forty's men crowded into the living room of a house in Nava, a small town on the scrubby outskirts of Piedras

Negras. One of the ranches would have been more fitting, not to mention more spacious, but on the day of the big race, Forty called the Piedras Negras plaza team to this safe house to watch.

The Company kept a few small safe houses in the area, places mostly distinguished for their lack of use; since the Zetas were rarely there, no one expected them to be there. Why Forty chose a particular safe house to gather for a particular occasion was usually a mystery, but those choices were never questioned. The safe house had what they needed anyway—beer, Internet access, and a fifty-five-inch flatscreen.

The crowd formed just as the start time of the All American Futurity approached: Forty; his brother Omar, Z-42; Poncho and his team of traffickers; and a squadron of sicarios. Security forces in armored trucks were parked on the nearby highways and on the narrow streets leading to the neighborhood, where even more armed guards roamed the street and protected the house.

Inside, the anxiety surged as they angled for views of the prerace coverage. The anxiety always surged when Forty was around. The Americans had recently offered a reward of five million dollars for information leading to his capture. Anyone here, or any of the soldiers outside, could tip off a U.S. agent to Forty's whereabouts and have a chance to cash in.

Even then, it was a long shot that Forty would actually get caught. The Americans would have to tip off the Mexican government, which would have to dispatch the nearest military squadron, the members of which Forty may or may not have on his payroll. There was always a chance he did. But some pockets of the Mexican military were more bribable than others, so the narcos in his presence worried that while the horses roared from the gates on the flatscreen, the Mexican Navy might storm the gates of their so-called safe house.

Then there was the anxiety of the race itself. Though only Forty owned the horse, Mr Piloto represented the Company in a way, and offered another small way to proclaim its dominance. Plus, if he won, they could count on Forty to throw a party. The horses loaded up and the safe house fell quiet.

■ ■ ■

RUIDOSO, NEW MEXICO
September 2010

The gates flew open. Mr Piloto was positioned all the way to the outside. He got out clean enough. But as the favorites bunched toward the inside, Mr Piloto swung even farther out wide, practically grazing the outside rail. The path created unnecessary distance for a horse considered one of the field's slowest, but before long he looked to be gaining ground.

The horses blazed through the finish line and bounced along the track, a murmur rippled through the stands: *Who won?* As the horses slowed and were led back toward the paddock, José walked onto the track and clutched Mr Piloto's reins. Along with everyone else, he watched the giant infield scoreboard that would display the finish order.

It was a minute that felt like ten, but eventually the scoreboard lit up, and someone let out a shriek, and there it was at the top: number 9. Mr Piloto had won by less than a nose, the second-closest win in the race's history.

José shook his fist and Carlitos bounded into view, his suit jacket soaring behind him like a cape. José reached into his pocket, pulled out his cellphone, and dialed.

■ ■ ■

NAVA, COAHUILA
September 2010

Forty and his men leapt into each other's arms, whooping loudly enough to make the house feel a little less secure. They stayed glued to the flatscreen, where José was taking his place in the winner's circle.

My brother, the bricklayer, Forty told the group. I bet he never thought he'd be there.

Forty called for wine and whiskey then, and they drank it hard and long enough that it made sense for them to just stay the night, crashing on whatever soft surface they could find.

■ ■ ■

RUIDOSO, NEW MEXICO
September 2010

After the race, Tyler left the track and drove into central Ruidoso to meet up with José. Mr Piloto may have been a long shot, but now he was another black-type colt that could one day stand as a stud at Tyler's resurgent stallion farm—*if* Tyler could stay in José's inner circle. Currently, that inner circle was on its way to drink and gamble in celebration, so Tyler was on his way, too.

He cruised down the town's main two-lane road, where West Texas tourists browsed boutiques stuffed with the chunkiest turquoise jewelry and geometrical-print clothes—inspired, if rarely purchased, by the Mescalero Apache Indians who once settled and defended these mountaintops. He passed chain motels and falling-down lodges where many of the workaday horsemen would sleep that weekend. He kept driving.

He pulled off the main road and climbed toward the Inn of the Mountain Gods Resort & Casino, a mountaintop resort on a 460,000-acre Apache reservation hidden in the trees that abut Lincoln National Forest. Celebrating with José required celebrating with Carlitos and Fernando, too, but Tyler knew it was good for business. Back in the winter, the group had shipped some more horses to Tyler's ranch in Elgin. Not long after that, Carlitos started visiting Elgin to check on them.

Where José tried to maintain the veneer of rookie horseman, Carlitos made no secret of his ambitions to rule Tyler's world. He'd approached the auction manager at Heritage Place and announced plans to put together a million-dollar buying syndicate for upcoming auctions. On Forty's behalf, he'd purchased multiple breedings to the sport's most expensive stallion, Corona Cartel, at thirty-five grand a pop. He crossed the border frequently, Tyler had learned, sometimes to deliver large cash payments to stud farms where he'd purchased breedings. Tyler knew him to bet big at the races, at the blackjack table, and on any subject that could be settled with a cash wager. For these purposes and others, he carried tens of thousands of dollars in his shaving kit. Once, Tyler had watched Carlitos pull a hundred grand from a backpack in the cab of the pickup he was driving. Tyler had seen several other backpacks in there, too. None of them looked empty.

At the casino, Tyler found the group, and they huddled around the craps table and celebrated—swilling drinks, throwing dice, and recounting the race. Even José was slowly shedding his modest-laborer's skin, talking up their success and allowing himself to bask in it.

But the group also had a business decision to make. The careers of great horses don't end like the careers of great human athletes, hanging on until the last fiber of ability is wrung from their bodies. There are calculations. The group needed to decide: Was barely winning the sport's biggest race enough to convince breeders to pair their best mares with Mr Piloto? If they decided it was, they would retire him, truck him straight to Tyler's ranch in Elgin, and start lining up breedings in hopes of turning out future winners. If it wasn't, they would run him again in one of the season's last races, the Golden State Futurity in California. They could also run him the next year as a three-year-old and maybe notch a couple more big wins—and cash a couple more of those big checks—before retiring him into the stud life.

The debate raged on. Tyler knew where he stood. Yeah, the horse had just won the All American. But he'd been the slowest qualifier among the finalists and was among the slowest winners in the race's history. Without some more impressive running on his résumé, potential breeders might smell a fluke and steer clear. So he told the guys: take Mr Piloto to California, run him there, and then we'll talk again. José agreed.

Carlitos had a different idea. Carlitos wanted to retire him right away and start racking up stud fees. After the craps game dissipated, Carlitos found José in the bar. He was sitting with a new member of the crew, whom Tyler knew only as El Negro. He seemed to be some sort of bodyguard or lookout, often ducking into rooms ahead of José to check them out. Carlitos waved them over, and they stepped outside. Tyler, who'd been gambling with them, joined the group outside.

As they debated the merits of each choice, Carlitos pulled out his phone. He was always on his Nextel. He never said whom he was talking to, but whoever it was seemed to be in charge. And whoever it was apparently had the power to settle the debate. He sided with José and Tyler: they would run Mr Piloto in California. For José, it meant another shot at a big win by a runner in his name. For Tyler, it meant another potential stud in his barn.

September 2010 had the makings of a good month for Tyler. In a few days he would touch down in Las Vegas for his bachelor party. Two weeks after that he would stand across from his girlfriend— a local girl who'd known him since his days under the lights at Wildcat Stadium—and become a husband, an important step if he wanted to prolong the Graham name and legacy. First, though, he'd finish his weekend of work, schmoozing his new clients in the sports bar adjacent to the casino.

The booze hit everyone a little extra hard in the mountains. It certainly seemed to hit José, who celebrated more than usual and looked a little wobbly. At one point, he took a stumble. An older guy, who looked to be a native Apache, tried to help José up, and José got defensive and swung his arms at the dude. The bouncer broke it up and threatened to toss José, but things settled down and everyone went back to their drinks. A little drama to cap a dramatic day. Even more so for Tyler, who was the only one in the bar who recognized the FBI agent sitting a few tables away.

# CHAPTER THIRTEEN

## FMES

CUE PEPPY BUT NONINTRUSIVE JAZZ MUSIC

INT. JAILHOUSE INTERVIEW ROOM—DAY

We see a young Hispanic man, the BAD GUY, slumped over a metal table in an orange jumpsuit. Across the table, we see a strapping, goateed DEA AGENT in khakis and a T-shirt that reads "DEA." He leans back in his chair, smirking in ecstasy.

> NARRATOR
> You love your job. They give you a shiny badge to wear on your belt, your own gun, and plenty of "bad guys" like this one to chase. Sometimes you even get to travel to Mexico, to tell important Mexicans what's wrong with Mexico. But sometimes . . .

INT. JAILHOUSE INTERVIEW ROOM—CONT.

Four more agents burst into the room. They look identical to one another, but each shirt reads something dif-

ferent: "FBI," "HSI," "IRS," and "CBP." The DEA agent
cranes his neck to see who's interrupting his special
moment. His chair tips backward; he falls to the ground.
Everyone POINTS and LAUGHS, including the BAD GUY.

> NARRATOR
Sometimes the pursuit of justice interrupts your moments
of ecstasy, leaving you feeling angry, possessive, and
petulant. But it's not you. It's your FMES—Fragile Male
Ego Syndrome. FMES is a proven medical condition affect-
ing 107 percent of male federal agents who work drug
cases. Symptoms include a refusal to share intelligence
or informants; nighttime urges to indict another agent's
informant; detailed thoughts of sabotaging colleagues'
cases; and a waning interest in truth, justice, and the
law.

INT. JAILHOUSE INTERVIEW ROOM—CONT.

The agents, bloodied from an apparent fight, are pointing their guns at each other now. The BAD GUY shakes his
head, removes a gun from an agent's holster, and walks
unnoticed out of the room.

> NARRATOR
So talk to your doctor about FMES. He will tell you
there is no treatment except retirement, and probably
not even that.

FADE TO BLACK

■ ■ ■

To understand just how high-stakes the game José, Carlitos, and
Fernando were playing in Ruidoso, it helps to know how it came to
be a gamble at all.

There was a time when their success as horsemen might have
been of little interest to federal law enforcement. A violent criminal
like Forty would have been a target of the Mexican government or

even the FBI. The cocaine he smuggled across would have titillated United States Customs agents, who until the 1970s were the federal government's main combatants in the still undeclared war on drugs. Once the coke made it to American streets, local drug cops may have busted some heads. But there existed few, if any, cops—local, state, or federal—who might have taken an interest in the shopping sprees of a few big-spending quarter-horse men.

That era is a quaint memory now, fading in the shadow of prairie-land prison towers. In the late 1960s, conservative politicians, led by President Richard Nixon, realized that cracking down on drug users—particularly black heroin users and long-haired pot smokers—scored major political points. They rolled back treatment programs and demonized users, but that was just their opening number. It was the invitation they extended to federal law enforcement that truly ushered in a new reality.

Congress passed laws beefing up the feds' wiretapping capabilities, and making it easier for them to seize money and property, and to target not only drug dealers but also their families and businesses. In 1973, at Nixon's behest, lawmakers created the Drug Enforcement Administration (DEA), foisting their political war on the Department of Justice.

Congress charged the new agency with hunting the biggest targets, but DEA agents struggled to move beyond street-level users and dealers, making mostly small-time possession cases. It was only as federal drug-enforcement spending swelled—from $65 million in 1969 to $719 million in 1974—that the DEA made its presence felt. They started in South Florida, the Colombians' preferred smuggling route at the time. By 1974, the DEA had so many agents in its overcrowded Miami headquarters that they overloaded its rooftop parking lot—and it collapsed, killing four employees inside.

The 1980s only invited more federal actors into lawmakers' cleverly choreographed stage play. At President Ronald Reagan's direction, the FBI for the first time enlisted agents in the drug war, where they would use expanded racketeering laws to work international drug gangs the way they did the American mob. Before long, FBI agents would be working drugs as much as any other crime.

So that brought the FBI to the battlefield, to chase Colombians around Miami alongside DEA narcs and Customs and Border Patrol agents. It was around then that Congress passed sentencing-reform laws that established "mandatory minimum" sentences for drug offenders, including life in prison for some drug dealers. That inspired more local cops to take their drug cases federal, knowing their targets would go down for longer periods. Meanwhile, Associate Attorney General Rudolph Giuliani recruited "hard chargers" to the nation's federal prosecutor offices, offering each new field agent a more aggressive legal partner on the way to serious convictions.

The result was a sprawling new sandbox for the nation's lawmen, brimming with colorful toys they could use to catch the Bad Guys. But it was still only *one* sandbox. So they fought. Along the border, Customs and DEA "thirsted for each other's blood, jurisdiction, and funding," writes journalist Dan Baum in *Smoke and Mirrors,* his searing history of drug-war politics. In New York and Texas, FBI and DEA agents working the same smuggling ring fought to an impasse that had to be settled in a sit-down with Giuliani. In Miami, the rivalry grew so bitter that a convicted trafficker was called before Congress to detail how the agents handling him had withheld intelligence from one another, jeopardizing their investigations in service of their egos.

Rather than admit the folly in using different agencies to investigate the same targets, the government expanded the alphabet-soup approach. Officials created a variety of interagency task forces, incentivizing cooperating with shared and increased funding. Among the biggest were the Organized Crime Drug Enforcement Task Forces, a Justice Department program that teams up investigators from every federal law enforcement agency in existence, plus local and state cops. Started in the early 1980s, the program now eats up a half billion federal dollars annually.

In the 1990s, cooperation became especially paramount along the southwest border, where Mexican cartels were thriving. But even cooperation couldn't be done cooperatively. The DEA, the Office of National Drug Control Policy, and the Department of Homeland Security—a federal agency founded in the name of fighting terrorism—each formed task forces with the goal of stemming the flow of drugs across the border.

The drugs kept flowing. So did the rivalries. Across the Southwest, many counternarcotics agents, current and former, don't even pretend to like or respect their counterparts. FBI agents, DEA agents, ICE agents, prosecutors—they're all armed with stories about the competing agent or prosecutor who refused to share intelligence, denied access to a source, or otherwise interfered with an investigation. A few years ago in Dallas, a defense lawyer orchestrated a meeting between his client, a trafficker, and some federal agents. When two rival agents couldn't agree over which questions were fair game, a "hold me back, bro" fight broke out in the parking lot.

Agents like to say they're just being protective of their sources, whose identity, safety, and usefulness could be risked by exposing them to other investigators. Which is often true. More often, the lack of cooperation signals a flare-up of Fragile Male Ego Syndrome, or FMES, as one former senior DEA agent calls it. (Despite the name, women agents can suffer from it, too.) It's a desire to be first, to be best, by agents who view their investigations as a televised blood sport in which they are the stars.

It fits with the image of agents that exists in popular culture, in which the "good guys" romp around soundstages "hunting bad guys," with body doubles standing by for the dangerous stuff. Too often, it turns out, the image mirrors reality, with agents using their interview rooms and courtrooms as battlefields on which they might add adventure and glory and some meaning to their lives. The pursuit of the actual justice is secondary, at best, especially when a Bad Guy like Forty happens to come loping into view.

# CHAPTER FOURTEEN
## CHRISTMAS TAMALES

W*ait, where are you going?* thought Special Agent Scott
Lawson, as the firefighter spun off his stool and
made for the door. It was Christmas Eve 2009, soon
to be Christmas Day, and now Lawson was alone again, but for the
beer on the bar in front of him.

Was he really alone at a bar on Christmas Eve? Was he really
alone at a bar on Christmas Eve in Laredo, Texas, a place he apparently lived now? And seriously, why did that firefighter just leave?

Lawson had harbored big hopes for his first few days on the border. Back at Quantico, most of the FBI's new recruits had made
plans to spend the holidays with their families before fanning out to
their new assignments. But right before graduation, Lawson received a call from his soon-to-be supervisor in Laredo. We got some-
thin' going, he said. We need you here before Christmas.

For all his anxiety about moving to the border, Lawson welcomed the news. He was a cop by trade, so he knew that any opera-

tion that required enough bodies to include him, a first-week agent, must be important. So while his Quantico friends headed home for their Christmas sabbaticals, he booked it back to his hometown in Tennessee, loaded up his things, and pointed his truck south.

It would be the first Christmas Lawson had ever spent outside Tennessee. But at age twenty-eight, it would also be his first opportunity to introduce himself the way he'd wanted to for so long: as FBI Special Agent Scott Lawson.

A few days before Christmas, he and a friend from Tennessee drove to Laredo, a fuming industrial landscape dotted with logistics centers and warehouses and tire shops—an entire metro area devoted to carrying things in and out of town and country. They dumped his things in an extended-stay motel, bought some new cowboy hats, and went out for drinks. Lawson dusted off his Spanish minor as he tried to order; the server appeared less than amused. "Dude," his friend said. "You're not gonna make it six weeks down here."

On his first day, Lawson found the FBI's offices, in an unmarked mid-rise right off the freeway, ready to go to work. His new boss met him at the door with the bad news. That thing he'd needed him there early for had been canceled. See you after Christmas, he said.

Lawson went back to his room and threw himself onto the bed. By the time he'd found ESPN on the TV, his anxiety about living and working on the border had settled in for the winter. His friend was already back in Tennessee. Christmas was two days away.

It was too late to get back to Tennessee to be with his family. So the next day, on Christmas Eve, Lawson sought comfort in one of the few places that was open, Buffalo Wild Wings. He lifted himself onto a stool at the bar, ordered a beer, and took in the challenge of his new job.

Detective work, the fun kind anyway, requires blending in. Laredo was 96 percent Hispanic, but Lawson wasn't sure he'd yet seen the other 4 percent. Even the gringos in Laredo could roll their Rs and stomach *tripas,* especially the small pocket of Jews, whose ancestors had emigrated from Europe around World War I and turned peddling into a borderland art form. Lawson was six foot five, had pale skin, and spoke with a Tennessee drawl. Walking around Laredo, he looked, as his friend put it, "like Big Bird in a cowboy hat."

Lawson was the only gringo in the restaurant. He did his best. He made small talk with a local firefighter, who couldn't believe Lawson was spending Christmas alone in Laredo. He asked Lawson what he did and Lawson fumbled for a response. He'd been toying around with different cover-story ideas, but he'd learned quickly that in Laredo, if you're white, you're probably a government employee. Border Patrol, most likely, but Lawson had a goatee, which was forbidden by the Department of Homeland Security. Oil-field worker was a decent cover, too, since the budding domestic-energy boom had drawn some gringos to town. But that required knowing something about working in an oil field. Lawson didn't.

He settled on FedEx driver, which was apparently believable enough. He and the firefighter drank beers together, eventually moving to a nearby bar. As they drank, something dawned on the firefighter.

Hold on, he said, and scurried out of the bar.

*Wait,* Lawson thought, but it was too late. A few minutes later, the guy came back holding a package wrapped in foil.

Christmas tamales, the guy said. A Texas and Mexico tradition that predates Texas or even Mexico. Welcome to the border, Big Bird.


Scott Lawson was born in Middleton, Tennessee, a working-class town cut out of thickets of trees and dotted every few blocks with steepled churches that alternated between Baptist and Church of Christ. About five hundred people live in Middleton. Growing up, Lawson knew most of them. Even more knew him.

His dad played a role in that. The son of poor cotton pickers, Mike Lawson had dropped out of high school and enlisted in the Army at seventeen. He served for three years, including long enough in the Vietnam War to suffer ailments attributable to Agent Orange.

(The almost four packs of cigs he smoked every day didn't help.) After Vietnam, he went to work for the local sheriff's office and managed to rise to the position of chief deputy. He also was elected county commissioner, becoming a kind of jovial, chain-smoking pillar in their rural county.

The other branch of Scott Lawson's family tree veered closer to middle-class, though barely. His maternal grandpa was a manager at the Dover Elevator plant, which was located in Middleton and employed much of the town. His stepdad and his uncle worked there, too, as did his mom, before she went to nursing school.

Scott's great-uncle, Bailey Howell, was a legend in town. He starred in basketball at Middleton High, played college ball two hours down the road at Mississippi State, and eventually won two titles with the Boston Celtics, under the tutelage of Bill Russell. He's in the Basketball Hall of Fame.

Genetically, Uncle Bailey explained Lawson's burly frame. He also served as a mentor, instilling in Lawson a zealous drive toward success in sports and life. The entire Howell side of the clan was marked by extreme competitiveness, led by his grandma, Bailey's sister, who played one-on-one with her brother on their outdoor hoop, and who, decades later, still liked to remind the Hall of Famer that she averaged more points in high school.

Scotty, as his parents called him, did his family proud. As a boy, he sang in the church choir and took care of the pony his mom bought him when he was ten, learning to give rides to the kids in the neighborhood. As a teenager, he was the starting center on the district-champion Middleton High basketball team, which played in a red-brick gym named for his great-uncle. Mr. Basketball, class president, Most Talented, Most Dependable, Most School Spirited, and Wittiest—Lawson was that kid who shows up on damn near every page of the yearbook.

He could do a lot of things after high school, including go to college, which no Lawson had ever done. But he wanted to be a cop. Lawson's parents had divorced when he was a boy, and his metered weekends with his dad were uncut introductions into the life of a small-town deputy. Lawson liked what he saw. Deputies streamed in and out of his life; on Christmas, his dad's table was filled with the deputies working through dinner.

On the long bus rides to basketball games, Lawson was usually one of only a few white boys; most of his teammates were black kids from Grand Junction, a small town down the road. He knew Grand Junction was a rougher place to live—poverty more rampant, crime and gangs more prevalent. So on the one hand, he understood why these boys, whom he considered friends, were so dubious of his dad and other cops, whom they had watched drag their friends and families out of their lives and into the backs of police cruisers. On the other hand, he thought, *My dad isn't the southern white cop you hear horror stories about.* He knew they existed—the patrolman who punished phantom resistance, the jailhouse deputy who broke up disagreements with particular fervor. His dad, Lawson liked to say, was the white deputy who got the warmest welcome when he showed up at the county jail.

Lawson's dad was proud of his work as a cop, but he wanted a different life for his son. His mom, meanwhile, preferred that Lawson go to college with his mind open to other careers. They forged a compromise in the end. Go to college. Do well. Be a cop for a few years. Then apply with the feds, the land of real salaries and generous pensions. It stung Dad a little, since it was the feds who always showed up late to crime scenes to piggyback and cherry-pick and generally annoy the hell out of the locals. Those pensions, though.

Lawson didn't just buy into the plan; he built his adolescence around it. As a teenager, he devoured the works of John Douglas, a former FBI agent who has written a dozen books about "hunting"—and understanding—violent criminals. Douglas has spent decades researching why the most violent criminals behave the way they do, drawing the same conclusions other researchers have: that a mix of native emotional distress and neglect has led them to act on fantasies and obsessions that others suppress. Of importance for his many fans in law enforcement, Douglas also lends criminals no moral quarter, no matter how severe their "mental problems."

"The crucial word is 'choice,'" he writes in *The Anatomy of Mo-*

*tive.* "With the exception of a very few truly insane (and generally delusional) individuals, these men choose to do what they do. . . . The fact that I can explain someone's behavior does not mean I excuse it."

For Lawson, a sheltered teen in rural Tennessee, raised in the conservative Church of Christ, Douglas's books helped square his religious upbringing with the realities of the world. *Some people,* he realized, *just make shitty choices.* But the books were also just engrossing tales of a diligent, process-focused cop—a cop Uncle Bailey would admire—chasing what Douglas described as unquestionably Bad People.

The books allowed Lawson to see what it would mean to apply his uncle's competitiveness to his dad's civic service. Douglas has said that he once chased a serial killer so long and hard that he worked himself into a coma, falling ill with a virus in his brain that doctors attributed to stress. Lawson read about that and thought, *That's what I want to do.* Minus the fried brain, if possible.

He studied computer networks at his local junior college, aware by then that the FBI, in the wake of the 9/11 terrorist attacks, needed more tech geeks than it did street cops. After transferring to Middle Tennessee State University, outside Nashville, he majored in psychology, hoping to learn to think like Douglas one day. He avoided drugs, knowing he'd someday have to convince an FBI-approved polygraph machine that he'd never smoked or snorted.

When Lawson was a senior, he applied to the police academy at several Tennessee sheriffs' departments. He knew rookie sheriff's deputies were typically assigned to jail duty, which was a turnoff; he craved the outdoors and longed to catch criminals, not babysit them. But from watching his dad, he also believed that the work of sheriff's deputies, who patrol more rural communities, was more service oriented than city police officers'. If he wasn't tracking a kidnapper, he'd rather dig a community out after a tornado than write a ticket.

The job he really wanted was at the Rutherford County Sheriff's Department, located in a suburb of Nashville where he went to college, but they insisted on jail duty. "I didn't do all of this to go do what you can do with a GED," he said in his interview, and that didn't go over well. He didn't get into the academy. In the meantime, he received a job offer from a telecom company he'd worked for briefly. It paid better than any cop job he could get, and he looked hard at it. His mom would be pleased, he knew. But then the major called him back, and Lawson walked into the office to find pants, boots, and a shotgun arranged neatly on a table. They don't give you a shotgun at the phone company.

It wasn't chasing serial killers till his brain broke. Lawson made about $32,000 with overtime and moved into an apartment in a low-end complex, receiving a discount off his rent in exchange for parking his patrol car out front and kicking drunks out of the pool. But he was a cop.

About a half-hour drive from Nashville, Rutherford County is about 80 percent white, part bedroom community and part college town. Crime is relatively low in most of the sheriff's department's nine zones, but some of the towns closer to Nashville, including Smyrna, were poorer and beset by more crime. "Not a war zone but not Mayberry, either" was Lawson's official description.

He started as a patrolman on the night shift. It didn't take long for Lawson to develop his theory of ten: that in any group of ten workers, there are three go-getters, four or five will-dos, and two or three won't-dos. He tried to announce himself as a go-getter, racing to domestic assaults and robberies in progress. Policing black and Hispanic neighborhoods, he also recalled the way his black teammates feared and resented the police, and he tried to present a different model. He gave warnings when he could, searched for common ground, and favored humor as his tool of de-escalation.

This was mostly useful with drunk drivers or ornery suspects, but it also came in handy the time he dove into the Stones River on a sleeting November night, after the call came in that a car had plunged over the riverbank. After Lawson swam to the car, only to discover it empty—it had been ditched by a criminal—his limbs locked up. His favorite K-9, Arak, swam to him with a rope, and the responding officers dragged him to the shore, where the paramedics frantically tried to cut off his pants and underpants to wrap him in blankets. By the time the paramedics started cutting at Lawson's underwear, a crowd had formed. "It's really freakin' cold in there," he deadpanned.

Through it all, Lawson tried to make residents see the police the way he saw his dad. His colleagues and superiors took notice, of both his temperament and his work ethic. He offered to ride with the interdiction team on his day off—a request that might have been annoying to the squad's vets if Lawson was an unrealistic or cocky striver, but he wasn't. He was a humble and realistic striver—one of the few young deputies people actually took seriously when he talked about one day working for the FBI.

Early on, he was called up to interdiction, the squad assigned to intercepting large shipments of drugs, fugitives, active criminals— anyone or anything moving through Rutherford County. He was too green for it, and things started slowly. The best interdiction agents are mechanical thinkers; they can see the inner workings of the trap car in their mind, and they know just where the drugs will be stashed. Lawson is emotionally intelligent, connects easily, can read the hell out of a room. But he couldn't build a doghouse with all the tutorials on YouTube. In his first few months on the squad, while his colleagues were taking down kilos and pounds, Lawson's bosses would be surprised when he found a joint. They started to think they'd brought him up too early.

He called his dad. Those were prime dad-calling days, those first few years on the job. His dad's age also made the calls feel more consequential. He was only fifty-six, hardly old, but he was ancient by the Lawson standard. Lawson's paternal grandfather and two paternal uncles had all died before their sixtieth birthday.

Scott Lawson tried not to think about what it meant for his own life span, though when he allowed himself the space to, he knew he lived with more urgency than a lot of his peers. Mostly he thought about what it meant for his relationship with his father. From the time Lawson was old enough to do the math, he had resigned himself to the idea that he only had Dad until he was sixty.

There was no puffy-cloud vision of heaven to fall back on, either. Despite his strict upbringing, Lawson's faith had been chipped away over the years, eventually deteriorating to the point that a concerned pastor would reluctantly ask Lawson if he was an "A-word." He was kind enough to label himself an agnostic, the more palatable of the two available A-words. But Lawson had no doubt that when Dad was gone, Dad was gone.

So Scotty called. They talked for several hours every week, with the elder Lawson preaching patience, empathy, that whole two-ears-one-mouth routine dads are so fond of.

It worked. Over time, the younger Lawson learned to apply his native abilities to interdiction. He learned to talk to people in a way that made the truth tumble from them like ripe apples from tree limbs, urged by only the gentlest twists. His first break came when he pulled over a car and found two of the three passengers pretending to be asleep. Nobody sleeps through a traffic stop, he thought, and soon he was pulling three thousand pills of Ecstasy out of the brake lights.

As his twenties progressed, some contradictions hardened in Lawson. He felt loyal to his Bible Belt swath of America, even as he began to question its reliance on, and the power of, the church. His political views skewed right, although he thought marijuana laws were probably too strict, and he balked at some small government intrusions, like seatbelt laws.

But from his dad—and from his time on the team bus—he was also stridently, reflexively pro-cop, maintaining a respect for lawmen that came with a profound respect for the law. From his mom and uncle, he valued order, will, self-reliance, drive, and reasoned decision making, regardless of how shitty a hand you're dealt. Showing up, in other words, even when the only job is in the fields, where one grandpa worked, or at the plant, where the other did.

He also simply craved the rush that came from certain types of police work. It wasn't that he didn't think a bank-fraud or insider-trading case didn't need attention; he just didn't especially want to work it. If he could do anything, he would chase murderers—the most violent criminals breaking the least ambiguous laws.

He knew those cases wouldn't be abundant with the feds, who

rarely work murder cases, and he did sometimes daydream about putting in for homicide and calling it a career. He'd be *happy.* But a deal was a deal, so after a few years on the force, just as he and his parents had planned, he applied with the FBI, ICE, and DEA.

A year passed. It was a good year. Lawson had always longed to find a woman to settle down with, to get right what his parents couldn't. But his obsessive drive toward becoming an FBI agent had made relationships challenging. Often he found himself frustrated with what he, in the sweat cloud of his own ambition, perceived as a lack of drive or passion in the women he dated. His colleagues marveled at the speed with which he started and extinguished relationships. Finally, though, just that year, at age twenty-eight, he'd fallen in love. She trained dressage horses, made a nice salary that offset his lousy one, and seemed to share his desire to achieve here and now.

They'd been dating about six months when they decided to head out to the lake. They were pulling his dad's Bayliner when the FBI called. He was in.

Lawson piled some clothes into his pickup and drove east. The rest of his stuff he either sold or stuffed into his girlfriend's garage, hoping that it, and she, would be waiting when he returned in twenty-one weeks.

At Quantico, between long runs and long classes, the agents-in-training talked incessantly about where they would be assigned and what kinds of cases they might work. Lawson remained drawn to both the physical and the intellectual adrenaline of investigating prolific, unquestioned criminals, the kinds of cinematic black hats that John Douglas chased across continents. A serial killer. A kidnapper. An especially violent bank robber. Any would do.

He knew those were hard to come by, so mostly he just hoped he wouldn't end up working Medicare fraud. One day, the bureau asked the agents to rank their geographical preferences. Lawson's first choice was Atlanta, a criminal emporium that happened to be a three-and-a-half-hour drive from his old stomping grounds in Nashville. It also happened to be the site of Douglas's brain-breaking investigation. But the agents often joked that their fate would be decided by whichever drunk monkey had hurled the dart at the map that day.

Orders Night came during week six, after a long day of classes. The trainees filed into a big meeting room to learn their fates. It was a stressful event, especially for the agents who were married or had kids, and who might not be able or willing to move to certain places. Sometimes agents quit altogether after Orders Night.

One by one they marched to the front of the class. The supervisor handed each recruit an envelope and told them what to do: announce where you want to go, what you want to do, and where you think you'll end up. Then, he said, open the envelope and tell everyone where you're headed. It was part light hazing ritual, part power play. There seemed to exist no correlation between where the agents *wanted* to go and where they were assigned.

Some assignments—Denver, say, or Nashville, big enough cities where a government salary goes plenty far—were met with groans of jealousy. Others were met with whoops that translated loosely to "You got fucked." Technically, they were dubbed "hardship assignments"—places like Puerto Rico, for its distance from the mainland, and Minot, North Dakota, for its distance from everything.

Lawson strode to the front of the room. I want to work violent crimes in Atlanta, he told his classmates.

The agent handed Lawson his assignment.

"San Antonio, Texas," Lawson read aloud.

He'd never been there, but it sounded like a decent assignment: a mid-sized city with a pro hoops team, low cost of living, and plenty of interesting cases. But the San Antonio field office encompassed some offices considered "hardships": the towns along the Mexico border. That night, one of his supervisors confirmed Lawson's fears. You're a rookie agent who speaks a little Spanish, the supvervisor said. He was going to Laredo.

Lawson retreated to his room and did what any twenty-something might do upon receiving word of a job transfer: he Googled. "Armpit of America," the Internet declared. When the Internet elaborated, it told Lawson of a city that had become a sort of municipal hostage to its southern neighbor. Nuevo Laredo was once Laredo's true "sister," a cultural change-up that was just a short walk away, where only fifteen years ago, parents happily let their teenage daughters walk alone to shop or swig margaritas or flirt with boys. Now it was, if you believed the Internet, an emerging battleground in the drug cartels' war over one of the border's most lucrative passageways.

Only a couple of months before, Lawson had been working good cases right outside Nashville, his favorite city in America, while spending his free time on a boat with his girlfriend. Now he was in a dorm room in Quantico staring at a five-year sentence in America's "armpit." Hit with the news back home, the girlfriend was already wavering: *Laredo?*

*What have I gotten myself into?* Lawson wondered. For the rest of his training, his classmates answered him: *You've gotten yourself into some shit.* In grappling class, they told Lawson he'd better pay attention, since he'd surely be mixing it up with narcos. In shooting class, they made sure to give him an extra round, since he'd be shooting it out with the sicarios.

The instructors got in on it, too. One day, the academy's gangs instructor invited all the border-bound agents to a special evening session in his classroom. Once they piled in, he proceeded to bombard their frontal lobes with images of brutal cartel beheadings—snuff videos so violent they existed not on YouTube but on the weird back channels of the Internet, alongside porn ads and videos of people being maimed by grizzlies.

They were often the same: a thin, blank-faced man, his tattoos shining in sweat, kneels in the grass, surrounded by rival cartel members, including one holding a chain saw or a machete. Lawson didn't understand all the words, but by the sixth or seventh video he could venture a guess: *Tell the people what you did,* they probably asked; and he probably said what he did—moved drugs on the wrong road, killed the wrong guy, whatever. Lawson didn't know for sure what the guy said, but he also knew it didn't matter.

Yank.

The next chain saw vroomed to life.


A few days after plowing through his Christmas tamales, Lawson finally reported to the Laredo FBI offices. He feasted on the scraps of some ongoing investigations, helping write subpoenas or otherwise execute grunt work the case agents were too swamped to deal with. The daily, weekly, monthly dopamine hits of working interdiction in Tennessee had been replaced by a job that required a phone full of code-named sources and patience measured by the kilo. Lawson had neither. Nor did he have his Tennessee girlfriend, who'd bailed after Lawson got shipped to Laredo. In those first several weeks, the theme of his calls to his dad was *What have I done?*

Meanwhile, he struggled to shake the feeling that he was some twangy alien walking around some foreign rock. Lawson had been on high alert when he first arrived, thanks to the dire warnings of his colleagues and instructors at Quantico. He was still moving gingerly through town when his mom drove down to help him outfit his first new house. On her way into town, she called: "I think I'm going over the bridge, Scotty." She described her surroundings and, sure enough, there she was, not a couple of miles from Lawson's new house but stuck in traffic on the World Trade International Bridge. "Do not cross that bridge, Mom," Lawson told her. He instructed her to make an illegal U-turn, traffic laws be damned.

Lawson was still reeling when, about a month in, a new agent arrived. Her name was María Medina.\* She was small, with wavy black hair pulled back to reveal round, almond-colored eyes that looked wide open—to the bureau, to the border, and to Lawson himself.

---

\* This is not her real name. With her family in Mexico, the agent asked that she be given a pseudonym. Hers is the only pseudonym in the book.

There were about thirty agents in Laredo, including local and state police who had been deputized as part of federal task forces. About half were devoted to corruption and white-collar crime. The other half were in Lawson's unit: Mexican criminal enterprise. When he arrived, he figured they'd all be knocking doors down together, local-cop-shop style. But he quickly learned how much of the agents' work was devoted to collecting intelligence. Especially post-9/11, the agency that Lawson associated with trailing serial killers and bank robbers had transformed itself into an international intelligence service more akin to the CIA than a cop shop, relying on a network of informants that had ballooned from one thousand in 1980 to roughly fifteen thousand when Lawson arrived. Good intel, questionable intel—it didn't seem to matter what the snitches offered up, so long as the agents could file it in reports to be corroborated with other intelligence to go into other reports. Lawson watched them work and thought, *I did not join the FBI to be an intel analyst.*

Medina seemed different. She was from the borderland, the daughter of Mexican immigrants. Her mother had moved to Texas as a teenager, in the 1960s, so Medina's grandfather could work on a pecan farm and her grandmother in a factory. Her father moved from Mexico after meeting and marrying Medina's mom. As a South Texas kid, Medina spent most weekends in Mexico with extended family, and she still had friends and family there. Spanish wasn't her minor but her co–native tongue.

Like Lawson, she'd always wanted to be a cop, for reasons she had trouble pinpointing. There were law enforcement agents in her family, but unlike Lawson's father, Medina's dad loathed the idea of his oldest daughter being in danger at work. When he dropped her off at the airport so she could fly to the Customs and Border Protection Academy, she saw him cry for the first time.

After five years patrolling the border, Medina got a job in the FBI's Miami office. And after putting in her time in South Florida, she moved back home to the border.

Not long after she arrived, Lawson asked her to lunch. He felt lost, and he didn't hide it. He asked Medina about her time as a rookie in Miami and the kinds of cases she eventually made. He asked whether it would get better, and when.

She urged patience. The sources will come, the cases will follow. It was the first of many lunches. Lawson usually dragged her to a chain restaurant called Luby's, the official state cafeteria of Texas, an interloper's sin she would never forgive. She liked him, though, so she always went along.

Not long into their friendship, Lawson and Medina teamed up on a case. It was the first in a class of cases that would become the most common in their time together: a kidnapping.

Kidnappings had always been commonplace in Mexico. Through the previous decades, they had typically been *secuestros exprés,* or "express kidnappings"—cheap, quick crimes of extortion often committed at an ATM. If a disappearance lasted longer or ended in death, the victim, it could safely be assumed, was involved in trafficking.

But as the Zetas and other cartel mercenaries grew in power, more innocent people were disappearing. The rate of kidnapping across Mexico had tripled in the few years after Felipe Calderón took office, and nowhere was the problem more obvious than in Nuevo Laredo.

The split between the Zetas and the Gulf Cartel was devolving into a full-blown turf war. Each had established checkpoints throughout Nuevo Laredo. Roll up to a checkpoint in a car they admired, and they might ask for it. Decline, and they might just take it, even if it meant kidnapping and eventually killing the driver and passengers. Among the victims were American citizens whose families had for generations crossed the river as if it were a railroad track, and who refused to be cowed into ignoring the southern half of what, to them, was one city.

An internal FBI memo from around that time warned of the Zetas' kidnapping prowess. Thirty-five American citizens had been kidnapped along the border in a twelve-month period, and twenty-eight of them had disappeared in Nuevo Laredo. Twenty-four were believed to have been abducted by the Zetas.

Working the disappearances was brutal. They were black holes of intelligence. Often the agents wound up showing grieving family members photos of their loved ones' beaten, tortured, sometimes beheaded, and always lifeless bodies. Medina took pride in her willingness to work those cases like multiyear conspiracies, however hopeless they might be. The moms, the wives, the sisters who kept calling her desk, wanting answers about their missing loved ones—she felt as if she knew them. They were immigrants like her parents and grandparents, habitual border crossers as she had once been and still longed to be. She worked their cases with patience and grace, taking every call, even when she had no more intelligence or solace to offer.

One kidnapping case dogged her and Lawson from the start. Two women came into the office and told their story. Their husbands had driven into Mexico to go dirt-bike riding and never returned. They had no ties to the drug trade, but they were in a nice pickup, something the cartels might like to add to their arsenal.

Lawson and Medina tried to find someone cooperative within the Nuevo Laredo police. That was always dicey for American law enforcement. The cartels were known to spend big, buying influence within local police departments. But it was still among the better tools. There was a time, maybe five years before, where Lawson might have been able to stick his gun in a drawer and walk across the bridge to interview sources and drum up leads. During Medina's time as a Border Protection agent, before she moved to Miami to join the FBI, she had crossed regularly, mostly to enjoy the simple pleasures of her ancestral homeland—lunch, shopping, whatever. Now, as it was for many civilians, Nuevo Laredo was strictly off-limits for FBI agents. The message from the bosses: Don't go.

As Lawson and Medina looked for leads, they began to hear more about the man believed to behind all those kidnappings: Forty.

For a few years now, sources had been telling law enforcement in Laredo about the growing power of Forty, and about his penchant

for snatching and violating and killing people. Lawson's new colleagues were obsessed with catching Forty. So were the DEA and
ICE agents who shared their headquarters.

It was an obsession fueled by proximity. Forty was known to
spend much of his time in Nuevo Laredo and the surrounding areas.
Members of Treviño's sprawling family lived less than two miles
from the FBI's offices, in a working-class neighborhood of small
brick cottages across the highway. It wasn't unheard of for an FBI
agent to eat lunch in the same restaurant as a Treviño relative.

Given the proximity, the Laredo agents worried about Forty's
disinterest in the traditional codes of the drug war. Law enforcement officers in the United States had always operated under the
assumption that they were off-limits—that the cartels would never
reach into the States to hurt an agent and risk the wrath of the
Americans. But Forty regularly flouted that code.

A few years before Lawson arrived, a Laredo police officer noticed he was being followed. He slowed down, swung *behind* his
pursuers, and tried to pull them over. They fled, and the officer
wound up chasing them down a dirt road along the Rio Grande. He
lost sight in a cloud of dust but heard the sound of gunshots coming
from the car. When the dust cleared, the car was crossing the border. The FBI suspected the cop had been targeted by "Zetitas," the
growing band of young criminals deputized by Forty to use his
group's name and do its dirty work.

Another Laredo detective had lived a similar experience, though
he wouldn't know it until later. His name was Robert Garcia, and he
was the homicide cop assigned to investigate the rash of cartel murders gripping Laredo. He was making inroads, too. Through an informant, he and federal agents had managed to trick Forty's teen hit
men into crashing at a "safe house" that was actually a DEA front,
outfitted with surveillance equipment. Eventually, he would put
several of Forty's teen hit men away, but not before they revealed
the darkest of their plans: to murder Detective Garcia. They had
followed him for days, and had watched him through the window
while he ate breakfast inside a Laredo diner. They were waiting for

word from Forty, but it never came. Still, to this day, Garcia reminds his breakfast companions, "Make sure no one follows you."

There was one FBI agent Forty especially despised. The agent, a hard-charging veteran named Arturo Fontes, had tossed his sister's house in Laredo a few years back. Forty apparently called the agent directly and threatened retribution. The agent became so convinced that Forty would send someone that he and his wife had taken to perching assault rifles next to their beds as they slept.

A year before Lawson arrived, Forty's mom got pulled into hard secondary as she tried to cross, despite having spent decades traveling seamlessly between Los Dos Laredos. She didn't see her son Miguel much—few people but his most-trusted fellow gangsters did—but she went to church with him some Sundays in Mexico. The feds had some questions when she returned. When Miguel found out they'd cuffed his mom to a wooden bench, in a holding cell with nothing but a squat metal toilet, he ordered his men to lob a grenade at the American consulate in Monterrey.

For his prolific drug smuggling alone, Forty had done enough to capture the attention of the country's counternarcotics agents, who have an uncanny ability to recite the precise quantities they've seized from which cartel. But over time, even the agents figure out what so much of the world already knows: no matter how many monster loads they seize, the trucks will keep coming. That's what made Forty so alluring to the agents. Beyond smuggling, he checked all the boxes that made them take notice. He kidnapped and killed Mexicans in Mexico: that was important, though it was baseline shit. Plenty of drug lords did that. He kidnapped U.S. residents and citizens: that was the next level, something the agents could cling to when they needed to get up for a fight. But targeting American diplomats and law enforcement agents? Here Forty was tapping directly into the cops' fierce tribalism, the place deep inside them they unleashed when they felt their shield had been disrespected.

There was, it seemed, a message implicit in each of Forty's enticements. On both sides of the border, the drug war had constructed an implicit hierarchy of lives, based on how valuable the war's architects considered them to be. The most valuable were the untouchable American law enforcement agents. Wealthier white Americans came next, to be protected at all costs. Poor blacks and Hispanics were worth mourning upon death but not nurturing in life.

The least valuable were the lives of ordinary Mexicans as Forty had once been. They were dying by the thousands with nary a shrug outside Mexico. They were worthless, it seemed, to the world and to Forty himself. With his threats against American cops, Forty was making sure they knew: *Your lives are just as worthless as ours.*


Needless to say, he was just the sort of criminal Lawson had longed to catch since he'd first cracked open John Douglas's *Journey into Darkness*. Along with Medina, he tried to zero in on Forty through his work on that first kidnapping and the dozens that followed. But in those early days, he wondered what difference he could really make. He was hardly the kind of agent who got to work a source entangled with Forty.

All across the Southwest, counternarcotics agents were intercepting thousands of kilos of cocaine that could be tied back to the Zetas. With every bust, more and more traffickers were ratting on Forty. They were driven by a mix of vengeance, self-preservation, and greed. Some were paid informants. Most were looking for a reduction of their own inevitable sentences. But many of them believed that Forty had blurred, then obliterated, the line between turf protection and killing for killing's sake.

These sources were almost always Mexican and Mexican-American drug dealers, many of whom spoke little English. They were guys like "Rocky Juárez," a code-named snitch who'd moved drugs for Forty. Forty had turned on him, beating and nearly suffocating him over some minor infraction. To retaliate, Rocky Juárez helped the DEA take down the crew of Zeta hit men who haunted Laredo. Another informant was a young Dallas drug dealer who met Forty on a hunting trip in Nuevo Laredo and eventually became part of Forty's inner circle. Forty turned on him, too, taking him captive for the crime of cutting out of a party too early. When the trafficker was finally released, he became an invaluable source for the feds.

When these informants started talking, the agencies typically used Hispanic, Spanish-speaking agents to handle them, since they could more credibly arrange phony drug deals with Zetas. These agents could be hard to find. The FBI had been struggling to diversify since at least the 1990s, when it was hit by multiple discrimination lawsuits by minority agents. The agency was 87 percent white and 6 percent Hispanic at the time but vowed to take steps to reduce bias in its hiring process. Two decades later, when Lawson joined the agency, it was still about 6 percent Hispanic.

Even so, many of the Hispanic agents did end up on the border, including Lawson's friend Medina, who was better positioned to work a Mexican source than he'd ever be. In chasing Forty, there just wasn't much work for a six-foot-five rookie from Tennessee.

■ ■ ■

ELGIN, TEXAS
February 2010

Lawson glided his hand across the horse's coat, which gleamed in the lights of the barn. It was late February 2010, two long months after landing in Laredo, and he was finally on the verge of getting a source of his own. This was no Forty ally with an axe to grind—no "Rocky Juárez"—but Lawson would take anything he could get.

A few weeks before, the FBI had received a tip. It was way out of left field, about some horse auction in Oklahoma City, where a straw buyer had spent more than a million dollars on behalf of an "undisclosed Mexican buyer." But this wasn't any undisclosed Mexican, the tipster said; it was Forty. And he'd done it with the help of his American brother José.

The feds had always thought they might get to Forty through his family—by following them to him, or by following his money to them. They kept a close eye on his mother—who moved between Laredo, Nuevo Laredo, and Dallas—and the rest of his siblings and nephews. But agents either didn't know about José or just didn't suspect him of anything. One Dallas DEA agent worked Zeta cases for years before even realizing Forty had a brother in Dallas; others looked into him, found nothing, and moved on.

Lawson's bosses in Laredo didn't know much about him. But they found it suspicious that bricklaying José was now bidding on million-dollar racehorses, even if he wasn't the one paying for them. A picture started forming in Lawson's head. It bummed him out. *Damn,* he thought. *He was poor, he tried for thirty-something years to do the right thing. He was just offered something that a poor man would have a hard time refusing.*

Who knows what would have happened had they knocked on José's door to ask him about it, or trainer Chevo's. But as they looked into this big horse auction, they learned that some probably oblivious rancher kid had helped José do it. They decided to knock on his door instead.

After his bosses told him about Tyler Graham, Lawson went home and rifled through the unpacked boxes that were spread throughout his new house. He dug out what he needed: snug jeans, a button-down shirt, and leather cowboy boots. That cowboy hat in the house somewhere, reserved for the nights Big Bird went two-stepping. He could wear it, but he figured it was more important to *feel* the part than to look it, and he didn't go two-stepping enough to feel comfortable in a hat.

The FBI called Tyler to feel him out, and even sent a more experienced agent to meet him. But they decided that Lawson—a young, white country boy, trying to make his way in the family business—might have better luck. So he and his training agent, an older agent assigned to help him learn the ropes, scheduled a meeting at Tyler's ranch, hoping to secure him as a source.

Lawson assumed Tyler wouldn't cooperate. People talk to save their asses, and by Lawson's estimation, Tyler's ass didn't need saving. He hadn't touched a brick of coke or an AR-15. He likely didn't even know whom he'd bought those horses for—not exactly, anyway. Even if he did know, it wasn't a crime unless he'd done it as part of some conspiracy to launder Forty's money.

Lawson could bluff and dangle a few years over Tyler's head. But he had a guess about how that would turn out: Tyler would lawyer up. That lawyer would instruct Tyler to tell the feds what little he knew and move on with his life. The FBI would then be back where they started, on the outside looking in.

Just knowing what Tyler knew wasn't enough. Lawson needed more. He needed Tyler to ingratiate himself to José, to let José continue exploring this new career while the FBI figured out how to connect it to Forty's drug business. It was a big ask, Lawson knew, but he would try.

He'd hoped to take an XL pickup to the meet, so they would look like fellow ranchers or potential customers. To keep their investigation quiet, it was important that only Tyler know they were FBI, not his grandpa, not anyone else on the ranch staff. Lawson also feared that Forty may have planted Mexican ranch hands at Southwest Stallion Station as lookouts. Best to blend in.

But the bureau didn't have a suitable truck. They ended up taking Lawson's personal car, a seven-year-old Chevy Impala in gold. It was about the most obvious G-ride ever to roll off an assembly line.

Whatever. Lawson needed a source. He and his training agent rumbled north on Interstate 35, Texas's narcotics superhighway, before detouring onto one of the two-lane highways that veer into the farmland east of Austin. Arriving in Elgin, they passed a strip mall owned by and named after Doc Graham and pulled onto Bitting School Road, an empty country road that bent and swayed, covered by an unruly canopy of trees.

The road did a down-and-out and the trees fell away like dominoes, giving way to lime-green pastures and, in the distance, a collection of metal barns. Lawson slowed down when he saw a long driveway framed by the silhouette of four horses and a red sign branded with "SSS," for Southwest Stallion Station.

In the driveway, Lawson stepped out and greeted Tyler. From the time their palms pressed, Lawson began to hope. Tyler was not flanked by a lawyer, as Lawson had feared, nor did he appear to be especially anxious about his meeting with the FBI. He led them into a barn.

Though showing up in a gold Impala hurt his chances, Lawson still thought it was important not to send out cop vibes, so he took his time in the barn. He felt at home there. After caring for his first pony, he'd graduated to a full-sized riding horse, and he and his mom took long rides through the Tennessee countryside. After years spent living in apartments, one of his most enduring fantasies involved moving back home, securing some acreage, and buying some tame riding horses like the ones he'd ridden with his mom.

They would be nothing like these. Accustomed only to the low-four-figure riding horses of his youth, he swept his hand down the long face of one of the horses. For all he knew, it was Forty's almost-million-dollar mare.

When Lawson finished playing rancher, they moved into an office attached to the barn. This was delicate. Over the years, Lawson had developed a direct, indifferent approach to enticing informants, laying out their options dispassionately and counting on them to choose wisely. "If you don't wanna do it, don't do it," he liked to tell them. "You get twenty years if you don't help me, you get ten if you help me. I don't give a fuck."

For Tyler, the choices weren't that stark. If Lawson leaned too hard, Tyler could tell him what he knew and be on his way. If he didn't lean at all, he might leave that ranch with no intelligence, no source, and no case. Lawson decided to play it somewhere in the middle, telling Tyler, plainly if vaguely, that he had stepped in some shit and that Lawson could help him clean up his boots.

It was around then that Tyler pulled up the photo on his computer.

■ ■ ■

RUIDOSO, NEW MEXICO
September 2010

Looking across the bar, watching Tyler swig beers with Forty's brother, the thrill of the All American still flush on their faces, Lawson could hardly believe that Tyler was doing this. Even after that first meeting in the barns, he'd half expected the next call to be not from Tyler but from some high-priced Austin lawyer. *My innocent and regretful client has cut ties with José and moved on,* the lawyer would say. *The FBI should do the same.*

Instead, Tyler had returned Lawson's calls. Tyler's relationship with José had already meant good business for Southwest Stallion Station. Tyler's ranch was owed $130,000 for boarding the horses he'd helped buy in Oklahoma. The longer the horses stayed, the more José would owe. If Tempting Dash or Mr Piloto started breeding at Southwest Stallion Station, it would mean not just new revenue but a new identity for Tyler and his family's ranch. José's business also might soon be good for Tyler's then fiancée: she was a local real estate agent, and she had been helping José look for a ranch nearby to serve as the headquarters for his new business.

Though Tyler would never publicly acknowledge it, these new business relationships gave him an obvious financial incentive to cooperate with the FBI, even if that incentive came loaded with risk. If he talked, he could keep doing business with José, the sport's new big spender. If he didn't, he couldn't, not without immediately becoming the subject of an FBI money-laundering investigation.

Lawson could understand Tyler's financial motivation, but he viewed his decision to cooperate as more complicated. He saw in Tyler a young man of privilege who believed that success and wealth were his for the taking. No one and nothing would stop him. Certainly not the government, not when Tyler believed, and the FBI seemed to believe, that he hadn't broken any laws. The way Lawson saw it, Tyler had been graced with an opportunity to do his business, and grow his business, while simultaneously helping out the Law and routing the sport he loved of some guys who probably needed routing. Why the hell not?

For many potential sources, the answer to "why the hell not" is: because I'll die. Across the criminal landscape, no act fuels violence like cooperating with the police. In Forty's Mexico, snitches get not stitches but their brains beaten in with a two-by-four, roaring chain saws to their necks, their own balls stuffed into their still-breathing mouths. But as far as Lawson could tell, Tyler wasn't scared. He seemed to intuit the drug war's value system, knowing in his bones that because he was a wealthy white rancher on American soil, the rules didn't apply in the same way.

Viewed from the right side of the border, this is the splendor of the drug trade. It's *big* business for ancillary interests—the bankers and the ranchers, the developers and the car dealers—who can turn around and flip when necessary with nary a scratch, even though their role in the trade is essential and knowing. The Mexican smuggler, the Colombian grower, the black kid selling rocks on the corner, the Mexican man plopping cocaine proceeds into gas tanks—they do their jobs at great physical risk. But for certain players, no less essential to the business, the risk is mitigated by their privilege. When HSBC Bank and Banamex got caught laundering millions for the world's most notorious, blood-soaked cartels, they found themselves before judges, prosecutors, and other professional-class peers unlikely to send them to hard time. When Tyler stumbled unwittingly into helping the narcos, the law arrived not with a wiretap or a door blown from its hinges but with Lawson, an FBI agent who was handpicked because of their commonalities, and who didn't dare lean too hard.

Together in that barn, whether they'd ever considered it or not, Tyler and Lawson must have intuited that in the drug war, their lives had value that those of poor Mexicans, even poor Americans, didn't, and a chat here and there couldn't change that. Which perhaps was why Tyler, in that first interview, had pulled up on his computer a photo from after one of Tempting Dash's big wins. Tyler was in the photo, there to recruit José. But what he showed Lawson was two of José's kids, Alex and José Jr., flashing hand signs for the camera: "4-0" and "4-2." Cuarenta and Cuarenta y Dos. (Alex and José deny this was the intended meaning.)

Lawson wouldn't pay Tyler for his work the way he might other sources. Nor did Tyler sign anything agreeing to work as a "source" or "informant." As Tyler saw it, he had merely agreed to take Lawson's calls and answer his questions truthfully. Still, according to Justice Department regulations, that was enough officially for Lawson to count Tyler as his first big CHS: Confidential Human Source. Lawson entered him into the FBI's source-management software, Delta, where the bureau's informants are registered and tracked.

Tyler took Lawson's calls as he'd promised, and Lawson and Tyler met several times over the next several months. Lawson had asked Tyler to keep their relationship a secret, so after that first interview in the barn, they started to meet in bars and restaurants around Austin. Time and again, they slunk into booths for long intro-to-quarter-horse sessions led by Tyler.

He told Lawson about José's recent activities, which included moving one of his brother's prized mares to Oklahoma to breed with famous Corona Cartel. He told Lawson how Ramiro Villarreal, aka the Horseman, was on the outs.

That could have been bad news for Lawson. If Ramiro and Forty were still in business together, Lawson could have used Ramiro to pursue Forty—either by tracking Ramiro, arresting him, or quietly trying to "flip him." But if Ramiro's fall from grace was bad news, it was offset by what Tyler told Lawson next: that Ramiro had been replaced by Carlitos and Fernando. They were the new Horsemen, Tyler explained, in charge of buying and caring for Forty's horses.

It was exactly what Lawson needed. The feds had been hunting Forty for five years or longer. The odds of Lawson, a rookie with no network of Mexican sources, identifying new links to the Zetas' leadership were slim. Now came Carlitos and Fernando, who not only connected directly with Forty but were also working with his brother José.

Better yet, Tyler had told Lawson just where and when Lawson could lay eyes on Carlitos, Fernando, and José: at the All American Futurity in the mountains of Ruidoso, New Mexico, over Labor Day weekend.

A day or two before the race, Lawson flew from Laredo to El Paso, tracing the scraggly border from above. Lawson's training agent didn't share the rookie's eagerness to travel, so another young agent, Raul Perdomo, joined him. A Cuban-American city boy from

Miami, Perdomo had landed in Laredo a couple of years ahead of Lawson, and he'd spent those years jumping at every chance to do out-of-town surveillance. He spent the four-hour flight calming Lawson's nerves over whether they could use a long-lens camera at the track without being noticed. No one will give a shit, Perdomo counseled.

In El Paso, they rented a Hyundai sedan, favoring the bureau's budget constraints over their desire to blend in. They drove north into New Mexico's Sierra Blanca, strategizing as they climbed into the thin mountain air. Though his surveillance and Spanish skills might be useful, Perdomo couldn't tell a Shetland from Secretariat. Lawson used the drive to help him understand the world of quarter horses.

On the morning of the auction, the agents invited Tyler to their room at the Best Western for a lowdown of what to expect. That night, they waded their Hyundai into the sea of king-cab pickups and lugged their camera into the auction house. They stood in the Coors-swigging ring of cowboys and snapped photos of Carlitos and José, standing not quite together and technically not bidding on dozens of horses. Lawson reluctantly texted Tyler for help identifying people, not sure how his new source would handle receiving and responding to texts while standing among the people he was informing on. From Lawson's vantage point, Tyler handled it like a cold-blooded pro.

On Labor Day, at the All American Futurity, Lawson leaned on the outside rail, waving a betting slip. (He would never say which horse he bet on.) He watched José and Carlitos and Fernando and Tyler across the track. He watched José's horse, Mr Piloto, cut a wide, weird path to a historic win. He snapped photos of José talking on the phone. Lawson assumed he was talking to Forty, though that was unlikely; they didn't talk on the phone much. People there that day believe José actually was calling home to Zulema and Alex.

Now Lawson, nine months removed from Quantico, was sitting in the bar at the Inn of the Mountain Gods, babysitting his prop beer, watching them celebrate. Watching, at least as Lawson saw it, the fading image of José as a humble bricklayer who'd fallen into a good horse. He was the owner of his sport's most prestigious title belt, and he was carrying himself like it, betting at the tables and drinking deep into the night. *Like a boss,* Lawson thought, as he watched José saunter through the bar. If he was a boss, he was an unusual one: a Mexican immigrant in a world dominated by old, white American money. Some might have seen a career mason and weary dad seizing a long-deferred moment to strut. Lawson saw José's preening as confirmation of the feds' long-held, never-proven suspicion that José was a narco-in-waiting.

He saw José fall, and he saw José swing on the old Native American who tried to help him. He worried that chaos might ensue, with him in the middle of it. He watched cooler heads prevail.

Last call came, and the group dispersed. Lawson and Perdomo drove back to the Best Western, talking the whole way, then holed up in a room, recounting the mission well into the night. They flew back to Laredo the next day.

There remained so many questions about what the group was doing, and how, and why. Lawson couldn't help wondering whether any of the intelligence he was gathering could lead directly to Forty himself. And what to do about Ramiro, the missing Horseman? Lawson didn't know. All he knew was that for reasons he didn't precisely understand, he had in Tyler Graham a very willing Confidential Human Source, and he was going to ride him for as long as he could.

# CHAPTER FIFTEEN
## WHERE'S PAPI?

NUEVO LAREDO, TAMAULIPAS
October 2010

Ramiro had smuggled enough horses across the border to know the terrain without seeing it—how long it took to get from the border to the highway, how the road swayed left and right, tracing the arcs of the river. But there were no horses on this trip. No drugs or booze or migrants. No money. Ramiro wasn't even the one doing the smuggling this time. This time, he was the product.

They were driving through Nuevo Laredo. He didn't know where exactly; the blindfold precluded that. The men Forty had sent had pulled one over his eyes before driving him to the meeting location. Now they were driving again, and everything was black.

Ramiro hadn't been at the Inn of the Mountain Gods after Mr Piloto won the All American. He hadn't been at the auction house or the races that weekend, either. He'd been buying horses for the Company for years now, spending millions of their dollars on hun-

dreds of horses. It would have been fitting to be in the winner's circle with them that day, or at the casino with them that night, or
asleep on the floor of Forty's safe house the next morning. But he
wasn't invited. So when Mr Piloto nose-haired his way to a win in
the All American, Ramiro celebrated at a bar in Mexico with friends.
It was Ramiro, after all, who'd picked up Mr Piloto at the auction
house. He could count himself among the horse's connections
whether he showed up in the winner's circle or not.

The Ruidoso sale was the first in years where Ramiro hadn't
been the point man—the guy studying the sales book, working the
phones, making the bids, and seeing to it that the horses got hauled
to the right ranch the morning after. Carlitos and Fernando were
the guys now. That much was obvious.

Maybe that was for the better. Ramiro had been thinking for a
while that he should get out of this business, and he had even taken
some steps to end his career as the Company's Horseman. To find a
way to be just a lowercase horseman again.

He knew it wouldn't be easy; you don't just put your two weeks
in with the Company. Recently, though, he'd met a guy who could
offer a lifeline out of the cartel's grips. There are guys like this—call
them fixers—sprinkled across the drug war's various battlefields, on
both sides of the border. Some are defense lawyers. Some are former agents, some Mexican and some American, who have retired to
a life of so-called security consulting. Some are both, and some are
neither. Some are former narcos themselves.

Whatever their official vocations, they all get paid to help guys
like Ramiro grease up and slip free of the cartels' clutches. One such
fixer, a former Mexican intelligence officer and prosecutor now living in the States, was known to charge narcos millions of dollars in
legal fees for helping them find work as informants. He then turned
around and charged the American government hundreds of thousands of dollars for the same introductions. The agents this fixer
worked with classified him, and paid him, as a registered informant,
and he did provide reams of information. But his real service was
connecting the agents with narcos ready to talk.

Ramiro's fixer was prolific. A former counternarcotics agent himself, the fixer knew investigators in every American agency working along the border, which was every American agency. Though the DEA would undoubtably be interested in Ramiro, the fixer worried that its agents weren't as cautious handling sources who required a little more care than typical traffickers. So instead, around the time Tempting Dash starting running in the States, the fixer introduced Ramiro to someone he thought he could trust: a Houston-based agent for Homeland Security Investigations, or HSI, the investigative arm of Immigration and Customs Enforcement.

Ramiro and the agent met occasionally in Texas, with Ramiro telling the agent everything he knew that might help the feds locate Forty. They started to build trust. Neither Ramiro nor his handling agent has ever acknowledged their relationship publicly, so it's hard to know exactly what, if anything, was promised. But Ramiro no doubt believed his cooperation would eventually lead to a life outside the money-laundering business, and maybe even a home in the United States. Witness protection was a possibility, though most informants couldn't handle being cut off from their families and their identities. More likely, the agent could help Ramiro secure immigration status in exchange for his cooperation. Ramiro could then safely lie low in the States until Forty was killed or captured. And though Ramiro wasn't believed to be a paid informant, he likely was in line to be compensated handsomely if he helped take Forty down.

Now Forty was fading Ramiro out. He was still involved enough to be useful as an informant, but it wasn't clear how long that would be the case. A couple of months after the All American, he had shown up at one of Forty's safe houses in Piedras Negras for a meeting. The usual suspects were there—Forty; his brother Forty-Two; Poncho Cuellar, the Zetas' chief trafficker for that territory; and Poncho's deputy. Ramiro's apparent replacement, kickback Carlitos, was also there. So was "the clean brother," José.

José wasn't one to make a show of things, but everyone in the room could see that he was beginning to own his role in this growing horse business. It was José, not Ramiro, who walked into the meeting with a replica of the All American Futurity championship belt and the trophy they'd received at the Ruidoso auction house.

And it was José, not Ramiro, who brought along an Excel sheet detailing the $1.8 million in outstanding horse expenses, spread across various companies. Poncho ordered one of his workers to retrieve the cash and get it where it needed to go.

By the time Ramiro left that meeting, it was obvious he was on the outs. But he was still in the horse business. So a week or two after the big win at Ruidoso, he boarded a plane to fly to Oklahoma City. It was Heritage Place's big fall sale. Ramiro would be there, but first he had a layover in Houston. That's where the DEA agents were waiting for him.

They held him for hours. The agents knew, if not then, then soon after, about Ramiro's ongoing relationship with the HSI agent. If he was already helping one agency, shouldn't the DEA let him go?

Not quite. The DEA had been hearing about Ramiro from sources, and hearing him on phone calls they were monitoring between other Zeta operatives. Then, about ten days before Tempting Dash won his first stakes race, a judge had given the DEA permission to tap Ramiro's phone, as well as the phones of his father and friends, just in time to hear Ramiro gab about Operativo Huesos with Forty-Two. From the phone calls, it was obvious Ramiro could lead the DEA directly to Forty.

By this time, Forty had solidified his position as the Zetas' second-in-command, below Heriberto "Z-3" Lazcano. After the racetrack murder of Carlitos's friend Fourteen, two more original Zetas had been captured by the Mexican military. The U.S. State Department believed they'd been betrayed by Forty. In a confidential memo to the Mexican government, revealed by WikiLeaks, State Department officials even claimed that Forty had bought off leaders within the Mexican federal police to help smooth his ride to power. Now, American officials believed, it was only a matter of time before Forty orchestrated Lazcano's killing or his arrest and took over the cartel.

At the airport, the DEA agents threatened to prosecute Ramiro if he didn't inform for them, too. They cut him loose, and he continued buying horses, now working for two agencies. As he flew from town to town, he sent short, cryptic emails in broken English to an email address set up by his DEA handler. "No talk more time with A and B and no see they," he wrote in one, using code names for Forty and Forty-Two. "The A called a few minutes of this number," he wrote in another, and gave up the phone number used by Forty.

Then Forty called Ramiro to Mexico, which was how he ended up in the car, blindfolded, on his way to see "A."

The instructions from Forty had been simple, and Ramiro followed them. He drove as instructed to a Walmart parking lot in Nuevo Laredo. Ramiro quickly realized he wasn't the only one called to meet Forty. There were others, guys he didn't recognize, waiting in the same parking lot, probably with the same hollow feeling in their stomachs.

An SUV arrived. Follow, the driver said, so Ramiro and the others followed, driving to a ranch not far from the border. Five more men showed up. They slipped black masks over their faces and picked up long-barreled assault rifles. Ramiro felt his heart thump.

"Where's Papi?" Ramiro asked. He had never wanted to work for Forty. Now he called him Papi.

"Don't worry," someone said.

The men loaded him and the others into an SUV. They drove about five minutes away, to a new ranch, where twelve more SUVs were parked, waiting, seemingly positioned to leave in a hurry. Then they left in a hurry.

Now a pickup pulled up. Ramiro looked at the bed. It was filled with fifty-five-gallon drums. The Zetas were known for disposing of their enemies' bodies by tossing them into oil drums filled with acid. Forty was especially fond of the practice. Ramiro studied them.

*I'll be killed soon,* he thought. *I'll be cooked soon.*

Ten minutes passed, if time can really pass when you're considering the mechanics of your own death. More likely, those minutes burrowed themselves deep inside everyone there, waiting. Waiting for Papi.

A caravan of fifteen more SUVs rolled up, brimming with men dressed in black fatigues. One pulled up close. That's when Ramiro saw Forty, reclining in the passenger seat of one of the SUVs, nursing some kind of leg wound. He'd shot himself, Forty said. Then he started talking about horses.

After a while, Forty assigned one of his grunts to take Ramiro for a drive. The grunt pulled a blindfold over Ramiro's eyes, and now they were driving through—Ramiro didn't know exactly, but they were getting farther away from his car, from the bridge, from the States. Everything was black.

The blindfold came off. Ramiro's eyes adjusted. They were at some kind of house. Forty showed up not long after and put racing on the TV. Forty was grumpy, Ramiro noticed, maybe because of the wound in his leg, but he answered Papi's questions as best he could. They went to bed eventually and spent the next day talking horses, while Ramiro considered whether and when the drums might come into play. That night, as the sun slipped beyond the hills of Coahuila state, Forty and his men dropped Ramiro off on the side of the highway.

Ramiro managed to get back to his car and back across the border and back into Texas, where he went to see his handler at HSI. Still coming down from his visit with Papi, he waited outside the agent's Houston office, chain-smoking and sweating through every strand of his designer shirt. He was, he knew, trapped in a maze with only dead ends. He could flee to Mexico and be killed; snitch in the States and be killed; or shut up in the States and go to prison, unless he was killed first.

The agent wanted to help, but his hands were bound in red tape. He'd been trying to get his bosses to pursue a money-laundering case, which might put an end to Ramiro's work as an informant. But his bosses would never bite. They preferred to use Ramiro to help the Mexicans capture or kill Forty, not so another American grand jury could indict Forty, a meaningless gesture so long as he roamed free. Few had direct access the way Ramiro did. And it was only a matter of time before Ramiro got called back across the border again.

A few days after meeting with Forty, Ramiro wrote to his DEA handler, describing the ordeal. I'm going through a "living hell," he wrote. If the government could help him escape it, they didn't offer. The next day, the DEA agent emailed Ramiro asking what he knew about Forty.

# CHAPTER SIXTEEN

## OTHERWISE
## ILLEGAL ACTIVITY

AUSTIN, TEXAS
January 2011

Not long after he got home from Ruidoso, Lawson drove north to Austin again, to present his findings to an assistant United States attorney. The case was starting to crystallize in his mind, including a growing list of targets he hoped a prosecutor could put away. At the top was José Treviño.

Lawson believed that José was what he said he was: a humble, hardworking bricklayer who'd steered clear of his brother's drug business out of respect for American law and decency. And he could see that what José was doing now—buying horses, breeding horses, racing horses—was not directly hurting anyone, except perhaps his rival quarter-horse men. Yet after tailing José through Ruidoso, he'd found himself disgusted with José's apparent choice to help his brother. To maintain even a benign familial relationship with a criminal of Forty's breadth was, to Lawson, questionable. To *help* him was abhorrent. And while Lawson wasn't yet sure how he'd prove it, he knew José's behavior was also criminal. He planned to

enlist the full force of the federal government to help prove himself
right.

First, he needed a prosecutor willing to work the case. There
were plenty to choose from. There had been ever since Giuliani enlisted more federal prosecutors in the drug war, and since the laws
were shaped to make drug money easier to seize—too easy, many
argued, because they could be seized and liquidated without a conviction, alleged property rights be damned.

With suspects in Dallas, Austin, Laredo, New Mexico, and California, Lawson could have plausibly asked prosecutors in five or
more cities to take on his case. But he'd settled on an assistant
United States attorney in Austin named Douglas Gardner. Gardner
had been a prosecutor for the United States Marines, with the close-
cropped hair and chiseled physique to prove it. He had a reputation
for taking on tough targets.

Lawson pitched it passionately, walking the prosecutor through
how the case could yield millions of dollars in seizures, take out
some of the Zetas' key money launderers, and maybe even lead to
Forty himself. Gardner was skeptical, if only because it violated a
day-one lesson from federal-prosecutor school. "You don't seize live
animals," as Gardner put it, "because then you're going to have to
take care of them." But in the end, he agreed to help. Horses, cash,
property—whatever they had to seize, Gardner reasoned, it would
help put a dent in the Zetas' flourishing business and send a message that United States industry was off-limits.

With Gardner on board, Lawson wrote a confidential report outlining what made the case worthy of the Organized Crime Drug
Enforcement Task Forces, which would mean more funding and
manpower.

[The] investigation targets the family members of LOS ZETAS
cartel leader MIGUEL ANGEL TREVINO MORALES (TREVINO),
who operate on his behalf in the United States," Lawson wrote.
"Specifically, the OCDETF targets the brother of TREVINO, JOSE
TREVINO MORALES (JOSE) and other associates, who are
laundering millions of dollars of illicit funds owned by TREVINO

through the AMERICAN QUARTER HORSE ASSOCIATION (AQHA) horse racing industry.

Lawson went on to detail how the alleged scheme worked, relying largely on what he'd learned from his surprisingly forthcoming informant, Tyler. Forty, Lawson wrote, is using straw purchasers, including José, Carlitos, and Fernando, to buy up the sport's most promising horses. They bid with no price limits and often overpay, Lawson noted, because the sellers know to artificially bid up the price. Once the horses are secured, he explained, they are placed into the ownership of various front companies, including Fernando's "Garcia Bloodstock." The group hires the sport's top trainers, including Chevo Huitron, to determine which horses to run in the sport's top races. The slow ones get shipped back to Mexico to occupy one of Forty's many ranches; no reason to risk drawing needless attention if they aren't going to make it big. But if a horse qualifies for a top race, Lawson added, its ownership is transferred to Tremor Enterprises, the front company owned by José. That way, if the horse wins big, like Tempting Dash or Mr Piloto, Treviño's American family reaps the benefits.

In his report, Lawson also appealed for the sanctity of an American sport that he saw as under siege. Industry insiders speculated that "Los Zetas are using bribes and extortion to affect the outcome of the race," including paying off gate starters and using performance-enhancing drugs. "The AQHA industry is normally comprised of long time horse owners, doctors, lawyers, and respected businessmen and women. JOSE was a 20 year [mason] by trade," Lawson wrote. As a result of this infiltration, "Many of the long time traditional members of the industry are considering leaving or already have left the industry."

Toward the end of his report, Lawson remarked that "through intelligence received, agents hope to obtain a valid location of TREVINO to give to the Mexican Military." Mostly, though, he concluded, he sought indictments of all of these horsemen. None was more crucial than José Treviño.

Around this time, Lawson also pitched the Internal Revenue

Service to come on board. He had never done a money-laundering case. Proving it would require not only towers of records but also agents with the patience and aptitude to go swimming in them, squinting till their eyes ached. Lawson knew that some agents see boxes piling high and think, *Yes*. He saw them and thought, *Ah shit*.

Lawson teamed up with a Texas-based IRS task force that specialized in using bank and other records to build cases against drug traffickers. They set up a war room inside the U.S. Attorney's Office in Austin, sent out subpoenas, and watched the boxes of records start stacking to the ceiling.

In the fifteen months since Tempting Dash's first win, Lawson figured that Forty had amassed at least a hundred horses across several front companies. In high-dollar broodmares alone—the ones Tyler had bought at the auction in Oklahoma—Forty owned a million dollars in assets, not to mention the future assets they could give literal birth to. According to Tyler, Tempting Dash and Mr Piloto were worth $2 million each. If they turned into top-producing stallions, they might one day be worth $10 million.

Lawson didn't pride himself on his math skills, but he knew Forty had piled up horse-related assets well into the millions, spread across various front companies. One way or another, many of those assets belonged to or seemed destined for Tremor Enterprises, the company controlled by José.

They'd never make it back to Forty or the Zetas. If you viewed José as a distant but loving brother, uninterested in the drug trade but loyal to his kin, those assets might be considered a gift or an investment. But if you viewed José as the FBI did—as a co-conspirator in a large-scale money-laundering operation—those assets were "monetary instruments" being laundered by and for Los Zetas. Eventually, José could sell them off and move the resulting proceeds through American bank accounts unchecked, creating generational wealth for himself and his family.

Viewed from a wide enough lens, what José was doing—collecting generational wealth through sweat and guile, by any means necessary, ethics be damned—was *supremely* patriotic, a page from the playbook of most every American empire. To Lawson, though, it was an affront to the law, to Forty's victims, and to law-abiding families everywhere.

Lawson knew that if they built the case right, they could take it all. They could also get a grand jury to indict any number of Treviños—Forty, Forty-Two, José, maybe even some of their wives and kids. Carlitos, Fernando, Ramiro, and perhaps dozens of others could go down, too.

What would happen to them then? If he was convicted of money laundering, José could land in prison for as long as twenty years.

That sounded fair to Lawson. He was starting to see how José was undone by some mix of loyalty and a longing to do better. He felt he understood what José had faced, which was not unlike what was faced by the poor families, black and white, he'd played ball with in rural Tennessee. Lawson, too, saw a system that valued the lives of HSBC bankers over small-time money launderers named José. But when it came to fighting violent drug gangs and their enablers, Lawson preferred to take them all on.

Given that, he felt fine with the prospect of sending José away for twenty years. If José wanted less, he could help take down his brother. If he wanted none—well, it was probably too late for that.

Lawson's feelings about Forty were even less ambiguous. But what might happen to him was anyone's guess. Given his penchant for shoot-outs, it seemed exceedingly likely he would be killed by the Mexican government. If he was somehow captured, it was unclear whether he would be turned over to the United States. This was years before before El Chapo would be extradited. In early 2011, the Mexican government was reluctant to hand over cartel bosses, because cartel bosses knew a lot about which Mexican officials took which bribes, and because extradition is a useful bargaining chip for the always outmatched Mexican government.

If Forty *was* somehow captured and extradited, Lawson knew he wouldn't likely face money-laundering charges in Austin—not with charges pending on trafficking and other charges that could land Forty in prison for life. Still, you never knew. They got Capone on tax evasion. Why not Forty on money laundering?

■ ■ ■

## ELGIN, TEXAS
January 2011

For Tyler Graham, things only accelerated after the races at Ruidoso. He got married a few weeks later, in the rugged hills south of Austin, among black-tied friends clutching red plastic beer cups. If he'd kept his promise to Lawson, none of them knew of Tyler's work as a Confidential Human Source.

Then it was back to work. José, Carlitos, and Fernando had shipped thirty of the horses bought in Ruidoso back to Elgin. Several had the potential to light up the tracks as two-year-olds in 2011. But since Tyler's ranch was built for breeding, not training, Forty was plopping down three grand a month for thirty stalls at a training facility down the road. He'd even sent in a team of five Mexican horsemen—including a one-eyed jockey named Parra—to break the horses before sending them off to Chevo, Fernando, or other trainers.

The horsemen were staying in a camper behind the training facility, apparently with a large stash of cash to be used on supplies and sundries. Tyler was still in recruitment mode, so he'd had dinner with them recently. They talked openly about the rules laid down by the *"principales"* back in Mexico: no drinking, no drugs, nothing to draw attention to themselves.

There were still plenty of horses at Tyler's breeding farm, too, including some expensive broodmares and racehorses. There was Tempting Dash, whom they hoped to start breeding soon, and Mr Piloto. He'd gotten hurt in California and retired to stud duty at Tyler's farm.

It all added up. In the last few months, the group had racked up tens of thousands of dollars in fees at Tyler's farm, and they had failed to pay their monthly bill for three months running. Tyler gently nudged them to pay up. He emailed Carlitos with the totals, and he reminded Fernando every time they spoke on the phone. He didn't talk to José as much, but José came by the ranch often enough, and they'd recently gone hunting again. Tyler uploaded photos to Facebook of José, snug in a camo jacket and ski cap, kneeling next to a bloodied whitetail buck.

Tyler made sure to tell Lawson all this whenever they met. In turn, Lawson made sure to bring Otherwise Illegal Activity (OIA) agreements for Tyler to sign. Though Tyler wasn't being paid for his work as a source, these agreements allowed him to commit certain illegal activities and collect the proceeds. It was a common practice and becoming even more so. The FBI, the only agency that reports the crimes of its informants, would allow sources to commit thousands of crimes that year, including selling drugs and making bribes.

If Lawson's suspicions were correct, Tyler's Otherwise Illegal Activity included laundering the Zetas' drug money. But laundering money required receiving money, and the group was slow to send it. It didn't do Tyler much good to keep working with this crew if they weren't going to pay their bills. It didn't do Lawson any good, either.

With the bill sitting at $35,000 in early 2011, Carlitos and Fernando finally called. They were ready to pay up. Could Tyler meet them in Laredo to pick up the cash?

For any other Texas rancher, it was a ludicrous request. It would require passing through Interstate 35's Laredo North station, the interior Customs and Border Protection checkpoint that had undone José's brother Kiko. To do that with thirty-five grand in cash required either declaring (and explaining) the money or lying.

Tyler the rancher couldn't agree to it. But Tyler the Confidential Human Source could, so long as he had a fresh OIA contract on file. But that raised another potential wrinkle. No one knew the $10,000 rule as well as smugglers, so why would they ask Tyler to break it? Could they know he had cover from law enforcement?

Probably not. Regardless, Lawson needed the drop to happen. If someone could deliver cash in Laredo, the money would likely come from Mexico. Lawson wanted to know who the someone was, and where the someone went after making the delivery. He asked Tyler to arrange the drop.

Sending an inexperienced operative would be risky, since Lawson would need to record audio and shoot photos of the drop. It was a risk agents routinely took with paid informants and drug-dealing snitches, but asking Tyler might send him running. So Lawson instructed Tyler how to play it. Tell them you'll send a laborer, Lawson said. Tell them the laborer will be waiting in a hunter-green Silverado near the plaza.

"It's very important that this deal go in the morning," Lawson wrote to Tyler the night before, eager to watch the money change hands.

"OK buddy," Tyler wrote back. "I got it."

■ ■ ■

LAREDO, TEXAS
January 2011

Downtown Laredo used to hum on a weekday morning like this, with throngs of people crossing Bridge One from Nuevo Laredo and walking straight into the downtown shopping district. Peddlers crossed, looking to shop wholesale. Shoppers from interior Mexico crossed, looking for a good deal on new American luxuries. Maids and servers and other workers who lived in Mexico but worked in Laredo stopped before catching the bus to their jobs. They popped into La Fama, the one-hundred-year-old men's clothing shop to buy a cheap dress shirt, or into a fifty-year-old electronics store to buy the latest Walkman, or into a cluttered shoe store to buy the brightest Nikes in stock. This was the bargain: Mexicans could cross easily and expect better wages and American shopping; Americans could cross easily and expect cheap, authentic Mexican treasures, and a little break from Texas conventions, most notably the legal drinking age.

By the time Lawson pulled into downtown Laredo that morning, the bargain was dying. Americans could no longer stroll into Nuevo Laredo for dinner; that was a given. The Zetas were fighting a multifront turf war over control of the Laredo ports. The Gulf Cartel, the Sinaloa cartel, and the Mexican government were all trying to keep Forty on the margins of the smuggling business. It had become so violent that people could hear the gun battles from the American side.

Retailers on the American side had been pummeled by a series of blows. Increased border security after 9/11 made crossing a nightmare. The availability of American goods in Mexico also made shopping in the States less of a novelty.

Through it all, one institution seemed to persevere, and that was where Lawson was now—parked across a grassy plaza from La Posada, Laredo's landmark hotel. The hotel and square were an oasis, quiet but for the birds chirping in the grove of trees in the plaza, draped year-round with strings of white lights. The hotel was the city's best place for a lunch or breakfast meeting, and the plaza was the city's best place to wait for that meeting, or for a ride, or for the right moment to say the right thing. If Laredo had one of those free weekly newspapers with the snark in front and the prostitutes in back, it would vote this plaza Laredo's Best Place to Wait.

Lawson could attest to that by now. He'd been waiting for a half hour. He picked up his phone and dialed "Tyler's laborer," the undercover in the Silverado. Call him, Lawson said into the phone, and the undercover agent picked up his phone and dialed.

It was a simple mission with a simple premise, but it was also their most stressful yet. Though Lawson believed that Tempting Dash and Mr Piloto had been purchased with drug money—that all of the horses controlled by José, Carlitos, and Fernando had been purchased with drug money—it wasn't clear how he would prove it. José had told everyone who would listen that his wife and he had saved up to buy the horse. The horses bought at auction had been paid for by seemingly legitimate Mexican businessmen. Were they being paid back with Forty's drug money? Lawson suspected so. Could he prove it? No.

That was where this morning's drop came in. Lawson figured he would eventually use bank statements, auction-house records, and other paper to trace the Company's cash from safe house to quarter-horse business—the "placement" stage of this apparent money-laundering gambit. But Lawson knew that the easiest transaction to understand—for him, for a prosecutor, and for a jury—would be one in which a Zeta operative handed drug money to a horseman.

Just as important was keeping Tyler on board. If the money dried up, Lawson figured, so might Tyler's willingness to continue working with the FBI. If Lawson could make sure Tyler continued his business with José, he could buy himself time to build the case.

On the plaza, Lawson kept waiting. A half-dozen other agents stalked the area on foot to secure and photograph the operation. Lawson's friend María Medina parked across the plaza in her G-ride. Raul Perdomo, the agent who'd accompanied Lawson to New Mexico, parked closest to the drop point, in the "extraction car," from which he would leap if shit went sideways. A half hour into the mission, Lawson was starting to worry that it already had.

The eleven A.M. meeting time passed, then another half hour. Then another. Lawson figured the courier had been slowed by typical bridge delays. For couriers carrying drugs or illicit cash, the delay was sometimes strategic. Customs used what they call a pulse-and-surge strategy, flooding one bridge with agents and K-9s for about forty-five minutes before moving on to the next crossing. Some smugglers dispatched lookouts to the American side of the bridge to study the enforcement patterns. If the agents were pulsing and surging, the lookouts lingering at the checkpoint alerted the smugglers to wait. That could have been holding up the courier, too.

Eventually, a young Hispanic man in his twenties approached the Silverado. Lawson watched and listened as the man handed over $27,000—$8,000 less than the group owed Tyler. He'd brought four female money mules with him, each carrying eight or nine grand. The last one had been detained. But don't worry, the courier said. They can't keep her because it's not $10,000. He walked back toward the bridge, pledging to be back with the rest.

Listening over the transmitter, Lawson worried. Yes, the law only required the women to declare amounts over $10,000. But it was also a crime, called "structuring," to strategically divide larger sums into smaller ones to avoid detection. If the agents discovered one smuggler carrying $8,000, they'd know to ask about the others. If they broke her, they could all get locked up, foiling the operation.

And if the Company's courier happened to get caught the first time he attempted to deliver cash to Tyler, what might the Zetas start thinking about Tyler?

Lawson radioed another FBI agent and told him to make sure that Customs let the woman through—that the FBI was working something bigger. Lawson hoped it would work but feared it wouldn't. Cooperation, he knew, was not abundant in the DNA of federal law enforcement.

They waited some more. The courier called back. OK, he said, they're across. A few minutes later, the courier climbed into the Silverado and handed over the final eight grand. Lawson listened in as the agent counted it and sent the guy on his way.

They had their money, which Lawson transported to the FBI offices to be inventoried. With a little sleuthing, they also had the courier's name. Lawson figured the courier wouldn't stray too far from his mules as they crossed, so he'd sent an agent to examine the crossing records. They narrowed it down and found their man: Victor Lopez, a Mexican who crossed several times a day.

There was one more thing for Lawson to do. A few days after the drop, he retrieved the cash from the FBI offices. Even with an Otherwise Illegal Activity agreement on file, the FBI rarely let drug money "walk." Snitches posing as dealers usually relinquished their proceeds; politicians-turned-informants never got to keep their bribes. But Tyler was different. For starters, they had no leverage—no charges to dangle over him in exchange for his continued cooperation. And they weren't paying him for his work as an informant. Since he needed the money to keep the farm going, they needed him to keep the money.

Lawson loaded the cash into a duffel bag and drove north toward Tyler's ranch along Interstate 35, the smuggler's favorite corridor. Technically Lawson should have declared that thirty-five grand at the checkpoint a few miles north of Laredo, but he just smiled and waved and cruised on through. In just a few hours he was in a parking lot not far from Tyler's ranch, watching Tyler count.

Every so often, Lawson would ask Tyler, "When are these guys gonna sell?" They didn't have to convert their assets back into cash to be considered launderers, but it would help complete the cycle, from "dirty" American drug money to horses to "clean" American dollars. But no matter how many horses the group bought, they never cashed out. They don't sell, Tyler always told Lawson. They only buy.

Then, one day, it happened. The annual Winter Mixed Sale at Heritage Place—the same Oklahoma City auction that put José and Tyler on the FBI's radar—was coming back around, and José needed Tyler's help again. This time, he needed Tyler to sell, not buy.

The horse was named Blues Ferrari. Ramiro had bought him the year before for $15,000, a good price for a colt out of the sport's best stud, Corona Cartel. Blues Ferrari had started his racing career with promise, winning an $8,000 maiden race for one of Forty's many front companies. Following the group's typical strategy, they then transferred Blues Ferrari into José's company, Tremor Enterprises, and entered him into a million-dollar race in California. He finished in last place by two full lengths.

Now José planned to sell him. He asked Tyler to act as the agent—a broker, basically, who would prep the horse and make sure he sold for the best price. Naturally, Tyler said yes. But José wasn't making it easy on him.

Most owners ship a horse to the selling agent weeks before the auction to allow time for prep—to feed the horse well and keep him fit, to pick his hooves clean of debris, to brush the shedding hair from his coat until it shines in the auction-house lights. José shipped Blues Ferrari straight to the auction house. Tyler didn't see the horse until the day before the auction.

The horse looked like shit. His bay coat was long, and his ribs bulged from his underfed trunk. He was three years old, in the middle of his racing career but without much promise. Why not race him again and hope they get lucky? And if José needed money that bad, why not give Tyler time to clean him up? He was only worth thirty or forty grand looking good; looking like this, he was worth even less.

Blues Ferrari clicked into the sales ring. Tyler knew the horse looked like hell; everyone did. They wondered why Tyler Graham, scion to the auction house itself, was selling a horse so poorly groomed. One breeder said the colt looked like "death eating a cracker."

As the bidding began, Tyler noticed a Hispanic man sitting in the arena. He had wavy black hair and skin whose orange tint indicated a life spent by the beach. But there was something else about his appearance that Tyler noticed: he looked as though he'd been in an accident. His hand was bandaged and swollen. His face was bruised like a picnic peach.

Tyler asked the guy: What happened?

And the guy said: Golfing accident.

If it was a lie, it was a terrible one, and the confusion only escalated once the bidding for Blues Ferrari heated up. Swollen Golfer was bidding, and someone somewhere kept coming over the top of him, and Swollen Golfer kept coming right back. Now the auctioneer was asking, "ThreetenDoIhavethreeten?" Swollen Golfer kept raising his hand.

Tyler didn't see Lawson in the room, but he could safely assume that the FBI was there somewhere, watching this strange scene unfold. He would tell Lawson all about it the next time they spoke. But even when they put their heads together, Tyler and Lawson couldn't exactly figure what had happened. Why did a man with a bandaged hand and a busted face just buy José Treviño's old, slow, mangy horse for $310,000, ten times what he was worth?

# CHAPTER SEVENTEEN

# OPERATION FALLEN HERO

BALCH SPRINGS, TEXAS
February 2011

Alexandra was home that morning, which would be a rare occurrence soon enough. She was nineteen now, with bangs that slashed across her round face, which was narrowing with distance from adolescence. It was going on two years since she'd graduated from high school, and Alexandra was still straddling childhood and adulthood. She spent a lot of time here, at her parents' cramped brick house in the Dallas suburbs, caring for her smaller siblings when her parents were gone. But she and *love of my life!* Luis were on a collision course with adulthood. In the last eight months, Luis had graduated from high school, enlisted in the Marines, and shipped off to train at southern California's Camp Pendleton. They planned to marry soon and move near the base. Alex, now a sophomore at the University of Texas at Arlington, would have to finish school in California.

With Luis thousands of miles away, Alex tended to her lovesickness by splicing together videos of the two of them and setting them to cinematic scores. There were shots of him in his fatigues, of her with a cooking pot on her head, of quick kisses and of wasted afternoons, of her searching high and low for his dog tags as he prepared to leave town. Of him quietly muttering to the camera, too low for Alex to even hear: "Babe, you're beautiful. I fucking love you."

Zulema was home that morning, too. She would head out soon to her job in downtown Dallas, a thirty-minute, traffic-snarled commute that ended in a dank parking garage that cost eighty-five dollars a month to access. First, though, she would help her four kids—eight-year-old Oscar, twelve-year-old Rebecca, seventeen-year-old José Jr., and nineteen-year-old Alex—get ready for school. Though it was solely Zulema, not José, whose days were now strictly defined by early mornings and grinding labor, she rose each morning with the burden of managing the house—of making sure the kids' school-lunch accounts were filled and that the bills were dutifully paid. They always were.

José was home that morning, too. It was just after sunrise. If he were still laying bricks, he would have been gone already, barreling to some dusty job site across town. Lately his life had been a little less rote, a little more chaotic. He was traveling more than he ever had, driving to Tyler Graham's ranch to check on horses, scouring CheapTickets.com for flights to California and Oklahoma to visit breeding farms and auction houses. But he was spending more time at home, too, handling his horse business from the family computer.

Money was an issue, as always. Technically, his company only owned a few horses, which he'd bought from Forty's front companies after they showed promise at the track. But his expenses were mounting. Before winning the All American, his company ledger showed Tremor Enterprises to be deeply in the red. His business checking account had fallen so far that José had been forced to write personal checks to keep it afloat, basically negating the occasional paychecks he'd afforded himself. As a result, his and Zulema's checking account had ended 2010 below two thousand dollars.

Winning the All American was a boon, but in the months since, his business accounts had tumbled back toward zero. The $300,000 check his company received from selling mangy Blues Ferrari had been manna from quarter-horse heaven.

Even more crucial was the new breeding season, which was just getting under way. Since the beginning, José had imagined his business outliving him, which almost assuredly meant outliving Forty, or at least outlasting Forty's freedom. José had said as much to Alex, whom he imagined one day taking the business over, not from this crowded house but from some spacious cut of American farmland. But if José wanted his new business to make it to the next generation, he needed revenue, and not the kind that relied on backpacks of cash or luck at the racetrack. He needed the kind that relied on diligence in the breeding barn.

That's where the real money was—the money that could truly replace the steady income José gave up when he quit bricklaying. A breeding business would allow him to pay himself better than the sporadic three-thousand-dollar checks he wrote himself. Breeding would allow Zulema to shop somewhere other than the Walmart around the corner from their house, or take their kids out to eat somewhere other than the fast-food joints they frequented. Maybe it would even allow her to quit her job at Ernst & Young, where she worked overtime just to push her weekly pay past five hundred dollars. She'd been helping with the horse business a little, managing bills mostly. Maybe she could work full-time for José one day.

For that, José needed his star horse to produce. After getting the bad news about Tempting Dash's disease, José and Tyler had worked together to make sure the stallion could at least fulfill his destiny as a breeder. Tyler used his connections at Texas A&M to research whether Tempting Dash could safely breed. It turned out he could. Though piroplasmosis could be transmitted from a mare to a foal through their shared blood, it could *not* be transferred from a stud to a mare through semen. As long as Tempting Dash was properly quarantined, state health officials would allow him to breed.

José chose Tyler's stud farm to breed him. Tyler had been there from the beginning, offering marketing advice, taking José hunting, diagnosing Tempting Dash, and now helping convince health officials that the horse was safe to breed. Perhaps more important, José had been working closely with Tyler for a year now. He trusted him, as much as he trusted anyone.

José and Tyler had spent the winter offering free breedings to handpicked breeders; they hoped that breeding Tempting Dash to some topflight mares would increase the quality of Tempting Dash's first crop. Otherwise, they knew, it might be hard to attract the sport's top breeders, since Tempting Dash's race record was as thin as it was impressive, and because questions swirled about how fast he truly was. He'd tested negative for performance-enhancing drugs after his two big wins, but the industry knew that inventive cheaters could find new drugs to beat the tests. A colt coming out of the blue to break track records naturally raised suspicions.

There were eager paying customers, too, whom José would charge $5,000 per breeding, a modest but not insignificant stud fee. Multiplied by the seventy-five paid breedings Tyler and José had lined up, breeding season could bring $375,000 in stud fees from Tempting Dash alone. And Mr Piloto was breeding, too, at $3,500 a pop.

With any luck, that money would fortify Tremor LLC, and might even one day help José and Zulema move out of this crowded brick house. José Jr. would turn eighteen soon, an occasion Zulema would mark by writing him a hundred-dollar check; Alex would be out of the house by spring. For now, though, things were still tight, with six people stuffed into fifteen hundred square feet, in a place, Dallas, where fifteen-hundred-square-foot bungalows were routinely bull-dozed and replaced with forty-five-hundred-square-foot Tudors.

*Bam-bam-bam.* A knock at the door, and not a ginger one. José Jr. pulled it open. A trim, handsome Hispanic man in a bulletproof vest stood on the porch. Beyond him were at least a half-dozen more agents lurking in the street, dressed for a fight.

"Can you get your dad?" the cop at the door asked in Spanish.

José found his way to the door, his bare chest leading the way, naked but for his work jeans. It wasn't hard for José to figure out what this was about. He'd always known the feds were on him. Recently, José had walked into his fenced-in front yard at four-something in the morning to find two guys in street clothes milling about near one of his trucks. They had told José they were just looking for scrap metal, and José didn't have any proof that they weren't. If he suspected otherwise, he was right: they were DEA agents, trying to put a GPS tracker on his truck.

If anything, the family probably should have expected the feds' visit a week before. After the news broke about the dead ICE agent.


Nine days before, two ICE agents from Laredo had been driving south through Mexico, headed to Mexico City on a "diplomatic" assignment. There was so much cover in that word, *diplomatic,* ten letters that allowed federal agents from every federal agency to operate in Mexico and feel some measure of safety. As long as they weren't caught carrying weapons, which was outlawed by a U.S.-Mexican treaty, they were good—allowed by the Mexican authorities to work and investigate, and generally not targeted by narcos, who knew how bad for business it would be to harm an American agent. There hadn't been a federal agent killed on Mexican soil since 1985, when a DEA agent named Enrique "Kiki" Camarena was kidnapped, tortured, and killed by narcos in Guadalajara.

The Zetas were different, though. Their original benefactor, Gulf Cartel boss Osiel Cárdenas, had once discovered a pair of American agents doing surveillance of his estate. He rolled up in a Jeep Grand Cherokee toting a gold-plated assault rifle and banged on the window of the Americans' armed SUV, apparently unmoved by the diplomatic plates on the bumper or the FBI badge gleaming through the windshield.  .

"You'll regret anything stupid that you might do right now," one of the agents said. "You are fixing to make three hundred thousand enemies."

"You fucking gringos," Cárdenas said, before driving off. "Don't ever come back."

Message delivered. Things were changing in the age of the Zetas.

The Zetas had only reinforced this since declaring independence from the Gulf Cartel. They'd hurled grenades at the American consulate in Monterrey. They'd made direct threats against American cops. They'd even killed an American jet-skier on a borderland lake, which they patrolled in boats like rifle-wielding pirates. Now this.

The ICE agents were driving through a remote patch of San Luis Potosí, between the American embassies in Monterrey and Mexico City. They knew that stretch of highway was controlled by the Zetas. They knew it from the most recent intelligence, which showed the Zetas taking control of the area. And they knew it from the SUVs that sped up on them, boxed them in, and ran them off the road.

Gunmen approached the SUV, which was, thanks to the work of a British defense contractor, well armored. But the contractor had overlooked one feature that could easily turn into a bug. When one of the agents, Jaime Zapata, threw the SUV into park, the doors automatically unlocked. How diplomatic.

A gunman opened the door. Zapata scrambled to shut it, and did, but accidentally rolled down one of the windows. A gun barrel appeared in the vacant space. Bullets exploded into the SUV, tearing through Zapata's thirty-two-year-old body. His partner tried to use the SUV's onboard distress signaler, but it failed, so he used his cellphone to dial the embassy. A Mexican helicopter would be sent to their aid, but not in time. Zapata bled out.

He was the first agent killed on Mexican soil since Kiki Camarena, and the gunmen escaped. In the months afterward, Zapata's murder would become intertwined with a widening political scandal, after it was discovered that the guns used in his attack had been purchased in the United States. In a series of undercover operations, including one called "Fast and Furious," federal law enforcement had allowed straw purchasers to buy and ship thousands of guns back to Mexico, with hopes of tracking them to cartel leaders. But the strategy had failed, and now the guns were being linked to the murder of an American agent.

In the days after Zapata's death, the feds sought payback. They dispatched hundreds of agents to hit any home with ties to the Zetas. The agencies tried to coordinate, though they couldn't even settle on one name. ICE called it Operation Fallen Hero. DEA called it Operation Bombardier. The FBI diplomatically called it by both names, clumsiness aside. Whatever the feds called it, it took them to José Treviño's doorstep.

Alex watched her dad politely wave the agent in. He was from the DEA. He asked José if his guys could search the house. José stepped aside. The agent asked Zulema and her four children to move into the cramped kitchen. They did, finding seats around their small kitchen table.

Once the family was in the kitchen, the feds flooded the crowded house and searched. The DEA agent, a veteran named Johnny Sosa, stepped outside with José.

"You know why I'm here?" Sosa asked in Spanish.

José's eyes went glassy.

"Why are you tearing up?" Sosa asked.

"Is it true about my brother?" José asked.

The Mexican media was reporting that José's brother Omar, Forty-Two, had been killed in a shoot-out. Later, it would be determined that Forty-Two was alive and well. But the DEA agent didn't know that yet, and he was operating under the same impression. He had even seen a photo of a body, though it was too ravaged by bullets to discern whether it was really José's brother.

"I'm hearing the same things," Sosa said. "Do you know? When was the last time you talked to him?"

"I haven't talked to my brothers in five years."

Sosa asked José what he did for a living. José told him how he'd laid bricks for so many years but had recently started racing horses. My wife and I saved up, he said. We got lucky, he said.

Inside, Alex watched as the agents swept the house—it didn't take long—looking for drugs, for weapons, for cash. When they were finished, they started to file out. Alex spotted Sosa, the agent who'd questioned her dad. She lit him up.

I'm a college student, she said.

I'm studying the law, she said.

Leave my family alone.

I know my rights.

You have no right to—

They did. José had invited them in. But they left his house empty-handed, with his daughter's rising voice tailing them out the door.

■ ■ ■

ELGIN, TEXAS
March 2011

It had been a year since Lawson first pulled his gold Impala into Tyler's long driveway, and here he was again, barreling up 35, carving past shuttered, wrung-dry ranches on his way to see his first and best CHS. He'd been in Laredo long enough now to have friends, so this time he borrowed a truck, something a little less conspicuous, and a lot less gold, than his Impala. Agent Medina went with him.

When he'd first trekked north to Elgin, Lawson had been thrilled at the idea of getting out of Laredo's industrial thrum and into the wavy terrain of central Texas. He liked the idea of hitting Austin, too, a mecca of fellow twenty-somethings, where, once off-duty, he could post up at a high-top, take down wings and a craft beer, and not be immediately pegged as a fed. They probably thought he was an insurance guy. He was fine with that.

A year later, as he and Agent Medina reached the outskirts of Austin, that thrill was muted. The FBI called Laredo a "hardship assignment," but Lawson and his colleagues could hardly imagine a better office for their first post.

First to go was his impression of Laredo as some sort of war zone. Lawson only had to read the FBI's own crime stats to know how overblown his initial vision of Laredo was. Despite having an entire cable series devoted to its bloodshed, Laredo was considerably safer than Houston and Dallas and not any more dangerous than allegedly idyllic Austin.

Lawson had also learned that the culture of Laredo was one uniquely suited to making him feel welcome. Ninety-six percent Hispanic, it was basically a northern Mexican town masquerading as part of Texas, a case study in the arbitrary nature of America's southern border. Most of its prominent and powerful citizens were

of Mexican heritage, and the smattering of Anglos tended to assim-
ilate to, and be welcomed by, the dominant culture. Raised mostly
by a conservative mom in a Bible Belt stronghold, he found himself
infatuated with the way big Mexican-American families threw open
their doors and their coolers and insisted that he sit and drink and
stay.

It also helped that the feds tended to assign young, single agents
like him to the border. They sent as many Spanish speakers as they
could, so many were Hispanic, though there were always a few
gringos like Lawson in the mix. Hispanic or white, they bonded easily over their circumstances. They played on sports teams together,
including the city's worst wood-bat baseball team. They watched
football on Mondays, played poker on Wednesdays, and grilled out
on Saturdays, before descending on a nearby bar.

Lawson and some of his fellow rookies were cautious at first
about going out. In a town that was nearly all Mexican and Mexican-
American, they were employed specifically to fight Mexican criminal enterprise; he figured that would make him a target. But he
quickly learned how naïve that assumption was. The city was brimming with law enforcement agents, including four thousand CBP
agents alone—more employees than almost any other entity in
town, public or private. That meant everyday Laredoans couldn't
help coming to know a cop or two, and those relationships naturally
bred a level of sympathy born of simple human connection. Lawson noticed it especially when the police and fire departments
squared off in an interdepartment football game. Thousands of
people showed up, and no one minded when the lumbering FBI
agent from Tennessee checked into the game. Nor did they mind
when he checked into their local bar.

Agent Medina made it out when she could, though she wasn't
precisely part of the group, since she was married with kids, and
already had extended family and friends sprinkled on both sides of
the border. For her, the border wasn't a hardship. It was home.

It was those and other differences that helped her and Lawson
work so well with each other. Lawson was hard-charging and hard-
headed, impatient with what he perceived as laziness among other

agents and scurrilousness among other agencies. Medina was collected, diplomatic, and destined to climb the bureau's ranks. Lawson could imagine a hundred different ways to set up a takedown or work a source; Medina could identify the most effective way, and the one least likely to get anyone killed or fired. Medina was happy to cede the spotlight, and maybe a little too willing; Lawson didn't mind getting credit and attention for work done well, and wanted it for Medina as much as he wanted it for himself. She was, as he liked to say, "somewhere between big sister, mother, and attractive coworker." But she didn't need a brother or a boyfriend, so they settled into an extremely close, and extremely platonic, friendship and partnership.

Working together, they had basically solved the initial kidnapping case that Medina had invited Lawson to work, though it was hardly satisfying. They confirmed through sources that the two dirt-biking brothers had been killed by the Zetas, probably after refusing to turn over their truck or dirt bikes. The agents also identified the hit man, and confirmed that he was dead, too. It was brittle closure for the victims' wives, one of whom happened to live down the street from Lawson and occasionally dropped by for updates. But it was good police work, so they kept teaming up, going on as many adventures together as they could.

After the American jet-skier was shot dead by Zeta pirates on Lake Falcon, they'd begged the Tamaulipas state police to search Mexican waters for the body. The Tamaulipas government was reluctant. When they finally put the chopper in the air, it became clear why: the Zetas tried to shoot it down.

With some cajoling, Lawson and Medina got permission to let the Mexicans land the chopper on the U.S. side. But by then the chopper was almost out of gas. So there were Lawson and a pregnant Medina, driving from the Laredo airport to the field where the chopper had landed, in a truck carrying jet fuel.

Today's mission, in Elgin, would be tame by comparison. But it was important. Tyler Graham had officially been a Confidential Human

Source for longer than a year. In that year, Lawson had grown surprisingly close to his first CHS. He had gone in hoping to forge a trust, a relationship, even a bond. It was among the many things he considered noble about being an FBI agent, especially when compared with DEA agents. DEA agents get informants because they dangle twenty years over their heads, Lawson thought. FBI agents could work more credible sources from less leveraged angles. They had better standing in the community, thanks to their work in public corruption, violent crime, and terrorism, to go with $8 billion in annual funding, compared with the DEA's $2 billion. More time, more resources, more juice—it all allowed Lawson to slowly cultivate a source like Tyler. Someone without the stick of heavy time hanging over him, but not without a few carrots to gain from his cooperation.

Still, the relationship had blossomed in ways Lawson hadn't foreseen. He spoke with Tyler on the phone, exchanged emails, and continued to meet him in bars and restaurants around Austin. What developed was not exactly a friendship; Lawson knew he shouldn't call it that. But it felt that way some days: two young country guys who loved beer and football and home, who were making their ways in their respective family businesses, who appeared flush with a sense of familism not unlike José's. One night at the sports bar, they stayed late enough that the bar started to transform into a party spot, and the music transitioned from country to some popular old-school hip-hop song. As country as they were, they were also young men raised in the 1990s. They rapped along in unison.

It was precisely these similarities—the kind of cultural proximity that existed between them—that had caused the FBI to send Lawson to see Tyler in the first place. They could have sent the more experienced Medina, not to Tyler's ranch but to Chevo's falling-down training center—offering Chevo a lifeline and letting Tyler Graham work his way into becoming a target. Chevo was inherently under more suspicion than Tyler simply because of their respective ethnicities. The FBI's own guidelines, obtained by the investigative website the Intercept, explicitly allow agents to use race when deciding whether to target someone: "Ethnicity may be considered in evaluating whether a subject is—or is not—a possible associate of a criminal or terrorist group that is known to be comprised of members of the same ethnic grouping, as long as it is not the dominant factor for focusing on a particular person." So they used Lawson, and through his Tennessean eyes they saw Tyler as their teammate and most everyone else as potential targets. That the two of them vibed to old-school hip-hop and colliding linemen only served as confirmation of their wisdom.

But there had been some tension between source and handler lately. Despite knowing about Lawson's relationship with Tyler, a DEA agent, Fragile Male Ego Syndrome apparently raging, told Lawson he planned to approach Tyler himself, to see if he could convince Tyler that he needed to cooperate with the DEA as well. Just as the DEA had done with Ramiro Villarreal.

Lawson's patience with his DEA counterparts was already thin. He'd watched the FMES understandably flare up after Jaime Zapata, the ICE agent, got killed. Lawson had known Zapata. The FBI and ICE share an office building in Laredo, so they'd occasionally trade head nods at the office gym. Lawson understood the desire for revenge, and even shared that feeling with the DEA.

He also saw a shortsightedness in their random search of José Treviño's house. The DEA swore it had asked the FBI's permission before it door-knocked José's house outside Dallas, and maybe someone had. But nobody had asked Lawson, because Lawson would have said no. The DEA knew the FBI and IRS were investigating José, and they knew that such an investigation benefited from its target's nursing a false sense of security. If José hadn't already known he was under suspicion, he did now.

And now the DEA wanted to flip Tyler Graham?

Lawson knew he couldn't lose Tyler to the DEA. The case could go on without Tyler, but then it would go on without Lawson. Back in their Austin war room, IRS agents were sifting through stacks of records, searching for evidence of a money-laundering scheme. But Lawson was no sifter; he knew Tyler was his only unique connection to the case, and that without him the case might slip away.

In some alternate universe, maybe this wouldn't have mattered to Lawson. Maybe he could have trusted the agents from the DEA, who as fellow Justice Department employees were essentially colleagues, to work the case thoughtfully and ethically, in search of only truth and something like justice. Maybe Lawson could have trusted the IRS to do the same. Maybe, as an agent of Justice, he would have been happy to step aside, even if it meant he didn't get to sit in a courtroom one day and watch people get locked away. Even if it meant he couldn't call his dad one day and say, Hey, Dad, I made this big case. But that alternate universe, where justice proceeded outside of self-belief and possessiveness, didn't exist, for Lawson or any other agent he'd met. The DEA? They'd fuck it up. The IRS? They'd put the jury to sleep. The truth? Lawson was on the verge of it. And the case? It was his, so long as he kept Tyler.

Lawson urged Tyler to ignore the DEA—to literally not answer the door when agents came knocking. Naturally, it pissed Tyler off that these two agencies couldn't even pretend to be on the same team. In the bar of the swanky Omni Austin Hotel, Tyler pushed back for the first time. He'd talked to an attorney, he said. The attorney had advised him that he hadn't done anything wrong. That he could bail on the FBI without consequence.

"I've saved your ass from the DEA and IRS trying to indict you," Lawson replied. "You need to know that."

They'd gotten past it quickly, but Lawson knew things were delicate. Every in-person meeting could keep them from coming apart. The presence of Medina offered an extra coat of adhesive.

Tyler filled them in. It was only March, still the early part of breeding season, but Forty's horse operation had already foaled fifty new racehorses, with fifty more on the way. That was good for the FBI, as it meant more potential assets to track on their way to becoming racehorses, breeders, and money-makers. Less good: most of the babies were being born to surrogates in Mexico.

Everything that happened south of the river made Lawson anxious. If it was in Mexico, it was untouchable—couldn't seize it, couldn't freeze it. You could indict someone in Mexico, but you couldn't arrest him.

Carlitos, their closest connection to Forty, was in Mexico now, too, Tyler was saying, and "not expected to cross anytime soon." That was bad news for Tyler just as it was bad news for Lawson; Carlitos owed Southwest Stallion Station eighty grand.

José was still in Texas. That was good. But he still had connections in Mexico. When he'd stopped by Tyler's ranch not long before, on his way north from the border, he'd pulled up in a white Cadillac CTS, new enough to still have paper plates, and his family from Nuevo Laredo had poured out: his mom, two sisters, and two other women. They were headed back to Dallas to celebrate José's mom's birthday.

Then there was Ramiro, the original Horseman. Since he was out of the business by the time Lawson came around, Lawson didn't view Ramiro as a target. And while Ramiro was cooperating with the DEA and ICE, Lawson hadn't met him and wasn't sure how helpful he could still be. Still, he and Medina knew that one day Ramiro might be useful as a source or as a witness against José and the others. But Ramiro, Tyler was hearing, had disappeared to Mexico, too.

■ ■ ■

NUEVO LAREDO, TAMAULIPAS
March 2011

Five months after he left Ramiro by the side of the road, Forty summoned his former Horseman back to Nuevo Laredo. He'd been basically out of the business, lying low, on his way, hopefully, to escaping the drug war's clutches unscathed. Now, though, another trip across the river to see Papi.

His friends urged him not to go, but Ramiro saw no choice. His family, including his parents, still lived in Monterrey, well within the Zetas' reach. Friends, as well as his fixer and handler, told him to move his parents to the States, to do anything to avoid crossing back into Tamaulipas. But Ramiro wouldn't listen. Mexico was home, for him and for almost everyone he loved. They were staying. He was going.

He went alone this time, crossing the Colombia Bridge, just

south of Laredo. Sometime after that, his car was found engulfed in flames at the bottom of a thirty-foot embankment. There was no ID on him, and he was so badly disfigured—by something heavy being slammed repeatedly into his face, and then by the car being sent over the cliff—that authorities had a tough time ID'ing him. But eventually they confirmed that it was Ramiro Villarreal, the original Horseman. The new Horseman, Carlitos, had stood by and watched Ramiro die.

# CHAPTER EIGHTEEN

## LITTLE BLACK DOTS

Not long after the colonists accidentally invented quarter-horse racing, their sport fell from favor. By the Revolutionary War, thoroughbred racing was the dominant brand in every American territory but those dusty, stubborn ones out west. For all the colonists' achievements, including their brutal conquest of an already inhabited land of historically unrivaled natural resources, they probably would have been sad to learn that future horse races would be not violent sprints but long, floppy-hatted affairs in which the horses just kept running and running.

But there is one thing those early breeders might have been proud to know: that *their* brand of horse racing would eventually become home to some of the most exotic, advanced, industrial, and downright weird breeding techniques in all of equine science. Compared with those in thoroughbred racing, the typical quarter-horse breeding barn looks like nothing less than the lab of some especially mad scientist.

Ruled by regulation-averse cowboys, the American quarter-horse industry has long been more willing to push an envelope, let a line blur, or otherwise ignore the uptight conventions of the sport of kings. It started in the 1970s, when the American Quarter Horse Association began considering artificial insemination. Critics argued that it would denigrate the breed by allowing stallions to mate with a wider selection of mares, watering down his bloodlines. That's why the thoroughbred industry hadn't allowed it and never would.

The cowboys at AQHA approved it, and they didn't stop there. In the 1980s, they voted to allow breeders to transfer embryos out of pregnant mares and into surrogates, protecting prize broodmares against the wear and tear of pregnancy. In the 1990s, they allowed the shipment of cooled semen, meaning a stallion's sperm could be transported to a nearby ranch to inseminate a mare. In the 2000s, they allowed breeders to freeze and ship semen cross-country, and to continue using frozen semen *after* a stallion died. Around the same time, they voted to allow multiple embryos to be flushed from a mare in the same breeding season, allowing mares to produce multiple foals a year.

Eventually, a Texas breeder successfully cloned—yes, cloned— a topflight rodeo horse, and tried to register the clone as a new quarter horse. The industry put its foot down over that. Still, over the decades, the rule changes have turned quarter-horse breeding into an exacting science, with a hundred little glass vials for every horny stallion.

How this plays out varies from farm to farm and stud to stud, but the breeding of Forty's prized colt, Tempting Dash, offers a good case study. His origins can be traced to a California ranch that was, at the time, the epicenter of the quarter-horse breeding world: Vessels Stallion Farm.

The farm was named for Frank Vessels, a Kentucky-born businessman who'd built one of the sport's premier racetracks, Los Alamitos, on a patch of farmland in Orange County, California. Not just content to host the races, Vessels wanted to win them, too. So he owned horses and bred horses, and over the years his family built one of the industry's most successful breeding operations. Like most breeding operations, Vessels was known throughout the sport for its best stallion, First Down Dash.

The sport's most prolific stud, First Down Dash was owned by a syndicate of thirty-three breeders from across the country who had paid $175,000 each for a share of the stallion's breedings. He lived his days roaming a paddock at the heart of Vessels Stallion Farm. Breeders or admirers who wanted to see him run were out of luck, unless the nearest farmhand had a bag of sunflower seeds handy. The farm's manager had become addicted to the seeds in the 1990s, when he was trying to quit chew, and First Down Dash developed a liking. Now the only thing that got the horse running was the sound of a shaking bag.

Life got busy for First Down Dash on February 1, the first day of breeding season. Because a horse's racing age changes on January 1, breeders prefer foals born earlier in the year. Since mares gestate for about eleven months, the best time for them to get pregnant is February.

So February, March, even April were the busiest months at Vessels, and the busiest for First Down Dash, who spent the spring chasing sunflower seeds back and forth from his spacious stall and the breeding barn. Things started to die down by May, but May was still breeding season. So one morning in May 2006, First Down Dash was led out of his stall and down the winding farm road, to the squat breeding barn at the center of the fourteen-hundred-acre ranch.

If First Down Dash had been a Kentucky thoroughbred, he would have been greeted there by a mare, her hormones raging after being teased by a flirting colt. But this wasn't Kentucky, so no mare waited in the breeding barn. To his right, there was a small lab cluttered with vials and microscopes. To his left, there was a brown leather cylinder shaped and positioned to resemble, vaguely, female companionship.

First Down Dash knew just what to do. He mounted the dummy, thrusting away, and eventually ejaculated some of the sport's best semen. He produced between seventy-five and ninety milliliters every collection, with 250 million sperm in every milliliter and 75 percent "progressive motility," meaning three-fourths of his sperm swam straight for the finish line. It was enough strong-swimming sperm to impregnate a dozen mares, maybe more.

First Down Dash went back to loping around his sprawling paddock, listening for the sound of a shaking seed bag. Later that day, some of his prized semen was inseminated into a mare named A Tempting Chick, who spent the breeding season at Vessels. She belonged to a Kansas City insurance executive who owned a share of First Down Dash's breedings.

A week after inseminating her, the Vessels staff examined A Tempting Chick. They hoped to find an embryo in her uterus. And they hoped to get it out.

Theoretically, the Kansas City breeder could allow his mare to carry her First Down Dash offspring to term, the way a thoroughbred mare would. She could spend her eleven-month pregnancy grazing the Vessels pasture, foal her baby into its dewy grass, and trot its meandering fence lines with her weanling nipping at her swollen teats. But then A Tempting Chick would be unable to breed again that season, and maybe the next. So instead, the mare owner asked the Vessels team to do what most quarter-horse breeders do: flush the embryo.

In the breeding barn, they squirted a liter of buffer solution through a catheter and into A Tempting Chick's uterus. They sucked the fluid back out. In and out, in and out. Then they slipped the filtered tip of the catheter beneath a microscope. They pressed their eyes against it, looking for a little black dot, less than 0.4 millimeters across. There it was: a seven-day-old quarter horse embryo, the latest offspring of First Down Dash.

The mare's day was done; she sauntered back to her stall. The farm had more work to do.

Vessels did keep some surrogate mares on site. But A Tempting Chick's owner preferred his foals to be carried by one of the "recips"—short for recipient mares—at a Colorado farm that specialized in caring for surrogates. So the Vessels team went to work.

They flushed the embryo in and out of a petri dish to decouple it from any uterine debris, and dropped it into a tube filled with holding fluid. They capped and sealed that tube and submerged it in a fifty-milliliter centrifuge tube. Then, as if they were handling rare gems, they placed *that* tube into a cooled case called an Equitainer.

Working quickly, they called a courier to pick up the Equitainer. The courier drove it an hour south to the San Diego International Airport, where a United Airlines cargo handler collected it and made sure it got to Denver by early evening. If all went well, the embryo would be in a surrogate by nightfall.

Vessels lost track of First Down Dash's newest offspring after that. That particular little black dot spent a month or so on that Colorado farm, growing into a fetus. When the surrogate and fetus were stable enough, they were hauled to a West Texas ranch known for raising some of quarter-horse racing's best runners.

It was then and there, ten months later, that First Down Dash's newest foal, Tempting Dash, wobbled to his feet. The grooms weaned him from his surrogate's udder and from her side, taught the weanling how to walk alongside them, how to take a bit in his teeth without kicking anyone in the ACL.

Eventually, Tempting Dash's owner, the Kansas City breeder, paid to have the colt hauled back to California. He consigned Tempting Dash to the Schvaneveldt Winter Mixed Sale, a boutique horse sale, hoping to make some big sales despite the crashing markets. The horse was young and skinny, so no one was quite sure what to make of him, but everything fell into place once Ramiro started raising his hand.

# CHAPTER NINETEEN

## FLUSH

It was Saturday, and it wasn't even eight in the morning, but Tyler Graham was up. He was always up this early—early rising runs hard in the Graham family—and on this morning, Tyler had news to deliver. He dialed Fernando, who was cementing himself as José and Carlitos's chief of staff, the man you needed when something needed to get done.

"What's up, buddy?" Fernando asked.

"We got two embryos out of Dashin Follies last night," Tyler said. The sleep clung to his voice, undermining the severity of the news.

"Oh shit, man," Fernando said. "That's *hella* good."

It was that time of year, when stud farms like Tyler's were busy flushing, squinting, looking for little black dots. Tyler's stud farm was the busiest it had been in years, thanks to Southwest Stallion Station's first in-demand stallion in years, Tempting Dash.

Tyler didn't talk to José on the phone much, but Fernando seemed to represent the group nowadays. They spoke often, and

there was an apparent bond between them, even if Tyler's relationship with the FBI complicated things on his end. They were both
young, both still finding their way in the business, both prone to
playful ribbing. When Tyler had updates about which horses were
being bred, which bill needed paying, he often brought them to Fernando.

Dashin Follies, the horse Tyler was talking about, was the
$875,000 mare that Tyler had helped buy in Oklahoma, drawing
Agent Lawson to his doorstep. At the crew's behest, Tyler had inseminated her with semen from Mr Jess Perry, one of the top stallions in the sport. The pregnancy had taken.

That wasn't all.

"We got a Tempting Dash out of Coronita Cartel last night,
too," Tyler said. Coronita was the *other* mare Tyler had bid on for
the group in Oklahoma. She was a quarter-million-dollar broodmare, technically owned by Carlitos, who had ordered Tyler to
breed her with Tempting Dash.

"Fuck yeah," Fernando said. "It's about time for Coronita, huh?"

"It's the first time we fuckin' flushed her," Tyler said. "She finally
fucking cycled. We got an embryo."

"Cool," Fernando said. "That's way good news."

It was for Tyler. Otherwise Illegal Activity or not, this was Tyler's chance to turn Southwest Stallion Station into a power again.
The ranch made a five-hundred-dollar farm fee on each breeding,
but more important than that revenue was the prestige. If Tempting
Dash's offspring turned out to run like he did, that would draw
more interest from mare owners. It could also potentially draw
more interest from stallion owners, who might suddenly see Southwest Stallion Station as a smart place to stand their studs.

Pregnant recips, wobbly weanlings, rambunctious yearlings, ail-
ing racehorses—all manner of quarter horses could find a place at
Southwest Stallion Station if Tyler could reclaim the farm's standing, and every day a horse spent on the farm meant more revenue.
It cost $450 a month just to board a horse at Tyler's place, not to
mention smaller fees for palpation ($15), shoeing and trimming
hooves ($65), administering ultrasounds ($80), and other services.

And even now, before Tyler had proven the place as a stud farm, he was billing tens of thousands of dollars every month to horses sent to him by José, Carlitos, and Fernando.

Tyler knew that many of the stud fees he was collecting were basically bullshit. Of the one hundred forty mares he'd booked to breed with Tempting Dash, he figured at least half of them were owned by Forty, even if their official owner was Carlitos or another associate. Same for the mares breeding with Mr Piloto. So when Carlitos (eventually) delivered the stud fees he owed—$5,000 a pop for Tempting Dash, $3,500 for Mr Piloto—Tyler turned around and gave them to José. The way José told it, that was because Carlitos was a client. The way Tyler and the FBI saw it, Forty was just paying himself and using Tyler as the washing machine.

Bullshit fees or not, Southwest Stallion felt like a real stud farm again. In a way, Tyler was starting to worry that it was too busy. It was this guy, Victor Lopez, the courier who'd dropped the cash with the FBI in Laredo, who had Tyler anxious.

It turned out he was more than a courier. He was a direct conduit between Forty and his American horse business. Like Ramiro before him, Victor never said who his clients were in Mexico; he dealt exclusively in generic pronouns. "They" needed this and "we" needed that. All Tyler knew was that every so often Victor the Courier called and said he needed some of Tempting Dash's semen. Then he showed up *in a taxi* at Tyler's ranch, after a three-hour ride from the border. The cabbie waited in the car and watched the meter creak toward an eventual four-hundred-dollar fare.

Tyler always handed Victor the semen and sent him on his way, then alerted Lawson so the FBI could put a tail on Victor. He always went right back to Mexico, where Forty and other traffickers were apparently running a breeding operation with their less prestigious mares.

Lately, requests from the Company's Mexican satellite were coming too frequently. You can overtax a stallion if you collect semen from him too often, and Victor the Courier's "they" and "he" back in Mexico were pushing Tempting Dash to his limit. José even thought so. He told Tyler to put a stop to it.

"Hey," Tyler told Fernando on the phone. "Victor and them were calling me last night about eighteen fucking times about midnight, and I didn't answer the phone because I was asleep, and they want semen today. José has told me, do not collect those horses on off days anymore."

"José told you already not to send them anymore?" Fernando asked.

"Not on a noncollection day. Tomorrow's a collection day. Not today. And they're wantin' it on off days."

"Get through to them," Fernando said. "They gotta understand, Tyler."

"I don't want to piss 'em off, but, I mean, fuck, they gotta understand I'm gonna fuck these horses up if I'm collecting 'em every goddamn day."

But there were worse problems to have than a stallion with semen in demand. And it wasn't just the demand for Tempting Dash's semen that could help the future of Southwest Stallion Station.

There is a perk that goes along with standing a top stallion at your stud farm. Along with breeding the stud to other people's mares, the stud farm is typically offered a handful of free breedings. For Tyler and his family, that meant a chance to breed mares to Tempting Dash without paying the five-thousand-dollar stud fee.

It was like getting to play the slots without pumping quarters. If the breedings were busts, no harm, no foul. If they were successful, in a few years Tyler might have a two-year-old runner to send to the tracks. Maybe that two-year-old runner could even grow into a lucrative stallion or mare. Was it unlikely? Sure. Winning the jackpot always is. But if pulling the slot-machine arm is free, you pull it.

Tyler pulled it. Early that breeding season, he learned that little black dots had revealed themselves in two of the mares he'd decided to breed to Tempting Dash. José's star stallion was officially a breeder now, and at least part of his first official crop belonged to Tyler.

■ ■ ■

## LOS ALAMITOS, CALIFORNIA
May 2011

The family arrived at the track early, dressed in crisp collared shirts and sport coats, as if they were interviewing for new jobs. José wore the same button-down and white cowboy hat he'd worn in the winner's circle at Ruidoso Downs. This time, he added a woven jacket. Zulema wore her hair in tight curls and slipped the collar of her white blouse over the top of her corduroy sport coat. Alexandra's hair swept decisively across her face, and in her coat, she looked well beyond her years as the head of Asswipe Studios.

This was a land that José, quarter-horse racing's ascendant royalty, had not yet conquered. He'd won Texas's biggest race, and he'd won New Mexico's. But José had never cashed in here, at Los Alamitos Race Course, nestled amid the swinging palm trees of southern California.

When Frank Vessels, the businessman who built the track, bought this four-hundred-acre plot, he told his neighbors he planned to grow crops and raise cattle. But he quickly discovered that the soil was alkaline, prone to becoming alternately waterlogged and parched. So he pivoted. The town was suspicious about whether Vessels ever intended to farm that land, or whether he'd wanted to build a racetrack all along. No matter. When California lawmakers, under pressure to exhibit wartime austerity, shuttered most of the state's thoroughbred tracks during World War II, Vessels started inviting the public to Sunday-afternoon match races on his property. He paraded the horses, his wife sold hot dogs prepped at home, and Orange County fell hard for "the quarters."

In the decades since, Los Alamitos had become quarter-horse racing's West Coast mecca. Under predictable SoCal skies, it offered high-stakes racing from January to December, including the most Grade 1 stakes races—the races determined by AQHA to offer the stiffest competition. The sport's sturdiest schedule meant its most reliable attendance, which increased the amount forked over at the betting windows. That, in turn, fed larger purses, including a Triple Crown series made up of two $1 million races and one $2 million race, not to mention a handful of races that offered winnings into the six figures. Plus, SoCal was SoCal. Ruidoso was cute, but Los Al meant ocean breezes, a short ride to Disneyland, and the occasional attention of the *Los Angeles Times*.

It was the one major track where the Treviños hadn't won big. That could change tonight, in the Kindergarten Futurity, a Grade 1 stakes with $340,000 in prize money. They made sure to dress for the occasion.

To win at Los Al, José needed a Los Al trainer, someone with the barns and the workers and the experience to win. At first, Forty had tapped Adan Farias, a horse trainer trapped in a lineman's body. Farias's goateed mug had been seen in so many Los Al winner's circles that ESPN had called him the sport's "wonder boy." Like Chevo in Texas, he was a young Mexican national whose ties to the country made it more difficult to tell the Zetas no. Like Chevo in Texas, he had also proven himself willing to risk his reputation in the long term to succeed in the short. He'd had dozens of doping violations, and he had been suspended four times in 2008 alone.

It was Carlitos who first asked Farias to train. Farias agreed, and soon Carlitos extended him an invitation to come to Mexico to meet "the boss." Farias wasn't exactly sure who the boss was, but he had a sense he wasn't someone he wanted to meet. He resisted at first, putting Carlitos off. But one day at the track, Carlitos strolled up and let Farias know the trip was not optional.

"Either you go," Carlitos said, "or I take you."

Farias flew to San Antonio as instructed and was picked up by one of Forty's men, who drove him across the border. They drove into rural borderlands—Farias had no clue where he was—and onto a ranch. Farias extended his hand to the short, thin man flanked by bodyguards. He introduced himself as "Cuarenta."

Forty led Farias around the ranch and asked him how the horses looked. Farias told him, and then Carlitos drove him to the next ranch, and the next, until they had seen more than a hundred of Forty's horses, each better groomed than the last. Then they sent Farias home to train several of the group's most promising horses, including Number One Cartel and Tamaulipas Boy.

By the time Farias got home, he had an idea of whom he was working for. He Googled the Zetas and learned as much as he needed to about their tactics. He realized he wanted to quit about as quickly as he realized he couldn't.

So he trained. Farias's horses performed OK that first year, qualifying for two of the three legs of Los Al's Triple Crown. But a few got injured, as horses do, and Farias fell out of favor with Forty. So this year, José had partnered up with another trainer. That's whose barn José's promising filly was in now, as he, Zulema, and Alex found their place in the Vessels Club, the upscale box that offered the track's best view of the finish line, along with its finest meal. In a way, this new trainer was like Farias and Chevo and the other trainers the Treviños had employed recently, among the best in the sport. He was unlike them in one way that stood out: he wasn't Mexican.

José's new trainer was Paul Jones, who strode through Los Alamitos's muddy backside as if he owned it. He leased a good portion of it. He was the winningest trainer at the track, and the winningest in quarter-horse racing history. He'd won the All American in Ruidoso three times, and had won every big race at every big track. But his home was the sea of rickety barns that formed the backside of Los Al.

Like his dad before him, Jones leased by far the most stalls at the track, enough for a hundred horses at any given time. He wore jeans like his southwestern counterparts, but everything else about him was true to his native SoCal. Instead of cowboy boots, he wore bright running shoes, better for hustling from horse to horse, and instead of button-downs he wore breathable golf shirts. He spoke passable Spanish, he took every call, and he answered every question without consulting a note or an assistant: *Run this horse here, shut this horse down, let this one be claimed,* and so on. He could juggle his horses' needs as well as he could recognize them.

Jones's relationship with José had started where many owner-trainer relationships do: at the auction house. Jones was in Oklahoma scouting horses when Carlitos approached with a proposition. Pick out any horse, he said, and we'll send it to you to train. Jones wasn't exactly sure whom Carlitos was working for. He hoped it was Francisco Colorado, the wealthy Veracruz businessman who sometimes joined Carlitos at the track. He figured, he had no way of knowing where the money would come from. All he saw was a great opportunity.

He picked out a $113,000 horse, took it to Ruidoso, and ran it well. Not long after that, he found himself at dinner with José, who asked whether Jones wanted to be the official West Coast trainer of the biggest spenders in his sport. Jones told him what it would cost: $45 a day for every horse in his barns. Soon after, José delivered forty-five horses to Jones's barns.

It was a boon for Jones's business. Suddenly he was training dozens of the sport's most promising horses, all from the top bloodlines. Whoever actually owned them, they were managed by Carlitos, who stalked the barns as if *he* owned them.

The backside of the track was an ecosystem thick with humility. Besides Jones, most of the trainers struggled to make a living. The gallop boys and grooms who kept up the horses were sometimes so poor they slept in the closet-sized offices that were jammed between the stalls, or even in the stalls themselves. Carlitos, by contrast, flew by private jet, wore designer clothes, and moved through the mud back there with his volume and confidence at full blast, like he was back at his dad's track in Villarín. (He did manage to keep his shirt on.)

For Jones, what mattered was that Carlitos brought great horses and he kept up on his bill. Sometimes it was $60,000 a month.

There'd been a brief glitch earlier in the racing season. Several of the group's horses had failed to qualify for a high-stakes race in

Oklahoma City, and José was *pissed*. The horses weren't even in José's name. Technically, they belonged to front companies owned by Fernando or Carlitos or others, at least until they won. But José couldn't help fuming, and he talked openly about wanting to fire Jones, the best trainer in the sport. Carlitos claimed that Forty had even talked of wanting to kill Jones, as impractical and reactionary as it sounded.

Jones turned things around, though, and now the best of the horses in his famous Los Alamitos stables was a $45,000 sorrel filly named Separate Fire. She was owned, at least in name, by José Treviño.

José and his family found their cushioned seats inside the members-only Vessels Club, a tableclothed antidote to the sticky concrete of the main concourse. Night fell. The track lights, visible from palm-studded suburbs in every direction, helped consecrate the evening's gravity.

This wasn't Los Al's biggest race, with only $142,000 earmarked for the winning owner. But José could use the money, as the expenses of his sprawling horse business continued to outpace revenues. His business checking account was down from its high point of a million dollars to around $10,000, and he owed at least double that to Tyler Graham and Paul Jones, among other vendors.

José would have preferred to pay his own bills himself—to keep the business self-sufficient, rather than have Carlitos sending mysterious wires or Victor the Courier delivering cash in $9,000 increments. He also surely longed to write himself another check. Zulema was still working, still shopping at Walmart, still dining out at Whataburger and McDonald's, saving what she could. But as they sat in their box seats, their checking account had sputtered below $1,400 again, with $2,000 bills from Alex's college looming on the horizon.

They watched the horses load and explode. Separate Fire stumbled out of the gate, and, for a moment, it looked as if José's California dreams would blow away again. Then the filly accelerated. Ten seconds later, she was streaking to a three-quarters-length win and a track record.

The Treviños hustled downstairs, hugged Jones, and waded into the winner's circle to celebrate the next horse in their hot streak, after Tempting Dash and Mr Piloto. A reporter stuck a camera in José's face. This had been happening every so often, starting with that ceremony back in Oklahoma. He felt so awkward and humble back then: "I got lucky." Now, even for all his troubles, he felt buoyant from yet another win, proof that he belonged. He gushed about his three youngest kids back home—they had school but might be watching on their computer—and then giddily retold his love affair with this filly.

"I liked her on the catalog page and I liked her at the sale," he said. For anyone who'd been paying attention, and especially for the FBI, it was a strange declaration. José had always maintained that he'd bought horses *after* the sales, which was technically true; he'd kept his name off big, public purchases, only quietly transferring ownership when the potential revenue spiked. Now, after the race, José was going into detail about how *he'd* bought the horse, and why. (Later, Lawson, who occasionally watched big races online, would catch a video of José's postrace comments and see a man "believin' his own bullshit.")

"I was happy to buy her for $45,000. Would I have gone higher? I don't know if I would have gone $50,000, to be honest," José said. "It's easy now to see her worth, but it's difficult when you're bidding at a horse sale. I'm just happy that she ended up going home with us."

About a month later, José and Zulema flew back to southern California for the Ed Burke Million Futurity, the first leg of Los Al's coveted Triple Crown. They made the trip on the cheap. They flew in the day of the race and out the next morning, staying at the Residence Inn across the street from the track. The kids stayed home.

The $142,000 from their first win at Los Al had helped, but already their accounts were scraping the red again. Winning this race offered José a chance at $450,000, his biggest payday since the All American. Separate Fire was the favorite.

It must have been a strange time to have the industry's eyes fixed on him. With José now dominating at Los Al, with help from the sport's top trainer, José's fellow horsemen were saying more openly what they'd long grumbled privately about: that José was a fraud. That he was buying his way into the sport's upper echelon, as if there were any other way to excel as an owner, in their sport or any other. Now, with his self-congratulatory press conferences, he was rubbing their sunburned noses in it.

Then there was the matter of whose money he was spending. Back in Ramiro's days, they hadn't minded all that drug money propping up their struggling sport—and filling their own pockets. They'd happily pocketed hundreds of thousands of dollars of that drug money in those otherwise lean years. But they weren't used to losing. There was a good-ol'-boys club of old white oilmen, ranchers, veterinarians, and career breeders who saw themselves as the natural heirs to each winner's circle photo.

Over time, word also wafted through the stables about exactly whose drug money they were losing to. And if the money belonged to whom everyone suspected, there was something especially disturbing about it. Especially for those who'd been reading the papers.

Though the Zetas' bloodlust in battle was well known, recently they'd revealed themselves as even more disturbingly violent than previously believed. Along a highway in José's home state of Tamaulipas, Zeta soldiers had yanked seventy-two migrants, most from gang-torn Central America, from buses under the cover of night. They'd herded the migrants onto nearby ranches and murdered all but one, who escaped to tell his story with a bullet lodged in his neck. It was not clear, and would never be clear, exactly why the Zetas massacred those migrants. By then they were known for trying to extort refugees fleeing Central America through Mexico, so officials speculated that the people were killed because they couldn't pay. But later, a Zeta operative would offer a different explanation: that the Zeta bosses feared their Gulf Cartel rivals were smuggling in mercenary reinforcements from Central America, so they killed them instead.

Whatever the explanation, the story had repeated itself during José's winning run at Los Al, with more bodies being discovered in mass graves along the same highway. It was impossible to think José didn't hear about the massacres. Two weeks before the Ed Burke Million, the *Houston Chronicle* carried a story that made international headlines. This time, it was almost two hundred people, yanked from buses as they skirted the Gulf of Mexico and moved north through the Mexican state of Tamaulipas, approaching the border with Texas. This time, only the elderly were shot at first. The young women were raped. The able-bodied men were given bats and machetes and forced to fight to the death, with an unwanted prize for the winners: continued work as a killer.

Soon enough, witnesses would identify the mastermind of the migrant death matches: Forty.

José never spoke of what he knew, or what he believed, about his brother's violence. But it didn't stop him from his ascent at the track. He donned his new black hat—a coincidence, surely, though a grim one—and found his way back to the Vessels Club.

This time, Separate Fire didn't stumble, firing out to a three-quarter-length lead and never letting up. Separate Fire was now a third of the way to winning Los Al's Triple Crown, a probably impossible feat that would come with a million-dollar cash bonus. Few horses had even come close, but Separate Fire's odds looked as good as any.

José and Zulema pushed their way back into the winner's circle, a familiar jaunt now, and hoisted a heavy glass vase that signaled their biggest win in months and $450,000 to Tremor Enterprise's bottom line.

They were joined by Paul Jones, their star trainer. By night's end, José and Jones would be toasting with champagne in the track's Ves-

sels Club. By season's end, they'd be flying across the country together in a private jet that belonged to Hubbard, the owner of
Ruidoso Downs.

"We're down-to-the-ground people," José said that night, in an
interview with one of the quarter-horse publications that were becoming accustomed to courting his quotes. "But this is a great moment and we will enjoy it."

■ ■ ■

LAREDO, TEXAS
May 2011

When he took a beat to consider it, Scott Lawson had to admit that
things were very much going according to plan. He'd started as a
small-time cop, just as his dad did, and quickly graduated to federal
law enforcement, just as his dad suggested. No, he didn't land an
assignment chasing serial killers in Atlanta, like his hero, John Douglas, but perhaps he'd landed somewhere better—in Los Dos Laredos, the hometown of Forty, who was revealing himself to be
multitudes more prolific a killer than anyone Douglas ever chased.
He was working the case day and night, with a focus and diligence
his Hall of Fame uncle could admire. His bosses admired it, too:
management ordered Lawson's supervisors to keep his slate clear of
kidnappings and other smaller crimes.

Despite surpassing his dad's career as planned, Lawson spoke
frequently with his father about work. It was never case strategy:
how to stage a takedown, where to place a wire. It was people strategy: how to win over colleagues, placate a manager, keep a source
on board. How to deal with assholes. Maybe most important? How
to avoid being one.

This, Mike Lawson always said, was especially important for an
FBI agent, since so many of them were assholes. Take a bank rob-
bery: In the elder Lawson's eyes, a typical bureau guy shows up to
the scene well after the police work has commenced, dusts for
prints, and starts taking credit. A good FBI agent—the kind of FBI
agent Mike wanted Scotty to be and that Scotty wanted to be—

walked straight up to the local detective on duty and said, "Man, you did a badass job getting the scene secured. Can you go with me to help me look for so-and-so?"

They'd been talking like this for years now. Now that Scotty lived nine hundred miles away—his first real time away from Tennessee, other than Quantico—he cherished their conversations even more. The calendar's relentlessness amplified the calls, too. *Sixty,* Lawson had kept forcing himself to remember. *I've got my dad till he's sixty.* Now, in the heart of Scotty's first big federal case, his dad was fifty-eight.

Dad was still strong in ways, and sometimes Lawson mistook that strength for the promise of extra years—of sixty-five or seventy, genetics and hard living be damned. Just the previous weekend, Dad had told Lawson about the deck he'd built in the yard that he was always busy landscaping.

Scotty knew it wouldn't last, though. He'd last seen his dad around Christmas. Scotty had planned to fly home for the holidays, finally atoning for having missed the previous Christmas as a rookie. But that winter, he blew out his knee playing basketball—four torn ligaments, a broken bone, and a dislocated kneecap. Scotty called his dad and apologized that he would have to miss Christmas again. "To hell with that," Mike Lawson said. "I'm coming."

They spent that whole week together. They were a mess. The elder Lawson was still smoking, even though his cough sometimes came with splatters of blood. Scotty was eating pain pills and waiting for surgery. They watched movie after movie, becoming especially engrossed in *Gone Baby Gone,* about an ethically conflicted private detective. At one point, Scotty mentioned how special the week had been. His dad started crying.

When Lawson's dad left for the airport after their Christmas visit, it felt like goodbye, but they kept talking on the phone. Then, one day the following May, Scotty's work phone broke. It wasn't a standard iPhone. It was a clunky black thing that was extra secure, among other differences that Lawson didn't understand, other than that it kept randomly resetting. Lawson left it with one of the techs at the office and headed out to lunch at one of the Mexican places he and Medina frequented.

His phone fired right up when he got back. That was good. He had several voice messages. That was . . . good? Maybe Tyler had an interesting update, or maybe the IRS's box hunters had come across a smoking gun. He opened the first voice message and heard his brother's familiar drawl. He was cussing him out, as brothers do, for not picking up his phone, but the crux of the message was simpler:

"It's Dad."

As the other agents filed in for lunch, Lawson broke down crying. Medina put her hands on his heaving shoulders.

*This fucking phone.* Had it been working over lunch, he could have made the early flight out of Laredo and been at Dad's side by nightfall. As it was, he'd have to wait at the shitty little Laredo airport for the next shitty little plane, hours upon hours with his dad hundreds of miles away—his heart having sputtered, his brain having gone black, all those cigs and all that whiskey finally having bloodied his body back into its corner for a rest.

Scotty scrunched into the plane, scrunched into the next plane, scrunched into the rental car, the tears turning on and off like his damn phone. He was supposed to have two more years with his dad—two more years of phone calls, of advice, of lessons in empathy and patience and getting along. Two more years of his dad's country chill balancing out his maternally gifted type-A tendencies. Two more years to make a big case and call home about it.

He landed in Nashville late and drove through the night. Medically speaking, his dad was still alive when Lawson finally got to the hospital the next morning. Lawson knew what was coming, though. He knew he'd take a few weeks off work, and that even in the middle of this big case, the bureau would be cool with that. He knew he'd hear some great old stories from great old cops, and that he'd have to try to tell a couple himself. He'd go back to Dad's house and sift through his belongings, a tear-fueled ritual helpfully disguised as tedium. Then he'd say goodbye to Tennessee and retrace his steps back to Laredo, to the case, to the river he shared with Forty. He'd do all that and more, probably. But for a while he just sat there and

talked to him like always. "I think I'm going to be a part of something big," Scotty said, and then he just held his dad's hand and
waited.

# CHAPTER TWENTY

## THE WIRE ROOM

ELGIN, TEXAS
June 2011

The eighteen-wheelers came rising and falling through Elgin, spitting straws of hay into the open-air oven of central Texas and wheezing up Southwest Stallion Station's long driveway. Tyler Graham welcomed them, needed them.

Five years after returning to Elgin, he could look out onto his granddaddy's pasture and see it was teeming with more than a hundred horses, too many to keep an exact count in his head. The same could be said for the farm's accounting records, which teemed themselves, with thousands of dollars in fees for the boarding, care, breeding, and feeding of those horses.

The trucks chugging to Tyler's ranch, lugging square bales of alfalfa, would help with the feeding. Those bales, tied off and stacked like bricks, were the lifeblood of this patch of Texas. But as the clouds continued to hold out, fewer ranchers were ordering up truckloads of alfalfa. Because fewer ranchers had animals left to feed.

It just wouldn't rain. Droughts were part of life in Texas. They always had been. Spanish explorers lost a herd of four thousand horses to a particularly dry spell in the 1700s. Drought killed the first corn crops of Stephen F. Austin's colonists in 1822. The 1850s brought a drought that some researchers considered worse than the Dust Bowl. The drought of the 1950s—the drought against which all Texas droughts were measured—devastated the state's agriculture industry so completely that it reshaped the state, forcing it to diversify its workforce and invest billions in water infrastructure.

The current drought was catching up. In the Austin area, where Tyler lived, it had rained only a few inches between February and April, the lowest rainfall ever recorded for that stretch of time. Reservoirs were nearing record lows. Cities and towns were scrambling to pass water-conservation ordinances, threatening the pristine lawns of suburban oases all across the state.

But it was the ranchers who were feeling most threatened. No water meant no grass for grazing, no creek or well water for drinking. The dwindling supply of homegrown hay meant ranchers had to import more hay from alfalfa farms. The waning supply sent hay prices skyrocketing, from $60 for an eight-hundred-pound bale to $115 in some parts of Texas.

Ranchers were struggling to keep their animals fed. They were trucking hay in from out of state and eating the transportation costs. They were cutting it illegally off highway medians. Some were even supplementing it with stale hamburger buns. They were slaughtering their pride and sitting in their King Ranch trucks under pink, cloudless skies, waiting for donated hay to be distributed at dawn like bread in a bread line.

Others just gave up. All across Texas, ranchers were cutting down their herds. Some sold off cattle to slaughter that weren't ready. Some sold their entire herds to ranchers in wetter states, like Montana and Nebraska, bailing on the cattle business altogether. To do what? Who knew. Some saw their futures in oil and gas, which in parts of Texas were being extracted at a record pace by new hydraulic fracturing technologies, or "fracking." In essence, they were trading an industry threatened by climate change for an industry happily married to it.

The Grahams kept their cattle business going and even benefited from the sell-off. They owned one of the auction houses where ranchers were desperately selling off herds at cut-rate prices. Across the state, auction houses were running late into the night, and the Grahams were there to facilitate the sale, a family well-practiced in the art of being on both sides of a deal.

But feeding the horses was getting expensive, and the longer the clouds held out, the higher his costs would soar. The higher the costs, the more he needed Forty's group to catch up on their bills, a feat that appeared less likely with each passing month. By the middle of summer, they would owe Southwest Stallion Station seven hundred thousand dollars.

Tyler called Fernando.

"¿Amigo?" Fernando said. "¿Qué pasa, cómo estás?"

"Bien, bien," Tyler said.

"What's up, Tyler?"

"Ah shit, man, just hoping we get some rain this week."

"Fuck, it's dry out there, huh?"

"It's terrible, man," Tyler said.

"So what's up, how come you don't call me no more? What the hell?"

"Huh? Well, I—" Tyler stammered. "Man, I ain't—I don't know. Ain't no specific reason, I just . . . Breeding season's kinda slowed down. I don't have any big news updates for you anymore. We're not flushing."

"I know, I know," Fernando said. "I'm just playing."

Tyler changed the subject to money. He'd just been in Manor, another cow town on Austin's outskirts, paying top dollar for alfalfa to feed the horses.

"What do you think your schedule is on your little brother to shovel some money in here?" Tyler asked, referring to Carlitos.

"He hasn't shoveled no money yet?"

"Ze-ro."

"What the hell," Fernando said. "I don't know, I haven't talked to him in a week. I've only talked to Victor."

They did this to Tyler a lot, flipping control and responsibility left and right, up and over, playing a shell game with their debts. Tyler's voice indicated a waning patience for it.

"I've talked to Victor, too," Tyler said. "He was here last week, and he said they were supposed to start sending some any day, but . . . anyway. I'm not worried about not getting it, but it sure would be nice to start getting some of it. . . . It's a pretty monstrous bill."

"I'll ask," Fernando told him.

"I'm startin' to get pretty far out there. I'm needin' to pay some bills myself, you know?"

"I understand," Fernando said.

"Hell, I just bought seventy thousand dollars' worth of alfalfa, you know?"

"Seventy thousand dollars' worth of alfalfa?!"

"Yeah," Tyler said through a chuckle, as in, *Yeah, man, horses cost money.*

"Fuck, how much was that? How many barrels or whatever?"

"That's ten loads."

"You mean, like, ten eighteen-wheelers or what?"

"Yeah, ten eighteen-wheelers."

"Damn, that must be a shitload of alfalfa."

"Yeah, it is," Tyler said. "But you got this many horses around here, and it's so dry, man. I gotta have it."

"That's fine, that's fine," Fernando said, but he didn't say anything about sending any money.

It went on like that all summer—more horses, more hay, no rain, no money. When a little money did come in, it was impossible to know which of the dozens of accounts to apply it to, even though Tyler knew they all belonged to the same guy. The main guy. And any attempt to simplify things was shut right down.

"Finally got some money from your buddies," Tyler said to José one day, after a payment came in.

"From what buddies?" José asked.

He was still acting as if Victor the Courier and Carlitos and Fernando were clients, not business partners. Tyler couldn't help letting out a chuckle.

"From our main, uh—"

"I got you," José said, cutting him off. But Tyler pressed, trying to confirm the existence of a boss somewhere in Mexico. It might be useful to Lawson if José acknowledged what they all suspected, but Tyler seemed more motivated by a desire to cut through the group's bottomless bullshit.

"From our main guy," he said.

"Dah-dah-dah-dah-dah," José said, trying to scramble Tyler's words after the fact.

Then José said, "That's good for you."

"It's good for both of us," Tyler said.

■ ■ ■

LAREDO, TEXAS
August 2011

Inside the FBI's Laredo offices, there is a room called the "wire room," where a bank of computer terminals are equipped with speakers and headphones. It's a land of tedium, where haystacks of idle chatter are piled atop needles of evidence. But the wire room is where many cases are made.

Stronger wiretapping laws are among the many weapons bestowed on federal agents during the Nixon administration, as Republicans searched for ways to get federal agents on the drug-war battlefield. In theory, securing a wiretap requires convincing a judge that the likelihood of a crime outweighs the invasion of privacy. In practice, agents can do it whenever they want. The year Lawson started in Laredo, agents around the country asked judges for almost twenty-four hundred wiretaps, 86 percent of which were for drug cases. It was the most wiretap applications in history. Every last one was approved.

That summer, Scott Lawson was spending a lot of time in the Laredo wire room. In a way, he had the DEA to thank. Over the course of his investigation, the Laredo DEA agents he knew had continued to pester him about the pace of his investigation and his aggressiveness with Tyler. *If we had a source like that,* they liked to say, bragging about the various pressure cookers they'd plop Tyler in—wearing a wire, recording his calls, and so on.

Lawson had tried to dismiss the chatter as a symptom of their FMES. He remained convinced Tyler hadn't committed a crime. But he was naturally competitive, so he couldn't deflect all their chiding. Eventually he started thinking, *Maybe I'm not asking for enough.* During one of his recent meets with Tyler, he'd tiptoed into the subject of allowing the FBI to record Tyler's calls.

Tyler agreed, no arm-twisting required.

*Shit,* Lawson thought. *I should have thought of that earlier.*

It wasn't a wiretap but rather what's called "consensual interception," which didn't require the charade of "asking" a judge for "permission." Lawson simply told Tyler which phone to get, where to get it, and what information—serial number, phone number, and so forth—the FBI would need to start recording.

Once Lawson had that information, he passed it to the FBI's tech experts, who worked with the cellular provider to record all the calls made to and from that phone. The cellular provider had no choice but to help. Under the 1994 Communications Assistance for Law Enforcement Act, telecom companies are required to design their networks to allow them to record, store, and provide to law enforcement conversations that they have permission—from a judge or from a source—to hear.

Permission in hand, Lawson now found himself a few times a week in the wire room, listening. Mostly, lately, he was listening to Tyler try to convince the Zetas to send him some damn money.

Along with football, horses, domestic beer, and old-school hip-hop, getting Tyler paid continued to be a shared interest between agent and source. For starters, Lawson just felt bad for the guy, in a way he likely wouldn't for other sources. Most sources this cooperative had committed obvious, punishable crimes, and were only talking in an effort to reduce the punishment. Lawson still wasn't certain exactly why Tyler was cooperating, but he knew it wasn't to avoid prison.

It was enough to ask Tyler to do business with Mexico's most murderous drug cartel for a year and a half, knowing that at some point they might learn that Tyler had snitched, especially given what Lawson knew about Forty's particular disdain for snitches. Lawson knew, for instance, that Ramiro had been murdered because Forty believed, correctly, that he was cooperating with the feds. Lawson also knew that many of Mexico's most gruesome killings were committed by Zetas against people suspected of being informants. Recently, two narco bloggers had been tortured, gutted, and left hanging from a bridge in Nuevo Laredo, along with a note scrawled on construction paper: *"Esto les va a pazar a todos los relajes de Internet,"* it read. The translation was crude, but it was taken to mean "This is what happens to all of the Internet snitches."

None of those victims had been white people in central Texas, but still, Lawson knew their relationship carried some physical risk for Tyler. He didn't want to compound it by risking the solvency of the Graham family stud farm. Then again, the reason the stud farm had any good studs to start with was Tyler's ongoing cooperation with the FBI. So maybe Lawson needn't feel bad for him after all. Maybe Lawson was as much a source of income for Tyler as Tyler was a source of intel for Lawson.

Either way, if the Zetas' money dried up, so might Lawson's access. So Tyler kept pushing for money, and Lawson kept listening in. He knew that the debt José and the others owed Southwest Stallion Station offered an opportunity to prove—to himself, to prosecutors, to a grand jury, and eventually to the courts—that the money was coming straight from the Zetas.

Victor the Courier called Tyler with the good news: We have your money. He told Tyler to call a guy named Alfonso del Rayo.

Listening in the wire room, Lawson felt his synapses light up: Alfonso del Rayo Mora was the Swollen Golfer who'd overbid so badly on José's mangy racehorse. Lawson had always found the purchase strange, but he figured del Rayo was simply helping José launder money. He'd have to connect him to Forty somehow, and the fact that del Rayo was now going to help the Zetas pay off their debt seemed to support that theory, even if his injuries remained mysterious.

The checks from del Rayo rolled into Southwest Stallion Station after that—one for $250,000, another for $300,000, bringing the group's bill down to $150,000. Del Rayo promised Tyler three more checks, though he said that he'd have to wait to deposit a couple of them. Lawson listened to their calls, searching for answers about who del Rayo was and why he was paying the Zetas' tab.

"I just want to make you feel sure that the money is going to be paid," del Rayo said in one call that rain-deprived summer. "Because you know, people in Mexico are pushing me, asking me if I already paid you."

The money came through, and Forty and his associates were all caught up. Then, just as quickly, they weren't. There were still a hundred-plus horses at Tyler's ranch. Their balance accumulated every day. They quickly owed Tyler another sixty thousand.

Lawson listened as Tyler kept pushing them for it. In late August, Lawson sat down in the wire room and opened a call between Tyler and Victor the Courier.

"I got your money, man!" Victor said to Tyler.

"That's good. Send it on up here!"

"Man, I can't make a wire."

"What's the deal?"

"The thing is, I have the money. I'm the only one here in Laredo. My bank account—it's not a bank account, it's not a business account. It's a personal account."

"Why don't you just send me a check?" Tyler asked, sounding baffled about how something so simple had been made so complicated.

"What do you mean, 'a check'?"

"If it's in your account, just send me a check."

"Take it to the bank for them to make me a check?"

"Yeah!"

"OK. How much am I going to get from you?"

"How much are you going to get *for* me?"

"How much is going to be my profit?"

He was joking, right? Victor did joke sometimes. And he was laughing. Then again, this was how Victor operated, skimming on every trade.

Victor steered them back on track, back to the money he had in the bank. But suddenly, it was no longer in the bank.

"So, can you come for it, to Laredo?"

Tyler had seen this play before: cash in Laredo, there for the taking. He knew what to do.

"Ah, man, there ain't no way," Tyler said. "I could maybe send somebody down there."

"But can you take back sixty?" Victor asked, thinking of the checkpoint.

"I probably could," Tyler said. "I'd rather have a check if I don't have to take cash."

"Hmm. Well, I have hundred-dollar bills," he said, the pretense of legitimacy floating clear out of view. "It's a small package."

"OK," Tyler said.


They arranged the pickup for a couple of days later at a mall just off the highway. Again, Tyler wouldn't have to show up for the drop; this time another informant would pose as one of Tyler's friends. But it still presented a risk to everyone involved. There were agents perched around the Laredo parking lot where the drop was supposed to go down, including some taking photos, and the undercover was wearing a recording device. If any of that was discovered, the Zetas would know that Tyler was an informant.

Fifty minutes after it was supposed to go down, Tyler still hadn't heard anything.

His phone rang.

"Hello?"

"Tyler, it's fifty-nine-seven-fifty," Victor said. Victor was obviously inside the car with whomever the FBI had sent to pick up the money. And he was two hundred and fifty dollars short of the sixty grand the guy was expecting.

"OK," Tyler said quickly. "That's fine."

It was his money, so that should have solved it. But the phone went quiet.

Tyler spoke to the silence: "Hello?"

A new voice came on.

"Yeah, this is Pickup Man," he said. It was the informant, the guy posing as Tyler's friend. He was calling himself "Pickup Man"? Hadn't they agreed to call Tyler's friend "George"? Listening in a nearby car, Lawson thought, *Fuck.*

Pickup Man kept talking: "Fifty-nine—"

Tyler cut him off and spoke almost without breathing. "Hey, George, yeah, fifty-nine-seven-fifty, that's fine."

"All right, buddy."

"All right."

Lawson delivered the money to Tyler soon after. It was all in large bills, just as Victor had promised.

On and on it would go, Lawson figured. So long as he had Tyler, so long as he had Tyler's calls in the wire room, and so long as Tyler had the Zetas' horses grazing in his paddocks and sleeping in his barns, money would roll in. Lawson still needed to trace it back to Forty. He suspected Carlitos's and Fernando's cash came from Forty, but he couldn't prove it. He figured the various Mexican companies that were wiring money to the United States were being repaid with drug money, but the only source who could ever confirm it, Ramiro, was dead.

In time, Lawson figured, he would develop other sources to prove these suspicions. But there was another potential wrinkle. Lately, José had been talking to Tyler again about starting his own stud farm. He wanted to move Tempting Dash and Mr Piloto and all those pricey broodmares and all those surrogates and all those babies, all hundred-and-who-knows-how-many horses, away from Southwest Stallion Station and off to Oklahoma or somewhere.

That worried Lawson. It would push much of the Zetas' operation even farther from Laredo. More important, it would cut off

Lawson's access to the inside information Tyler had been feeding him for more than a year and a half. Without it, Lawson worried, the case would stall.

Then again, José had been talking about starting his own farm from the beginning, and he'd always come to realize that it made more sense to trust Tyler and keep his name off things. What were the odds that the Zetas' drug cartel would try to open its own stallion farm in the middle of middle America?

■ ■ ■

OKLAHOMA CITY, OKLAHOMA
September 2011

It was more of a hobby for Bill Pilgrim, if something as time- and money- and hay-consuming as owning racehorses can be considered a hobby. He was a builder by trade, and he had built enough to afford the simple life he lived on a flat patch of southern Oklahoma.

He was north of there now, at Heritage Place, Doc Graham's auction house in Oklahoma City. He drove up every so often to the quarter-horse auctions, to see which breedings were selling for what. Occasionally he picked up some horses to haul back to his ranch in Lexington, which along with Purcell formed Oklahoma's quarter-horse alley, a strip of rolling pastures cultivated by the industry.

Pilgrim wasn't a big player, but he had the space to stay involved: sixty acres adorned only with a small three-bedroom house, a thirteen-stall mare barn, a two-stall stud barn, and a hay barn.

Lexington was best known for its whiskey distillery before prohibition and its Navy gunnery after it. The biggest day of the year was 89ers Day, an annual commemoration of the 1889 Oklahoma Land Rush that allowed settlers into the new Oklahoma Territory. The land rush was an imperialist knife twist to the Native Americans who'd been resettled there on the promise that their land would remain Indian territory. It was celebrated in Lexington with fried food and carnival games.

Pilgrim's ranch was only a couple of miles from downtown.

Across the street was the Old Dog Gun Shop, a one-room storefront stocked with assault rifles and 9mm handguns and manned by a congenial old man in overalls. Down the road was Pilgrim's neighbor Cliff, a retired Army colonel who was always walking the neighborhood in a sleeveless Dri-FIT.

It was another neighbor Pilgrim had been thinking about lately. His neighbor to the north was talking about selling. That property was even bigger than Pilgrim's, closer to seventy-five acres. It had several structures, but the crown jewel was its brick mare barn stretching the length of a football field, with enough stalls for eighty horses. It had been designed and used by D. Wayne Lukas, a trainer carved into thoroughbred racing's Mount Rushmore, and it had once been home to Lady's Secret, a champion thoroughbred that eventually sold for four million dollars.

Lukas had stopped training horses there years before. It had been sold a handful of times since, the realities of a horse farm that big never living up to the vision in the owner's head. Now it was for sale again. Pilgrim wondered who his new neighbor would be. The whole town did. Then, that day at the sale, the new neighbor walked up, shook Pilgrim's hand, and introduced himself as José Treviño.

José told Pilgrim the plan. He was already buying his neighbor's land, the one with the world-class mare barn. He was interested in buying Pilgrim's place, too. Would he sell?

Pilgrim said he wasn't interested. But José started calling him after that, once a day, then multiple times a day, urging him to sell. Then José showed up at his house unannounced. Pilgrim kept saying no, but conversations with friends made him start to reconsider. These friends told Pilgrim who José's brother was; Pilgrim told these friends he was now sleeping with a shotgun.

The trucks came soon after that. Back on his little corner of old Indian territory, Pilgrim peered over the fence and watched trailer after trailer trudge up José's long dirt driveway, past the sloping pastures and thick grove of trees that fronted the property. Ten horses per trailer, every day for weeks. Crews of workers brought the property to life, mowing, painting, and erecting an even bigger barn to hold what would soon add up to hundreds of horses.

It was too many, Pilgrim thought. His wife and he had always said that if they were going to own horses, they were going to do it right. They were going to have plenty of space and resources to keep the animals clean, nourished, and healthy. Now he was worried, for himself and for his animals. Pilgrim's land shared a fence line with José's, which was practically overflowing with horses. Since José was known to ship horses back and forth across the border, Pilgrim could safely assume that some of them had at one point been in Mexico, where diseases like equine piroplasmosis spread more freely than in the States.

And the flashlights. That was weird, wasn't it? The way José's laborers would be out there at night with flashlights? Pilgrim knew they were just checking on the horses. He probably knew, or could have found out, that night watchmen roam the stalls with industrial flashlights at every major breeding farm, every night of the year, to make sure six-figure horses aren't experiencing colic, which can be deadly, or going into labor. But when his new Mexican neighbor did it, it spooked him.

It was around Christmas that José asked Pilgrim again: Are you interested in selling? It was clear that José wanted the property badly. He needed the pasture, and Pilgrim's parcel contained both a barn for José's stallions and a brick home for him and his family. So they agreed on a price, $500,000. José asked if he could pay in cash installments, probably hoping the money would show up when it needed to. He also told Pilgrim he hoped to avoid using a title company to transfer ownership, or a bank for transferring funds. Pilgrim rejected all that, which didn't appear to go over well with José; he'd gotten heated at the title company. But they agreed to the sale, and in the meantime, José asked Pilgrim if he could board one of his stallions on his property.

Sure, Pilgrim said. So one winter night, another horse trailer lit up the two-lane road that raced past the men's farms. This time, the horse trailer pulled onto Pilgrim's property. It was raining pretty hard as the hauler led the 2010 All American Futurity winner, Mr Piloto, into José's new stud barn.

# CHAPTER TWENTY-ONE

## HOMESTEAD

ELGIN, TEXAS
December 2011

The trailers rattled up the long drive of Southwest Stallion Station. The man they called El Negro did the hauling. Tyler watched as each hulking racehorse and clingy weanling clopped up the ramp, into the trailer, and out of his life.

At first, Tyler had expected José to take just a handful of horses to his new farm in Oklahoma. That seemed prudent, given José's inexperience caring for and breeding horses, and it seemed to be what Carlitos and Fernando wanted. They didn't trust José's horsemanship, and though they still never mentioned whom they worked for, they intimated to Tyler that whoever was in charge didn't trust it, either. The new farm, a handful of horses—that would be José's way to prove himself worthy of his own breeding business.

But somewhere along the line, someone's mind had changed. El Negro kept coming back, and now Carlitos and Fernando were saying that José was coming for basically every last horse. With Carlitos's and Fernando's help, José was collecting them from stables all across the country. Nearly the entire operation, now more than four hundred horses, would be in Oklahoma before the following breeding season. That included the All American–winning stud Mr Piloto. If José's first breeding season in Oklahoma went well—and if he could secure the permits required to move a horse with piroplasmosis—he might soon come for Tempting Dash, too, Southwest Stallion Station's most valuable resident.

Each horse that clopped on board represented a step closer to the end for Tyler. To his two-plus-year relationship with José Treviño, with Carlitos and Fernando, and with the FBI. It also meant goodbye to hundreds of thousands of dollars in revenue and to many of the horses that had helped Tyler rebuild Southwest Stallion Station's reputation. If some of Tempting Dash's offspring turned out to be runners, at least Tyler could lay some claim to their success. He'd also proven that he could manage a bustling stallion farm. But if José took every horse, Tyler would be right back where he started, or close to it: the manager of a stud barn with no name-brand stud to breed. He could always rebuild it again, but who knew how the industry would react when they learned it had thrived thanks to twin business deals with the Zetas and the FBI.

If José was going to take his horses, Tyler was going to make sure he got every last penny he was owed. Over the previous two years, whenever José and this group had fallen behind on bills, Tyler cut them plenty of slack. They had scores of horses on his farm, and they needed them fed, and bred, and cared for. That meant they needed Tyler. They'd pay up eventually.

Now many of the horses were gone, and trailers kept showing up to take more, despite the revolving debt the group kept with Southwest Stallion Station. The conversations around that debt and those horses were sounding tenser, the language more loaded.

Like when Victor the Courier had called recently. Tyler hadn't even finished saying hello when—

"Tyler, it just went through. I already checked my account," Victor said.

"It just went through?" Tyler asked. It didn't make sense; the bank had said it would be a few days, which was why Tyler had told them not to come pick up their mares until—

"I don't have my money no more."

"It cleared your account?"

"Check your account, check your bank," Victor said, the desperation leaking through the phone. "So you should let 'em go, OK?"

"What's the big deal about today?"

"I don't know! They're putting pressure to me."

Tyler let out a breath. *Pressure.* He must have felt it, too—the pressure of an unyielding business, a new marriage, a punishing drought, unpaid accounts, and a two-year-old gig as a Confidential Human Source for the FBI, a job perilous enough that the FBI's internal reports referred to him only by number, never by name. Tyler dug in.

"The problem is," Tyler said, "they need to be calling me before they're coming to the ranch, case I'm not at the ranch, and I don't have anyone there to load mares. . . . You need to tell Negro, Saltillo, whatever"—the guy who picked up the mares had a lot of nicknames—"that I need to know before they just show up, wanna pick mares up, and they don't have all their damn bacon right, you know what I'm sayin'?"

They worked it out and trucks kept coming. But they still owed money, and Tyler wasn't backing down. Especially when José called.

"Did you zero out my account or no?" he asked Tyler on the phone one day that winter. Tyler was constantly receiving money from Carlitos, Fernando, Victor the Courier, and other operatives he believed to be associated with the Treviño brothers. He viewed all of their accounts as one and applied it however he was instructed. But he hadn't applied it to José's because he hadn't been told to.

"No, I haven't," Tyler said. "Do you want me to do that with the next money that comes in? Victor didn't tell me anything."

"But you did do it last time you got all the money?"

"No," Tyler said. "I never put anything against your account."

"No, but remember last time, it was, uh, like, in June or July, we had that big account; you zeroed me out that time, didn't you?"

"Oh, yeah-yeah-yeah-yeah, we might have way back then, but . . . it's been building back up, I guess."

"How much is it right now, do you know?"

"No more than fifty thousand."

"Oh shit," José said.

With the horses leaving and the end in sight, Tyler kept pushing back. As breeding season approached, he told José that he would no longer accept stud fees from Carlitos. On paper, José owned the studs, and Carlitos owned many of the mares he was breeding with. But Tyler believed that Forty owned them all—that they were just using his ranch to "layer" the money on the way to José.

You're paying yourself, Tyler told Jose. He suggested José just collect the money from Carlitos directly.

José balked at that. Apparently he didn't want to chase Carlitos any more than Tyler did. They made plans to hash it out in person, and Tyler told Lawson about those plans. They would be valuable to the FBI, because the meeting would take place somewhere the FBI had yet to see inside: José's new stud farm.

■ ■ ■

LEXINGTON, OKLAHOMA
February 2012

The tractor's roar filled the quiet, and there was José, in the driver's seat, dragging his pasture as if it were the infield at Yankee Stadium. The sun sliced through the trees at the eastern edge of the property, and the filtered morning light elevated the contrast between the grass trampled one way and the grass trampled the other, forming stripes in the pasture. For José, it was a morning ritual, no foreman or trowel in sight.

It was February. A new breeding season. José and Zulema had moved into Bill Pilgrim's old three-bedroom home tucked onto the corner of the property, a mix of espresso-colored brick and horizontal redwood. Zulema had finally quit her job at Ernst & Young, despite glowing performance reviews that seemed to have her on a fast track to more money and responsibility. José's mother had moved into a double-wide at the far end of the property, along the freshly painted fence line he shared with the retired Army colonel.

José's brother Rodolfo had moved into another trailer on the property. They'd been building stuff together since they'd followed Kiko to lay bricks in Dallas thirty years before, and they were at it again. With a crew of laborers, they painted the mare barns the color of artisan chocolate. They installed industrial floodlights to trick the mares' reproductive systems into thinking it was spring, waking them early from their winter hiatus. They planned to build two more fifty-stall barns, a specialty barn for their highest-priced mares, and a racetrack where they could line up the runners and watch them fly.

José had enrolled his school-age kids in the local elementary school. He'd bought José Jr. a new truck in Norman and enrolled him in farrier school, so he could learn to trim and shoe horse hooves. Alexandra, whose fiancé was deployed overseas, came back to work on the farm, too. They were all together again, family and extended family, working for each other, caring for each other. Oklahoma didn't have nearly the terrain or the romance that northern Mexico did, but it still recalled the life José's dad had once built in rural Tamaulipas. Only José was no vaquero. Despite his limited experience with horses—despite thirty years laying bricks—he'd trampled right through his father's footsteps on the way to being *el patrón*. Some of the workers called him Don José.

It was the farthest José and his family had ever lived from Mexico, but maybe that was for the better. Lately the violence seemed to compound month over month, as if Forty was testing the limits of the public's desensitization. Most recently, the stories had been pouring out of Piedras Negras, where José had first met Poncho Cuellar under the palapa and talked about horses, and where Forty had celebrated José's million-dollar win at the All American.

Now it was under siege. Poncho and his crew had apparently flipped, agreeing to cooperate with the DEA in exchange for help escaping the Zetas. They'd provided the DEA with information about Forty's whereabouts, and the DEA had told the Mexican authorities, hoping they could use it to track down Forty. Instead, someone within the Mexican government had tipped off Forty that his former employees had snitched.

Poncho and his guys fled across the border and into the waiting arms of the DEA. Forty sent sicarios to Piedras Negras, where they rounded up the snitches' families, friends, and neighbors, and "disappeared" them. Some of their bodies were found shot to death; others were found incinerated in oil drums. Many were never found at all. Hundreds of people had been taken to a local prison that, under the control of Forty, investigators would discover, was used as a makeshift death camp.

José didn't make it to Mexico often, probably for good reason. Between the Jaime Zapata murder, the bus-passenger massacres, and these latest killings, the Mexicans and Americans were reportedly cooperating at unprecedented levels to locate Forty, who was living even further off the grid than usual. If José traveled these days, it was usually to California or New Mexico for horse-racing business. And there was plenty to do in Oklahoma.

Most mornings he rose early, mounted one of his tractors, and rode it down the hill to drag his pasture, breaking up and spreading the manure. There was a lot of manure. He had around four hundred horses, so even with an extra barn and multiple grazing spaces, they often ended up crowded in the pasture that sloped down from the main barn toward the road, loping in the shade of a thick canopy of trees. By the time José was done, the pasture looked smooth and ready for grazing.

After that, José often found his way into the offices sandwiched into the middle of the mare barn. From these headquarters, José's business was starting to look more like the miniconglomerate of his mentors, the Grahams. Zule Farms, named for Zulema, was the breeding farm. Tremor Enterprises, named for the family, was the horse-racing business. The ranch itself was named 66 Land and Cattle, after the famous highway.

The margins were thin. Tens of thousands of dollars flowed in and out of those accounts every week—revenue from stud fees and the occasional horse sale, expenses for new horses, equipment, feed, travel expenses, and salaries. His brother Rodolfo worked on the farm. Zulema worked in the office, trying to keep up with the bills. José's mother collected occasional checks—six hundred dollars here, four hundred dollars there—for working in the office, too.

José wrote himself the odd bonus check for a few or even several thousand dollars, though never enough to let his personal account soar much higher than it did when he was laying bricks.

From the office, it was a few steps into the mare barns, where José conferred with his new vet, Shalyn. She was his business's most prized human asset. She'd been recommended by a vet at Texas A&M, where she'd studied before moving to a high-end breeding farm outside Dallas. Recently, she and her family had migrated to Oklahoma, and she'd begun looking for work.

José offered her seventy-five thousand dollars a year, and soon she was in his barns, tending to some of the most valuable mares in quarter-horse racing. She had pale skin that turned pink in the summer and wavy chestnut hair that turned auburn, especially the strands exposed to the sun when she pulled them into a ponytail. She was a former Miss Rodeo Oklahoma, which explained her ease around the horses, but it was her technical savvy that made her so valuable to José.

As she worked, José studied her. When they'd first met, he had given her the impression that he knew enough to run a farm this big. Over time, he let her see that he didn't—that he knew a lot about some things and nothing about others. He was learning, asking seemingly every question that passed through his brain.

His family was doing the same. His two smallest kids were around in the afternoons, after school, asking little-kid questions. Alex, the farm's breeding manager, spent every day at Shalyn's side, inputting the medical records of each horse. Who knew how long she'd do it. Luis had proposed, and they were planning to get married that spring. But for the moment, Alex was what Tyler Graham had once been: the next generation, throwing herself into the work and soaking up what she could.

Spring came. José and his family were a fixture in Lexington. In the afternoons, his dozen or so workers hopped the fence, crossed the empty two-lane road, and ducked into the Old Dog Gun Shop, where they perused the selection and took the shop's overalled owner up on his offer of cold water. In the evenings, smoke often rose from the property, as José's family and the workers gathered in the yard for cookouts—"just enjoying life," as the neighbors who walked past in the evenings put it. On 89ers Day, José got dressed up in a pressed shirt, leather cowboy boots, and his white cowboy hat, and led his family through the crowd, chatting with neighbors and celebrating the land rush that let white men claim José's new home state just as it had his old one.

As he built out the farm, José made regular trips to a nearby feed-and-supply shop. In the aisles, he chatted up Jessica, a young woman who worked there. He could tell she knew her horses, and he could tell she wanted something more from her life than stocking the shelves at Equi-Mart. So one day he asked her, "Why don't you come work for us?"

She did. Alex was moving to San Diego, where Luis was stationed, so Jessica replaced her as breeding manager. She helped Shalyn palpate the mares and kept detailed notes about ovulation schedules. José mostly left them alone, but one day he took Jessica out on his John Deere Gator. They were checking on yearlings, but José also wanted to check on her.

He asked her what she wanted from her life.

She said she wasn't sure.

"You're a really smart girl, you're going to go really far," José said. Jessica seemed to take it the way José seemed to intend it: like the advice of a loving father whose daughter had just moved away. The Gator rumbled across the pastures, and José looked at Jessica and said, "You have to go after what you want."

■ ■ ■

LAREDO, TEXAS
February 2012

With most of the horses now in Oklahoma, Lawson knew his handle on the case was tenuous. Without Tyler, it would be hard to know what José and Carlitos and Fernando planned to do next, or when. He started to urge the prosecutor in Austin to take the case to the grand jury, so they could indict their targets for money laundering and arrest them before they caught wind of something and fled to Mexico.

In the meantime, he continued to duck into the wire room to listen to Tyler's calls. He heard one that made him wonder if his CHS understood what he was saying, and to whom.

It was a call with Victor the Courier. Victor had sent Tyler a check for twenty thousand dollars, to pay down the forty thousand dollars they once again owed Southwest Stallion Station. Tyler deposited the check, but then Victor called back.

"Hey, Tyler," he said, his voice lower than usual. "They're saying if I can get the money back, because that wasn't for the deal."

"What was it for?" Tyler asked.

"I don't know," Victor said. "We just make a mistake and send it to you. It was for somebody else."

Lawson had never gone deeply into specifics with Tyler about Forty, the Zetas, and their lust for show-stopping violence. But Tyler had to know. The whole horse industry knew. So Lawson figured now, if ever, would be the time Tyler relented. He had the Zetas' money, and the Zetas wanted it back. It wasn't that much, and the bill would get paid eventually. It always did.

"Hmm," Tyler said. "Well. What about the bills that they owe me for?"

"I'm not sure," Victor said. "I'm not sure how much they owe you."

"It's about forty thousand, so . . . I don't know," Tyler told him. "The money's already in the bank."

"I think it was for another person," Victor said.

"Hmm," Tyler said. "I don't know. Tell 'em that they owe and I need the money paid. I mean, their accounts are so far behind. I don't really have any motivation to send 'em their money back."

Lawson couldn't quite believe what he was hearing. Apparently Victor couldn't, either.

"Want me to give you another bank account for you to deposit back to me?"

"No, that's what I'm saying!" Tyler shot back. Then he laughed a little, as if he couldn't believe he'd have to tell the Zetas no for the second time in a minute. "I'm not gonna deposit back to you. I mean, they *owe* me the money."

"All right," Victor said coolly. "Let me call them and tell them."

"Yeah, I mean, just tell them, Hey, what's mine is mine, you know?"

"OK," Victor said, done negotiating. "I'll tell them."

The recording clicked into silence. Listening in the wire room, Lawson thought, *Does this guy know who he's dealing with?*

# CHAPTER TWENTY-TWO

## TRIPWIRES

NUEVO LAREDO, TAMAULIPAS
February 2012

Victor the Courier walked across the Laredo pedestrian bridge in the dark that morning, this time at a reasonable pace. It could take hours for him to cross and often did, but not at ten to six in the morning.

There was no express lane for cartel operatives like Victor, though some days he must have felt that there should be. This was important work, shuffling money across for Forty and his Zetas, who by February 2012 were the de facto bosses of Nuevo Laredo. They owned businesses and collected pisos from the businesses they didn't own. They owned the roads, in the form of checkpoints where armored vehicles could randomly harass anyone for any reason at all. They no longer owned the Nuevo Laredo police, but that was only because they'd so thoroughly owned the Nuevo Laredo police that state officials had disbanded the force.

With all that power, you'd think they could just build Victor the Courier an express raft across the river or something. He made the trip twice a week. Sometimes twice a day.

Victor the Courier was Victor Lopez. He was thirty-one but looked and sounded and *seemed* younger, as if the world were spinning faster than the blood pumped through his veins. His dad was Mexican, his mom American, and Victor enjoyed both citizenship and life on both sides of the river. He spent plenty of time with family in Nuevo Laredo, but he lived in a tattered shoebox apartment in central Laredo, across the street from a Catholic church and not far from Bridge One. His cousin "Yo-Yo" worked for the Zetas, too, in a role of increasing importance: the bookkeeper for Forty's quarter-horse business. When Carlitos or Fernando needed money to pay a trainer or buy a horse or pay Tyler's ranch, they (eventually) emailed Yo-Yo. Yo-Yo (eventually) got the money from Forty's accountants and (eventually) made sure it got where it needed to go. Often, that meant calling his cousin Victor and asking him to deliver it.

Once Victor got the money, he crossed this pedestrian bridge with rubber-banded stacks of hundreds. He kept a bank account on the American side, at a Wells Fargo branch where he routinely deposited cash in amounts of just under ten thousand dollars. Then he withdrew cash or wrote checks to veterinarians, breeding farms, and racetracks all across the Southwest.

If he was carrying more than ten thousand dollars, the work was more complicated, since it involved dividing it into smaller chunks and sending it across strapped to currency mules. In that regard, this morning's delivery was simpler—just five thousand dollars in cash to be hand-delivered to one dude.

In another regard it was more complicated, in large part because of the identity of that dude: José Treviño. Forty's brother.

It was well known that Forty was an obsessive family man. He'd ordered those grenades chucked at the American consulate in Monterrey after ICE harassed his mother. He'd threatened to kill the American FBI agent who tossed his sister's house in Laredo. A few years back when his baby brother Fito had been gunned down by El Chapo's sicarios, Forty rounded up his killer and his killer's brother. According to a Zeta assassin who witnessed the murders, he'd forced his brother's killer to watch while he shot his brother in the head.[*]

If he wanted to send the message that his family was off-limits, it didn't take. Later, the state police in Coahuila gunned down Forty's nephew Alejandro, the son of his big brother Kiko. Kiko was nearing the end of his twenty-year sentence for his marijuana trafficking operation, which looked cute compared to what his little brothers had built. But after Kiko's conviction, his kids, Forty's and José's nephews, had wound up in Mexico working in the drug business. Now, one of those nephews was dead at the hands of the Coahuila police. Forty responded by having the governor's son assassinated.

So Victor knew he couldn't fuck up this thing with José's brother. Especially after he'd fucked up that last thing with Tyler, sending him money he wasn't supposed to send him. After Tyler refused to return it, he'd asked Tyler to break off a piece of the cash and send it to José. But Tyler said no. So here Victor was, on his way to hand-deliver the cash to José. In Oklahoma.

Getting to Oklahoma required Victor, once he crossed the border, to endure something professional smugglers don't like to do: flying. There were the typical post-9/11 indignations not unlike the ones Victor faced each day when he crossed the border by foot, the snaking lines and the searching looks by federal agents. Even worse was the airlines' willingness to pass information to law enforcement. It was cooperation born out of a nation's fear of plane-related terrorism, but it had become a favorite tool of drug-interdiction agents, who used their friends at booking counters to track their targets' movements around the friendly skies. They call them "tripwires."

After crossing, Victor took a cab to the Laredo airport and boarded a plane and flew to Oklahoma City. He strode through the airport with only a small bag and found José, looking studious in eyeglasses and a plaid shirt, sitting on a bench near baggage claim.

---

[*] This is chronicled in *Wolf Boys*, a 2016 book by journalist Dan Slater about the lives of Forty's teenage sicarios.

They walked outside into the cold, found José's blue pickup, and climbed in. Victor pulled out the cash, handed it to José, and walked straight back to the terminal, a weight lifted—however much five thousand dollars weighs, plus the knowledge that he'd completed the work. He was back inside the terminal, wading back into the security line, by the time José saw the lights flashing in his rearview.

■ ■ ■

## OKLAHOMA CITY, OKLAHOMA
February 2012

Seeing the lights in his rearview, José pulled his truck off the highway not far from the Oklahoma City airport. *Finally,* he must have thought. At least they had the decency to announce themselves.

After the DEA showed up at his door, José always assumed the feds were behind them, sitting back in traffic somewhere, disguised and lurking. He could seem fantastically paranoid about it, seeing cops in the shadows when there weren't any. Once recently, he'd been tooling around Oklahoma with Fernando when he saw a car that looked suspicious.

"Look," he said. "They're following us."

Fernando looked. "It's some lady with a kid in a car seat," he said.

"They do that now," José said.

They did not do that, not for José anyway, but his paranoia was hardly unjustified. HSI at the bridge, DEA in his yard, half the government sweeping his house while his family gathered in the kitchen—and those were just the times he knew about. He didn't even know about the time Lawson and Medina picked up his tail at the bridge and followed him around Laredo for two and half hours, while he and his sister shopped for jeans and ate lunch at Long John Silver's.

The cop in José's window now said he'd pulled him over for crossing the center line, but it wasn't hard to put it all together, even if the precise details wouldn't come until much later. It wasn't hard to trace it back to Victor.

It turned out that Victor the Courier had been flagged by Homeland Security as a probable drug or money smuggler. That had prompted a Laredo-based HSI agent to set up a tripwire at the Laredo International Airport ticket desks, alerting him whenever Victor Lopez purchased a ticket. The HSI agent either didn't know or didn't care that the FBI was already on Victor's tail.

The airline had called HSI that morning. By the time Victor weaved through the security line and made it to his gate, the HSI agent was in the airport security office, watching Victor on a monitor. Once Victor boarded, the plan went into motion: to have agents trail Victor through the Oklahoma City airport and to the site of his drop, and then conduct a "pretext stop" of whomever he delivered the money to.

José pulled right over and allowed the cops to search his car. He could assume that they had pulled him over because of who his brother was. Even though it was a local cop who conducted the stop, the feds were probably around somewhere. The feds didn't like to announce themselves until absolutely necessary, so they used local cops as their fronts in exchange for cutting them in on whatever they seized.

As it turned out, the feds were around, but it wasn't because of José's brother. *These* feds didn't know anything about José or Forty, or why Victor had delivered José five thousand dollars in cash. They only knew Victor. To Homeland Security, five thousand dollars was no score at all, not even enough to seize. José had told them it was for horse expenses, and they'd sent him on his way.

It was a big deal for José, though. He'd spent his life trying to keep his distance from his brothers' drug business, and he'd spent half his morning in the back of a squad car holding five thousand dollars he knew was only a step or two removed from "our main guy," as Tyler had called him, prompting José's panicked shushing: "dah-dah-dah-dah."

After getting pulled over, José explained all this to Carlitos, and Carlitos told José what he knew. The story got worse. Victor had apparently been stopped on his layover in Dallas, by a different DEA agent, who was unaware of Lawson's investigation *and* the Laredo agent's. The Dallas agent had his own tripwires in place, and he'd been triggered simply by Victor's itinerary—a there-and-back flight from Laredo.

The DEA had let Victor the Courier go, too, and he found his way back to Laredo and back into Mexico. Having just accidentally alerted half the federal government to his relationship with Forty's brother, he probably should have just slipped into the night then, and taken a bus to Mexico City, or maybe Pittsburgh. But he opted for the loyal-soldier routine. He told his cousin Yo-Yo that he'd been stopped on his trip to deliver José money.

They came for Victor a few weeks later. Forty had put together a team to hunt down Victor, so escape was never an option. The only option was mercy in the way it was done, no oil barrel or rusty chain saw, no two-by-four or steep embankment or fiery blaze. Just a single bullet to Victor the Courier's thirty-one-year-old brain.

■ ■ ■

LAREDO, TEXAS
March 2012

There is a tension that exists between agents and prosecutors over when to drop the hammer on a conspiracy. Over when and how that hammer's blow should strike. Over whom it should pulverize, graze, or miss altogether.

Agents often push early to take their case to the grand jury, the secret panel of jurors who determine whether there's enough evidence to indict. Prosecutors often play the role of brake-pumpers, knowing that when the hammer drops, the conspiracy stops and the lawyering begins. Better to go slowly, gather more evidence, and arrive at the grand jury with the best case possible.

Lawson had felt this tension throughout his investigation, particularly whenever he thought the Zetas could catch on. When Ramiro was killed, when the DEA door-knocked José, when HSI stopped Victor the Courier at the border or at the airport, when

José found himself in the back of a squad car—every time, Lawson wondered whether they should just take it all down and hope they had what they needed to prove that José, Carlitos, Fernando, and the rest had conspired to launder Forty's money.

When Lawson pushed, the prosecutor pulled, vowing patience. Lawson and Medina kept hustling, kept stringing Tyler along, kept saying and believing that something would happen soon. Finally, by March 2012, "soon" at least had a date attached: August. The prosecutors were planning to take the case to the grand jury that summer.

Then, one morning, Lawson got a call from a source in the quarter-horse industry. That was good. Lawson had been slow to develop sources in the industry, where gossip spreads like an exotic virus. Eventually, he'd made some connections with people who worked in the offices at tracks and auction houses. He figured they weren't as embedded in the rumor mill as the groomers and trainers who milled around the backside, filling the time with their shit talk.

Usually the sources' info amounted to minutiae of varying importance: so-and-so had entered this horse in this race under this name, and so on. But what he heard that afternoon qualified as a bombshell: the DEA was at Los Alamitos Race Course.

Driving around Laredo, Lawson scrambled to figure out what was happening. He felt the paranoia rising. The horses leaving Elgin, the heat on José—it had all led Lawson to believe he was operating on limited time.

To make matters worse, Lawson had recently heard from a quarter-horse industry source that a *New York Times* reporter was sniffing around, working on a story about the Zetas' infiltration of the sport. Her name was Ginger Thompson, and Lawson respected her feat. During his time in Laredo, reporting on the drug war had become fraught with danger and compromise. The cartels routinely bribed low-paid Mexican journalists, securing favorable coverage with that three-word utterance so familiar to politicians and policemen across the country: *Plata o plomo.*

Those who resisted were being attacked more frequently, and more violently, than ever. Hundreds of journalists were being attacked every year, and by some estimates, as many as ninety had been murdered. The result was precisely what the cartels craved: silence. Around the time Lawson learned of the snooping *New York Times* reporter, the Zetas shot up the Nuevo Laredo offices of *El Mañana,* the town newspaper. The paper stopped printing news about the drug war after that.

In theory, life was different for a reporter like the *Times's* Ginger Thompson. In theory, she operated with the same privilege afforded to American agents and wealthy American informants, safe in the knowledge that the cartels would never attack an American journalist, just as they wouldn't an American agent or informant. Again, though, Forty didn't seem to play by those rules. Another American reporter, the *Dallas Morning News's* Alfredo Corchado, had tested that unspoken treaty between narcos and American journalists with dogged stories about the Zetas, including ones about Forty's rise. He'd found himself chased from Mexico City with an apparent price on his head.

Still, Ginger Thompson was pressing, calling around the industry with questions about Forty and his horses. *She's calling the right fucking people,* Lawson thought. *And some of these people she shouldn't know to call.* He knew that the moment her story blew, and maybe before, his targets would abandon the business and disappear into Mexico. He had again found himself nudging the prosecutor toward action, only to have the prosecutor preach more patience.

Now this call from a source. The DEA had rumbled onto the grounds of Los Alamitos, apparently hunting for Forty's brother Omar, Z-42. *He was* never *there,* Lawson thought as he heard this story, a tide of panic lapping at his throat. The Treviño brothers hadn't been seen in the United States in years.

Lawson texted Tyler, who within a couple minutes had confirmed Lawson's worst fears. Then Lawson called his counterpart at the DEA in Laredo. He'd butted heads with Laredo's DEA office over the years, but there was a new agent there now. He was a young Philly guy who, like Lawson, had been shipped to Laredo for a few years in the shit before he could be transferred somewhere more desirable. They'd arrived within a month of each other, and they'd relied on each other for deconfliction—the act of making sure one agency didn't dance all over the other's toes. Eventually, he'd been assigned to the Organized Crime Drug Enforcement Task Forces handling Lawson's investigation.

Lawson called Philly in a panic. Philly called a colleague in Mexico, who confirmed what Lawson was hearing: that the DEA, who believed Forty-Two was at Los Al, was still at the track trying to flush him out. They'd been searching the barns for hours, apparently, moving up and down with guns drawn, looking for a drug lord but encountering only sleeping grooms and spooked quarter horses.

The DEA agents had also detained some people for questioning. The agent in Mexico sent a photo to Philly, and Philly sent the photo to Lawson, and Lawson's gut clenched when he saw the image of a man sitting on a curb, messy hair suddenly more a mishap than style choice, looking as if his world had caved in.

*No,* Lawson thought. *Not Carlitos.*

Carlitos knew as much about Forty's whereabouts over the last couple of years as anyone. Until about twelve hours before, Carlitos had been sitting in an apartment in Orange County, unaware that Lawson or anyone else was on his trail. If prosecutors could have quietly secured an indictment, Lawson figured, he could be sitting across an interview table from Carlitos by August, offering him a way to save his ass in exchange for information about Forty. Now Carlitos would surely slip back across the border and into Mexico, never to be seen again. The others might not be far behind.

Philly told the agent in Mexico about the ongoing investigation. He pleaded with them to temper their FMES, and to avoid shaking too many more branches on the tree Lawson had been tending to for years. That calmed Lawson down a little. But he was still hot when he dialed the prosecutor and started begging.

"We have to indict!" he hollered into the phone. He pressed, again, to take the case to the grand jury sooner than August, which was five long months away. "They're going back to Mexico," Lawson said, a promise more than a prediction. "They're going back to Mexico."

# CHAPTER TWENTY-THREE

## CARTEL WEDDING

DALLAS, TEXAS
June 2012

Any other night, any other crowd, and this would be squarely in Lawson's wheelhouse: a long, slow evening at a hotel bar in a city bursting with opportunities for adventure, including no shortage of adventures soundtracked by pickup-and-jeans country. He was high on a leather stool and hunched over a bar on a Saturday night, bartender at the ready, king room reserved, and his prevailing thought was *This is such a waste of time.*

After the DEA's botched raid at Los Alamitos, Lawson had persuaded his bosses to reach out to Ginger Thompson, the *Times* reporter who was threatening to blow up his case. Thompson had been reluctant to cooperate. She was sitting on a prize-worthy scoop. In the end, though, she had agreed to hold the story until the FBI indicted and raided the targets—provided that they did it soon. The *Times* wouldn't wait forever.

In May, three months ahead of schedule, prosecutors had taken the case to the grand jury in Austin. Grand juries convene in secret, with no press or other citizens allowed inside; the transcripts are rarely made public. The targets of the investigation—the people prosecutors hope will be indicted as a result—aren't made aware of the proceedings and play no role in them.

Lawson's testimony alone took several hours. After establishing the case's basics and identifying the main targets—Forty, Forty-Two, and José—he worked through a lengthy PowerPoint presentation, which began with a tutorial on cartel violence. If they ever went to trial, a judge might prohibit Lawson from detouring into the Zetas' general bloodlust, to avoid prejudicing jurors and distracting them from the narrower accusation of money laundering. In a grand jury, no such limits existed.

"They're the ones that do the public hangings, the beheadings, the—they call them *narcomantas*—the banners on the bridges that threaten all of the townspeople," Lawson told the grand jurors. "And, basically, very few people will cooperate against them because they were kind of the first cartel to not just kill drug traffickers; they kill your neighbors, your wife, your kids."

After Lawson detailed the money-laundering scheme, the prosecutor asked the grand jurors to indict fifteen people, some more predictable than others. They indicted all fifteen. They charged both Forty and his brother Forty-Two, who were untouchable in Mexico. They indicted José, Carlitos, and Fernando. They indicted Veracruz millionaire Francisco Colorado, who'd fronted the money for so many horses, and Victor the Courier, who the feds didn't yet know was dead. They targeted several trainers, including Chevo Huitron, who'd trained Tempting Dash; Adan Farias, who'd trained their horses in Los Angeles and visited Forty in Mexico; and Felipe Quintero, who'd trained Mr Piloto during the All American. Every one of them, from Forty to José on down, faced up to twenty years in prison for "conspiring to launder monetary instruments," or money laundering.

The prosecutors also asked the grand jury to indict one person whose inclusion appeared motivated by strategy rather than justice: José's wife, Zulema. She also faced up to twenty years for money laundering, despite her limited involvement. The specter of prison

time for her felt like something dangled in front of José to get him
talking.

The prosecutor did not ask the grand jury to indict Paul Jones,
the only white trainer to work with the group's horses. They didn't
try to charge Tyler Graham, whom Lawson had rescued from his
involvement with the Zetas. There were plenty of other wealthy
white people in the industry who had played crucial roles in the
Zetas' horse business, from auction-house managers to insurance
brokers to breeders. None was indicted.

Lawson knew that could stir controversy in the press, and offer
a tidy narrative for defense attorneys one day. The term *implicit
bias* wasn't yet part of the cable-news lexicon; a Justice Department program to train agents to confront *unconscious bias* was a
few years away. Still, Lawson knew that white people, including
white cops, silently, sometimes unknowingly assigned stereo-
typically negative characteristics to people of color. So he knew
some people might wonder: Why did the FBI choose to approach
Tyler Graham, a white Austin horseman who appeared to
have fallen into business with the Zetas, and not Chevo Huitron,
a brown Austin horseman who appeared to have fallen into
business with them? And why did they present the name of one Los
Alamitos trainer, Adan Farias, to the grand jury and not another,
Paul Jones?

Lawson dismissed the notion that bias infected this or any other
decision, by him or most any cop. Like prosecutor Gardner, he believed in his ability to sift out his own prejudices and look only at the
evidence. Take Farias. Lawson told the grand jury that the trainer
"received several structured deposits from [Victor] Lopez. He
helped the group pick out horses at auction. He is currently under a
lifetime ban from California for being caught doping horses on nu-
merous occasions. Next slide."

But Jones, too, had received structured money, a stream of $9,900
deposits sent by Carlitos. He'd helped pick horses at auction, too,
and trained more horses than Farias ever did.

Besides their ethnicity, one difference between Farias and Jones
was that Jones had cooperated. Lawson, Medina, and agents from

the DEA and IRS had met with him in southern California before the grand jury, and Jones had told them all about his relationship with José.

Maybe Farias would have done the same, but Lawson had deemed Farias too risky to approach, since Farias had traveled to Mexico to see Forty. He also was deemed untrustworthy because he had been caught doping his horses. Jones, by contrast, told the agents during their meeting that he had "never cheated." He apparently didn't count the sixty-day suspension he'd received two months earlier, after a horse he trained tested positive for a banned substance.

So, next slide. Farias was indicted. Jones kept training—and kept every cent of the hundreds of thousands of dollars he'd earned training Forty's horses.

The indictment was sealed and the grand jury sworn to secrecy, which meant the people targeted by it had no idea they were facing charges. That gave the feds time to plot their takedown—the time, place, and manner in which they would arrest these people and seize their most valuable assets.

This date, this night at this elegant hotel in downtown Dallas, was the first that sprang to mind. It so happened that a week after the grand jury returned the indictments, José's daughter Alexandra was getting married.

Still worried about his targets fleeing to Mexico, Lawson and Medina had briefly discussed organizing their takedown around the wedding. There would be practical benefits. José and Zulema would obviously be there. People from throughout the quarter-horse industry had been invited, including Tyler Graham and his grandpa, so surely business associates like Carlitos, Fernando, and Francisco Colorado would be there. Lawson knew it was unlikely that Forty or Forty-Two would attend, but if anything was going to draw them offside, it was the wedding of their niece.

There could be other benefits, too. Though he knew he still had to prove it, Lawson had a deep, abiding faith in the fact that José and his wife were knowingly, deliberately washing Forty's money and helping him infiltrate the American horse-racing business. He was pissed about it, and he liked the idea of stopping it in some spectacular way, especially knowing that the *New York Times*'s story would likely drop the next morning as negotiated. There would be innocent people there, family and friends and associates whose nights would be ruined by the spectacle of Lawson dragging José and others out in cuffs. But he viewed the evening's festivities as a "cartel wedding." And busting up a cartel wedding on a Saturday night in downtown Dallas would feel *good*. And look good to the public, too, the image of a SWAT team storming the dance floor at what he considered a Zeta party on enemy territory. That, Lawson hoped, would teach the cartels to fuck around on this side of the river.

And yet. It was all so very dumb. Lawson knew it almost as soon as the idea flew out of his mouth, and Medina knew it, too. It was too soon. The brothers wouldn't be there. The hotel and the wedding and the streets would be flooded with boozy, Saturday-night chaos, making it easier for the targets to disappear into the city or for someone to get hurt.

Then there was the Carlitos factor. He'd gone off the radar after the Los Alamitos raid, which was exactly what Lawson had feared. By then, the feds had compelled a judge to let them access several email addresses used by the organization. Under federal law, service providers like Microsoft and Google are required to store customer emails and turn them over to law enforcement. Like agents hoping to tap a target's phone, agents hoping to read private email must first convince a judge. In this case, like most, the judge agreed, and the Internet companies coughed up thousands of pages of correspondence. The emails sent after the raid had revealed a swell of panic.

"Toss your cell," Forty's Nuevo Laredo bookkeeper, Yo-Yo, had written to Fernando after the raid. Then, addressing a more contemporary concern of the cartels, he urged Fernando to ditch his well-kept Facebook page, which featured photos of him working Forty's horses. "Get rid of your Face," Yo-Yo wrote.

But Forty's most pressing concern was the whereabouts of Carlitos. Carlitos had seen things, Carlitos *knew* things, and no one had heard from Carlitos since the raid at Los Al. "Why does the kid not answer?" Yo-Yo wrote in an email to Felipe Quintero, one of the other Los Al trainers. "The dude isn't answering and people are concerned." The emails went on like that for days—"Sweetie, tell me-e-e-e something"—but there was no sign of Carlitos.

Lawson wanted to know, too. He asked Tyler to look into it and then found his way to the FBI's wire room to listen for clues. Clues to Carlitos's whereabouts, and clues to who all might be at the wedding.

"Hey, you going to Alex's wedding next weekend?" Tyler had asked Fernando, who was in Ruidoso prepping the new class of two-year-olds.

"Yeah, that's the plan. You gonna be out there?"

"Ah man, it sucks, I can't," Tyler said. "My best friend has a damn wedding the same day, and I gotta be a groomsman in it."

"Ah fuck. That same day?"

Tyler changed the subject. "Where's my little brother Carlos at?"

"He's in California!" Fernando said.

"What the fuck, he don't want to come hang out with us anymore?"

"I guess not. Fuckin' little sucker hasn't called me in forever."

So Carlitos hadn't gone to Mexico after all. That was good. But he wouldn't be at the wedding. No Carlitos, maybe no Fernando, almost definitely no Forty or Forty-Two, and a big-ass headache if things went sideways. So they wouldn't raid it.

But what if Forty *did* show? They had to be there. Just in case.

Lawson coordinated with the Dallas FBI office to get some agents into the hotel that night. They convinced hotel security to let them install cameras at the entrance and outside the room José booked for his family. And they booked a room upstairs—partly a staging area, partly a place to monitor the feeds from the cameras downstairs.

Throughout the night, the agents rotated in and out of the hotel bar, which was tucked near a corner of the lobby. Upstairs, a DEA intelligence analyst lay on the bed and waited for photos to come through from the surveillance cameras; she'd been digging up dirt on the Treviños for years and knew their faces as well as anyone. In the streets, a SWAT team waited for word they figured would never come. Two more DEA agents, there on the way-off chance that Forty would show up, watched movies in their car and waited.

At the bar, Lawson babysat a beer. He shifted his eyes between the door, looking for the ghosts he knew wouldn't show, and the il-luminated painting above the bar, of two Labradors chasing away a hawk. A message lit up his phone: "Parking garage."

He slipped into the heat of the garage, heart jumping a little, and found his colleague, who pointed out a middle-aged Hispanic guy. Nah, Lawson said. Not anyone of interest. Back to the bar.

The night carried on for a while like that. Lawson followed a few partygoers to a nearby corner store, which allowed him to snag a Red Bull to help him make it through the night. At one point, he saw José step into the warm spring air to have a cigarette and make a call. Lawson followed him, lurked, and learned nothing.

By around eleven, he had given up on the idea of anything inter-esting happening. He had begun to think more distinctly about the night of sleep that awaited him at his own hotel. Then the bus pulled up.

He could see it through the hotel window. It was one of those gleaming tour buses, windows black as night. He watched the front entrance as a stream of Mexican men flowed into the lobby, past the palm plants, each toting black instrument cases. They were dressed in identical tuxedos, black on white. The only color came blaring from the side of the bus, which Lawson could see through the win-dow, idling in the glint of downtown light: "Banda el Recodo."

Lawson wasn't up on which Mexican bands were popular with which cartels, but he did know how intertwined popular music and criminality were across the river. Bands had been writing corridos about smugglers since smugglers existed, and in recent years, war-ring cartels were known to commission corridos and claim certain bands as their own. A popular norteño band called Los Tigres del Norte was said to have played the Company's end-of-year posadas, and its songs were banned from Mexican radio.

Banda el Recodo was less hip-hop-influenced than some of the younger gangsters' favorite bands, leaning instead on the polkaesque rhythms of *ranchera* music. As the band moved into the ballroom where the Treviños were celebrating, Lawson texted a source in Mexico.

"That band's there?" the source texted back.

And then:

"They're like three hundred grand a night."

And then:

"That's Forty's favorite band."

A gift, Lawson thought, from one brother to another. They streamed into the ballroom, and their trumpets blared into the bar, where Lawson lingered for as long as he could. They were still playing when Lawson left for the night.

■ ■ ■

LEXINGTON, OKLAHOMA
June 2012

The tractor would roar again soon enough, breaking up the manure and spreading it thin, that little magic trick José liked to do to make the shit his business threw at him disappear. For now, though, José had shut down the farm for the night and retired to the brick house with Zulema. It was about the same size as their place in Balch Springs, fifteen hundred square feet, with three bedrooms, a living room, and windows looking out over the pastures José tended to like a golf-course superintendent.

He was *proud* of this place. Of what he'd built. He'd told Tyler that when Tyler came to visit recently. If all went as planned, José would be free of Tyler as soon as he and his family could prove themselves capable quarter-horse men. Free of Carlitos, too, apparently. With Carlitos off the radar, Forty had promoted Fernando, whose discretion and demeanor José had always preferred anyway. Fernando had gone into Nuevo Laredo to meet with Forty about it—middle of the night, dozens of armed guards, a quick meet in the car, that whole routine. Fernando's knowledge would come in handy the next year, if José could succeed in ditching Tyler and moving Tempting Dash up to Oklahoma.

For now, though, he still needed Tyler. He'd offered him a tour of the ranch while they tried to smooth out their differences. He showed him the house and the barns and the pastures, and he told Tyler he was "living the American Dream."

Before Tyler left, José pointed across the two-lane road that fronted his new horse farm, rising and falling like the one that fronted Tyler's ranch. There, across the street, were about six hundred acres of empty prairie, adorned only by swaying grass, the occasional tree, and a rusty barn that could be knocked down and hauled away in one afternoon. I'm going to buy that land, too, José said.

At home with Zulema that night, he must have been proud of his family, too. They'd had the wedding nine days before. Alex looked gorgeous in her dress, her wide-open smile showing off her clear braces. Luis was on leave from the Marines, but he wore his dress uniform, white gloves and all.

José and Zulema had played the role of hosts admirably, moving around the ballroom to connect friends from the disparate corners of their life—this ad-sales lady from *Track Magazine* to that beloved teacher from Alex's high school to this quarter-horse insurance broker, and so on. Dr. Graham, whom José considered a mentor, had "the best time in the world," later calling Banda el Recodo's performance "educational." But he headed to bed early, and was up and dressed and heading back to his farm by four in the morning. The party was still going.

After the wedding, José's new, Alex-less clan—himself, Zulema, their three younger children, José's mother, and his brother Rodolfo—returned to the farm. The sun fell, and the prairie went quiet. Never had José's mom been so far from Nuevo Laredo. From

Miguel and Omar and her other children. But she was here with Rodolfo, and she was here with José, "the clean brother," her good, hard, honest worker, as he would probably remind her the next morning when he fired up that tractor and started painting lines in the pasture.

# CHAPTER TWENTY-FOUR
## LAND RUSH

LEXINGTON, OKLAHOMA
June 2012

Lawson could hear the horses if he listened closely. He was standing outside the black-iron gate with the horse silhouettes, at the bottom of a long driveway that led up to José's brick homestead. It was a little after six in the morning, the earliest moment the court would allow them to raid without a judge's permission.

*The phones,* Lawson thought, the professional silence occasionally interrupted by the neighs of horses in the nearby pasture. *We gotta get the phones.* Then the crack of a megaphone and a voice, booming into the lightening sky. Time to go.

Lawson had flown up from Texas the day before. After hitting the ground in Oklahoma City, he walked into a briefing room at the local FBI office and was greeted by 250 federal agents and local cops. They were all waiting for him.

He silently vowed to keep it short; he could see in their eyes the same glazed-over look he'd felt in his own over the years, brought on by severe allergies to meetings.

Besides, they'd been planning this since the day they secured the indictments. They'd written search warrants for several sites across the country—the trainer Chevo's house in Austin; Fernando's childhood home in Mission, Texas; Carlitos's apartment near Los Alamitos; José's house in Balch Springs; the stables at Ruidoso Downs; and here, in Oklahoma, at José's ranch.

Lawson sped through his grand-jury presentation and tried to keep it vaguely motivational, hoping they wouldn't tune him out but figuring they would. "We're a long way from the border," he told them, "but you're going to put a hit on a lot of guys who do some bad things down there."

After the briefing, Lawson went out for a steak and a beer at a restaurant swimming with cops and agents he recognized from the briefing room. They nodded at each other knowingly and made small talk about anything but. Lawson was in bed by nine. The wake-up call seemed to come the moment he closed his eyes. The clock read 3:45.

He slipped into his raid gear: khaki pants, collared shirt, FBI raid vest, and a thigh holster carrying his firearm. They met at the National Guard Armory in Lexington, then quietly rolled down José's street, forming a perimeter, while the SWAT team moved onto José's property and the sun rose. Across the road, the owner of the Old Dog Gun Shop, who lived next to his gun store, heard the commotion and stepped out of his house. He was shirtless under his overalls and toting a loaded shotgun. He asked some agents what was happening. They politely shooed him back inside.

"This is the FBI," the voice from the megaphone boomed. The SWAT leader urged José and Zulema to exit the house with their hands in the morning sky. Lawson jogged up the driveway and toward the front door. On the way, he passed José, shirtless, and Zulema, in her nightgown, sitting in the grass with their hands on their heads.

Later, Lawson would hear from Agent Medina, who was back in San Antonio, eager to give him updates when he called in. In Austin,

Tempting Dash's trainer, Chevo Huitron, had been dragged from his house and shouted at by FBI agents to not speak to his family in Spanish. ("I'll speak whatever fucking language I want," Chevo said, in English.) In Ruidoso, Fernando had been pulled out of a dusty Mazda 6 that José had lent him. In Santa Ana, Carlitos had been found in a posh apartment with his wife, his mother-in-law, and his newborn son. He hadn't returned Forty's calls in weeks, and he was working on getting his family immigration status in the United States.

Lawson wanted to hear all about it. First, though, he wanted inside José's house. He burst through the front door and went straight for the master bedroom.

He knew that everything inside, everything on the property, would be valuable for his case. He knew it would be part of his life for years, through trials and appeals and enough meetings to make him long for his days intercepting loads on the interstate. He knew there were truckloads of cowboys, contracted by the IRS, scheduled to arrive at the ranch later that morning. They would move through the stables, looking for the most valuable horses, which would be seized and moved to various ranches, while the Department of the Treasury waited to auction them off. He knew the same was happening in Ruidoso and Los Alamitos and elsewhere, and that every horse, every shred of paper, would be meaningful eventually.

But the phones were actionable today. The phones would, he hoped, allow the FBI to access BlackBerry PINs and Nextel numbers used by Forty in Mexico and could theoretically be used to track his whereabouts. If they could find him, they could alert the Mexican authorities and maybe see Forty captured or killed. He found the first phone in a drawer in José's bedroom; it had one phone number programmed into it, with a Mexican area code. He dropped it into a bag and kept searching.

José sat, waiting for the same waterfall of questions he'd been drowning in for years. He was inside the FBI office in Norman, Oklahoma, a half-hour drive from his ranch. After being lured half dressed out of the house, hands on head, they'd been allowed fresh clothes before being driven here.

Later, José would learn that some agents had asked his thirteen-year-old daughter, outside the presence of any adult, about her uncle Forty, which didn't sit well. He would also learn later that they'd pulled Zulema into an interview room like this one.

She hadn't told the agents much. It was José's idea to buy Tempting Dash, she said, and they'd used money they'd inherited from Zulema's mother. They'd gotten lucky with that horse, and lucky with Mr Piloto, too. The business took off from there. Miguel? Maybe some of the horses they bred at the farm belonged to him, but she wouldn't know. "José is not proud of being their brother," she told the agents.

Now the same two agents walked into the interview room where José was sitting. One was in charge—a big white guy with a scruffy goatee. He sat down across from José, introduced himself as Agent Lawson, and read José his Miranda rights. Then he started talking about a subject that had never come up in José's stops at the border, in his many long and fruitless interrogation sessions with the feds: horses.

José told them his story: how he'd worked hard for everything, made his children do the same. How he was an American like them, how he respected their uniform and what it stood for, even if it was men in those same uniforms who'd made his life hell for years, because of the actions of his brothers in another country.

I can pick my friends, he told the agents.

I can pick my associates.

I can't pick my family.

Besides, this horse business was his and his alone. It all started with Tempting Dash and grew from there. Carlitos, Fernando, these guys the feds said were friends with José's brothers in Mexico—they're just clients, José told the agents. Business associates. Not partners. Never partners.

The feds would never believe it—he had to know that. How much even he believed it would remain a mystery. But that had always been the story he told, to the world if not to himself: That he'd gotten lucky. For Tempting Dash to fall into Forty's lap; for Forty to decide to tell Ramiro to sell it to José; for Tempting Dash to keep winning; for Mr Piloto and Separate Fire to win, too; for this ranch in Oklahoma to become available, and then the one next door. So many chaotically bouncing balls had to fall snugly into place for José to have been sitting in that brick house this morning, with four hundred horses in his care, a dozen employees, a calendar packed with industry events to attend, and not a masonry job in sight.

How secure it would make his family remained to be seen. His mounting expenses had drained so much cash from his business bank accounts he'd been hit with a series of overdraft charges. That meant he couldn't pay himself or Zulema much for their work on the farm, even as they planned and paid for Alex's wedding. As the wedding approached, their checking account had fallen to $958.28, and they'd been forced to pay the hotel in cash.

Still, José could hardly deny their fortune. He'd played the ponies and won this life for his family—not for his code-named brothers in Mexico but for the people here with him at Zule Farms, his wife and kids and mom and brother. Who knew where they were now, or what hell they would soon face.

After José told Lawson his story, Lawson told José one of his own, about an Excel spreadsheet. That wasn't so worrisome: of course José kept detailed ledgers of how much money was owed to what auction house, to what vet, to what trainer. Every horse farm did. But then the agent claimed he had in his possession a spreadsheet that José had personally delivered to Carlitos and Forty in Mexico, outlining the expenses from Forty's horse-racing operation. José decided now would be a good time to stop talking.

# CHAPTER TWENTY-FIVE
# PAPER CHASE

DALLAS, TEXAS
June 2012

The day after the raids, I arrived at work early and picked up that day's copy of the *New York Times*. I'd been doing that lately, trying to build a habit of it: arriving first at the office, clicking on the lights, and laying claim to the lone copy of the *Times,* before another reporter could squirrel it away in his messenger bag, never to be seen again.

It was a powerhouse front page, with stories about an Obama-Romney fundraising sprint; a promising gun-safety measure foiled by the NRA; and an enduring conflict in Syria that, the *Times* reported, was showing "signs of mutating into a full-fledged civil war." I didn't read any of them.

My eyes instead darted to a story below the fold. I was drawn in by the prominent photo, of a middle-aged, round-faced man wearing a white cowboy hat and clutching a gold trophy, flanked by a beaming jockey and a guy in a sharp black suit. I was further intrigued by the story's author, Ginger Thompson, who had a reputation for shedding harsh lights on the role American agents played in

Mexico's drug war. But it was the headline that clinched it: "A Drug Family in the Winner's Circle."

As promised, Thompson had waited until the government's takedown to publish her story. But despite holding off, she'd held nothing back. Her story detailed how the government believed Forty had used José to launder money through quarter-horse racing, and how deeply embedded in the sport the Zetas were. She also broke the news that Ramiro had been murdered while working as an informant.

Looking back at it, Thompson's story was smart, nuanced, and ferociously reported, and it raised important questions about how traffickers use their money and agents use their sources. At my desk that morning, though, I just read it as, like, the coolest narco story *ever*. I saw a "self-described brick mason" who'd helped his savage drug-lord brother "launder millions" through American industry—an "operation," officials told the *Times*, that "amounted to a foothold in the United States for one of Mexico's most dangerous criminal networks."

Wasn't I smitten. And wasn't I lucky: José's suburban Dallas house was twenty minutes east of where I worked, at a weekly Dallas newspaper. Lone Star Park, the site of Tempting Dash's first big races, was twenty minutes west. The sprawling ranch that the feds had raided the previous dawn—"sending several helicopters and hundreds of law enforcement agents," the *Times* reported—was an arrow-straight, Chick-fil-A-studded, three-hour drive north on Interstate 35, the narcotics superhighway that practically ran through my office.

Naturally, I had questions, though I'd come to wonder whether they were the right ones. I wanted to know how this obvious narco—this "self-described brick mason"—had so thoroughly fooled these American horsemen into thinking he belonged. I wanted to know how unraveling this scheme might lead investigators to Forty himself. Mostly, I wanted to know who these investigators were—these racetrack-infiltrating, badge-waving cowboys who'd stormed José's barns like SEAL Team Six on an Al-Qaeda safe house.

In time, I made progress. I searched court filings for thrilling details, interviewed experts and defense lawyers, and got a money-laundering tutorial from the IRS agents who'd gone swimming in the boxes Lawson so loathed. But things took off when I got a call from the FBI. I'd requested an interview sometime before and been rebuffed. Now the bureau's answer changed. Lawson wanted to talk.

We met for breakfast, in a city he asked me not to name. Lawson was courteous and generous, in that meeting and the several that followed. He had a gift for self-deprecation, but he wasn't overly humble about his work. He was never boastful, just honest.

That morning, over eggs, biscuits, and a river of coffee, I asked how he did it, and he told me. He told me what he knew about Laredo before he landed there: "Cartel bad, border dangerous." How the case fell to him, based on his and Tyler's parallel backstories: "Tyler's a country boy, and he's young." How he fended off the DEA: "When I first started, I just could not believe the competitiveness. I didn't like it. I didn't understand it. You realize if you're ever gonna make a case, you have to be protective." How he staked out the races, rendezvoused with sources, orchestrated the drops, and fake-boozed while Alex got married. How he felt about the investigation: "It was sexy. . . . We just wanted to show that if you let these people roam free, they're going to control different industries. They don't want to just be a part of it, they want to dominate."

For almost three hours, I got the how. We didn't talk much about why. We did laugh a lot, though.

The story I published essentially chronicled Lawson's sleuthing. It had a slick title, "The Rookie and the Zetas," and featured a photo of federal agents staring distantly at the land they'd just seized from José, like Sooners basking in their industrious thievery. It was *The Untouchables*, with Lawson as Eliot Ness, Forty as Capone, and money laundering standing in for tax evasion.

But as I researched this book, my view of Lawson's caper started to muddle. It's a pretty common experience for reporters first delving into the drug war, their preconceptions forged by harried American journalism and bingeable cable dramas starring agents who, dirty or clean, always end up right. Like the real-life agents themselves, journalists who dig a little deeper tend to fling mud into their own virgin eyes.

I hardly immersed myself in the Zetas' world the way some journalists have, especially the Mexican reporters who have risked and lost lives. But I did share many meals, trade some prison emails, and otherwise pick the brains of former Zeta traffickers, money launderers, operatives, and snitches, along with their lawyers. To a man, they described lives devoid of opportunity, upended by a Company job offer that was hardly optional.

I spent time with federal agents and prosecutors, current and former, Anglo and Hispanic, across every letter in the soup. Each fell somewhere different on the path from idealistic to thank-God-for-retirement, but they all loved their work. Not one seriously questioned the underlying, prohibition-obsessed policies that made their jobs so possible—and so much damn fun.

As Lawson and I kept talking, I tried to pepper my *hows* with *whys*. He remained generous and patient, but I could tell he felt the ground shifting under his feet. We laughed less. We talked about "root causes," drug laws, sentencing laws, implicit bias, and how he sifted the potential targets from the potential cooperators. More than any law enforcement agent I asked, Lawson was open to the idea that something other than better enforcement could reduce the flow of drugs into the United States. He also at least acknowledged the existence of unconscious biases, in himself and others, and though he thought he was able to disregard them, he did acknowledge that their unconsciousness was precisely what made them difficult to disregard. He recognized the role diversity and training might play in helping to overcome them.

In other words, his view of things was muddled, too. Yet he saw this case in starkly simpler terms. Whatever choices his targets did or didn't have in their lives, Lawson believed they'd clearly opted into helping Forty, perhaps the most violent criminal in the history of Mexico's drug war. For that, twenty years behind bars or more seemed fair to Lawson. If they wanted less, they were welcome to flip, help find Forty, and try to atone for their missteps.

He also remained confident that he chose the right horsemen to secretly indict and which to secretly enlist. So many people played roles in Forty's business, and they all had the same incentive: to make money. How did you know, I asked, who was part of the conspiracy, who was along for the ride, and who was just scared out of their minds?

He told me.

"A lot of the judgments that I made were, real simply, based on: Who did their role out of fear and continued with life the same way? And who did that role and then started acting like a boss?"

"Yeah, yeah, yeah," I said, to this and so much else.

"In my mind, that's how I separated the two," Lawson said.

"You gotta do it somehow."

It's the sort of subjective litmus test detectives probably deploy every day, and it may even serve them well sometimes. In this case, the prosecutor, IRS agents, Medina, and all of their supervisors agreed with Lawson that they'd correctly identified and targeted the real culprits. But the subjectivity of that test seems to introduce obvious flaws. As I sat with it, I (eventually) realized that some of the people who "continued with life the same way"—Tyler, Paul Jones, and other upper-crust horsemen—had no reason to *act* like bosses. They already *were* bosses.

Lawson had never had much doubt about José's role as Forty's partner. But the agent's like-a-boss litmus test further sealed José's fate as a prime target. After all those years of building schools and houses and entertainment venues for the bosses of the world, José had finally become one himself.

Who knows how long he might have stayed a boss, had Lawson's cavalry not shown up on José's farm. Forty's tainted seed money would have dried up when he was killed or captured, which seemed inevitable. José would have been forced to make the business last on his own, with family investments of a different sort: sweat and time from wife and kids and brothers like Rodolfo. But if that was José's version of the American Dream, Lawson's was to crush it, and he didn't plan on losing much sleep over it. "He bought into his new placement in life," Lawson said, and so the hammer fell.

I hoped to ask similar questions of Tyler—how he did it, and why. Why he didn't just hire a lawyer, refer José elsewhere, and try to catch the next wave. I wondered whether he was scared to turn them away—the narcos *and* the FBI—or whether he considered himself, as one cartel operative put it to me, "ten feet tall, ten feet wide, and bulletproof." I wondered if he just thought, *Hey, the rest of the industry has been taking suspected drug money for years. Why shouldn't I?*

Lawson promised I would strike out, that Tyler wanted no part of the press. He was right. Tyler didn't return my calls, letters, emails, or Facebook messages. So one day, I found him on the grounds of Ruidoso Downs, surrounded by friends and associates. I tried to be discreet, introducing myself as the guy who'd been calling and sending letters. He clearly saw me, and he clearly heard me, but he acted, convincingly, as if my questions and I didn't exist. He looked away, continued the conversation that I'd interrupted, and didn't stop talking until I'd stammered my apology and slumped away.

For all my curiosity about Tyler's and Lawson's choices, I somehow felt I knew the contours of José's story. From the moment I read "A Drug Family in the Winner's Circle," I assumed this "self-described brick mason" had always played some role in turning his family into a "drug family." They'd popped him for what they could prove, I figured, not what they knew. Surely they knew more.

My first meeting with Lawson chipped away at those presumptions. As far as Lawson knew, José truly was "working his butt off for small wages and living like that." In every subsequent interview, I expected to find the one law enforcement agent who knew, or who at least suspected, that José's involvement in Forty's business went deeper than managing horses, and went further back than Tempting Dash. But it didn't. "We tried for years to start a case on him for drugs," one DEA analyst told me. They wouldn't have needed much to pull the trigger, but they found nothing.

People from the trafficking world said the same, to me and to investigators. It left me wondering about whether, or how, or when José made his choice to give in. For so many years, he lived on the right side of American law but the wrong side of American society. Then, just like that, he switched sides. Did he even view it as a choice? Did he think he was helping his brother, or that his brother was helping him? Did he understand that providing or accepting that help could land him in prison for twenty years? Did he not care about twenty years if it meant a foothold for his kids? Did he know they could seize the foothold, too, even before they convicted him?

I assumed José would never answer these questions, at least not with me asking them. But when I saw his smiling face on the front of the *Times,* I did wonder whether he'd ever tell anyone. Maybe now, finally, with his freedom and his family and his "American Dream" in the balance, an agent would convince José to answer all those questions about his brother. But as I devoured the rapidly expanding record of José's case, it became clear that José had chosen to tell his story not to the feds but to a team of defense lawyers who could help shape it, sell it, and use it to set him free.

# CHAPTER TWENTY-SIX

## INTERVENTION

AUSTIN, TEXAS
March 2013

There is a rule, unwritten but often spoken, in American law enforcement: Don't seize anything that shits or eats. Money can be deposited. Property can be sold. Cars can be auctioned off or added to the fleet. Drugs and guns can be laid out on tables in media rooms and ogled by the zoom lenses of America's finest pack-chasing journalists. But animals? Horses? Horses need to be fed and groomed and cared for, and horses make manure that needs to be hauled away or spread out dutifully by a man on a tractor. What did the Treasury Department know about all that?

The rule had dogged this case from the jump. In Houston, where Ramiro first started cooperating with ICE, word had spread throughout the agency that management would never pursue the case because it didn't want to seize horses. In Dallas, the DEA claimed they knew all about the horse-racing business, too, but had no interest in taking possession of live animals. In Austin, when

Lawson showed up to pitch prosecutor Doug Gardner on the case, Gardner almost turned them down because of the horses. In Los Angeles, after the DEA raided Los Alamitos in search of Forty-Two, the agent who led the raid heard only one concern from his supervisor: "Please tell me we're not seizing anything that eats?"

There were 466 horses in the United States that the feds had identified as the Zetas'. Treasury officials knew that seizing all of them would cost money and man-hours they didn't have. So they forged a compromise. They told the agents to seize eleven of the most valuable horses, to make sure they maintained their value until the courts gave Treasury permission to auction them off. They could deal with the rest later.

Arriving at José's ranch, the contract cowboys had moved through the barns in search of the most valuable studs and mares, checking their markings against photos and descriptions provided by the government. They loaded up Mr Piloto, the All American Futurity–winning stud. They loaded up Dashin Follies, the $875,000 mare. They loaded up Separate Fire, the horse José and trainer Paul Jones had ridden to fame in southern California.

They didn't need to load up Tempting Dash. He was safe down in Elgin with Tyler. It was still breeding season, so the government had contracted Southwest Stallion Station to continue breeding Tempting Dash.

That left 455 horses that needed to be cared for. Several of them were at Ruidoso Downs, in a cluster of stalls on the track's scraggy backside that had become known as "the Zeta stables." During the raid on Ruidoso, an IRS agent asked a young trainer to care for the horses the IRS planned on leaving behind. He agreed at first, but then he heard the same rumors everyone on the backside was hearing: *The Zetas are coming for their horses.* The kid bailed.

The Zetas never came back, but the trainer never did, either. The Treasury Department wound up taking them all.

Most of the rest of the horses were on José's ranch, and that's where they stayed in the weeks after the raids. Prosecutors had asked a judge to approve an unusual arrangement: to allow the staff at the ranch, including José's brother Rodolfo and son José Jr., to continue caring for the remaining horses while the case was adjudicated.

The judge agreed, but within weeks it became clear that the plan was doomed. José's prized vet had gone looking for new work; his beloved breeding manager, Jessica, had heard about the raid and never gone back. José's family and staff lost control of the overcrowded ranch. A pneumonia outbreak killed six horses. Twenty others, mostly foals, died of natural causes. Others suffered from persistent diarrhea, untreated injuries and wounds, and poor hoof care that could threaten whatever racing career they might have left. Meanwhile, the Treasury Department had apparently discovered how much work, and money, José had poured into keeping up his farm: the government had already spent half a million dollars caring for the horses, and the horses' value was dropping—fast.

Prosecutors asked the judge for a do-over. They proposed that they start auctioning off the horses immediately and put the money aside, to be returned to José and his creditors should he be vindicated. The judge agreed. The horses, whatever was left of them, were safe.

That was a relief for Lawson, for whom the case had rekindled a childhood interest in horses. But even with the horses secure, his mind swam. The trial was scheduled for April, ten months after the raids. He and Medina started driving to Austin every Monday, checking into a hotel, and working through the week, watching the boxes of records stack higher in their Austin war room. The records seized in the raids were coming in by the dollyful, to go with the thousands of pages of bank records that had been subpoenaed by the IRS.

Some of the IRS's and FBI's best minds were working through those boxes. As the trial approached, Gardner, the prosecutor, would carefully remove each record and hold it over a projector. The team would stare at it, their eyes burning, trying to decode its meaning, debating its merits like a family prepping for a garage sale. They kept more than they needed.

But Lawson knew it would take more than boxes full of records. Their main targets had lawyered up in big ways. José Treviño had hired a former federal prosecutor who'd remade himself as one of Dallas's most feared defense lawyers. Carlitos had hired a Miami attorney whose client list included a gangster nicknamed both Big Mike and Fat Michael, and Panamanian dictator Manuel Noriega. Francisco Colorado, the Zetas' alleged front man, had hired a Houston law firm that had defended multiple United States senators, famed cult leader David Koresh, and Robert Durst.

Lawson knew that whatever those boxes revealed, the defense lawyers would have compelling stories explaining it away. He knew they needed a compelling story of their own—a vivid scene that would play in the jurors' minds when their eyes went blurry from the bank records. He didn't know exactly what it was, but he knew it needed to start with drug money in Mexico and end with that money in the hands of American quarter-horse men. For months now, he had found himself wondering, *How do I prove that the same dollar bill that bought a cocaine piece went to this drug dealer, who sent the money to pay for this horse?*

■ ■ ■

AUSTIN, TEXAS
April 2013

The deputy marshal in the driver's seat couldn't have known it, but the route they took that morning, out of the county jail and west toward the awakening city, was more than a little familiar to the prisoner in the backseat. A left on Farm to Market 20 and they would be, in twenty-five minutes or less, kicking up gravel on the way to Chevo's training center, the site of Tempting Dash's first stateside sprints. A right on 95 and they would be rising and falling over the lime-green hills on the way to Elgin. In no more than a half hour, jail-cell door to stud-barn door, they could be standing on Tyler Graham's ranch, pulling out José's 2009 Colt of the Year. He might belong to the Treasury Department one day, and he might be with Tyler today. But for now, Tempting Dash still technically belonged to José.

The deputy marshal went straight instead. The hills east of Austin rolled them into and across downtown, to the federal courthouse, in a trendy patch of town near a combination bike shop–coffee house. The marshal escorted José into an interview room for a meeting with his lawyer.

José's family in Dallas had found the guy. His name was David Finn, and he was considered one of the city's best defense lawyers, with a client list that included accused murderers and white-collar criminals. Among other victories, he'd recently cut a deal for the CFO of Stanford Financial, for his role in a seven-billion-dollar Ponzi scheme.

Finn knew that money laundering could be hard to prove. The government would have to show not only that the money was drug money, and not only that José *knew* it was drug money, but also that he *knew* he was helping launder it. Finn also knew a good story when he heard one, and this was a good story: butt-busting American with no criminal record, charged with a crime too complicated for some lawyers to understand, let alone a workaday bricklayer. He took the case.

Then Finn showed up at the jail to meet José. He walked into a lobby packed with families waiting to visit their loved ones, approached the window, and announced to the guards that he was there to meet a client: "Tre-vi-ño Mo-ra-les."

Those six syllables upended the place. The marshals cleared everyone out and told them their visits with loved ones would have to wait.

José and Finn managed to shake hands, but everything else about them fit oddly. Finn was all puffed chest and clever metaphors; José was a talks-least-says-most kind of guy. On that visit and all others, he wanted to talk about only one thing: his family.

His wife, Zulema, was facing up to twenty years in prison for her role in the businesses. And in the months after the raid, the prosecutors had sent another aftershock rippling through José's family: they'd charged Alexandra.

"We recovered a chat log through our search warrants that we'll show here in a minute, basically, where she is proving that she knows everything her family now has came from Miguel and Omar," Lawson told the grand jury. "And she received a weekly check from Zule Farms for working as an office assistant at the ranch. So she knew about the conspiracy, received money from the conspiracy, and joined the conspiracy."

She had worked only a minor role for just three months at the farm, and it would be difficult to convince a jury to send her away for it. Prosecutors didn't need that, nor did they especially seem to want it. More likely, they wanted exactly what they were getting: a place inside José's head.

In their jailhouse meetings, Finn assured José that Alex and Zulema would cut deals and never serve a day. No prosecutor would go to trial with a wife and daughter sitting at the defense table, drawing waves of compassion from the jury. Not with the young woman's newlywed Marine husband in the gallery. Or, worse, unable to attend due to his prior commitments on some far-off military base.

But as the trial approached, José noticed that Finn's puffed chest was slowly leaking air. Finn couldn't necessarily see how the feds would prove beyond a reasonable doubt that José didn't pay cash for Tempting Dash, common in the quarter-horse industry, and then use his winnings to build a multimillion-dollar business, with Carlitos and Fernando and Colorado as clients. If José *was* laundering Forty's money, Finn wasn't convinced the prosecutors could prove José knew it. There was no wiretap on José's phones, and the only calls the FBI recorded between José and Tyler revealed no knowledge of a scheme. No emails or records, either. There was that five-thousand-dollar airport cash drop from Victor the Courier, but how could the feds prove it was drug money, especially since Victor the Courier was dead?

So what was Finn so afraid of? Eventually, José realized that his lawyer's confidence was under attack from the six syllables that he dragged with him every time he showed up at the jail—the same six syllables José had been dragging across the river for all those years.

"Tre-vi-ño Mo-ra-les."

"You're telling me to swim across the English Channel with weights on my back," Finn told José in the jail as the trial approached. "I don't walk on water, but even if I did . . ."

Finn believed what José believed: they couldn't get Forty, so they were coming for José. He urged José to consider pleading guilty in pursuit of a lesser sentence.

No deal, José said.

Finn approached the prosecutor, just to test the waters. "Can you offer ten?" It was half the maximum twenty, for a guy no one had ever accused of moving a kilo or firing a weapon. It would save the government time and money. And maybe they could convince José to cooperate against defendants *other* than his brothers.

The prosecutor was interested. Certainly he, like Lawson, wanted José in an American prison, as penance for helping the Zetas infiltrate American culture and commerce. Like Lawson, though, what he wanted most was Forty in a Mexican prison. Or, even better, on a plane to the United States. Or, if it came to it, slumped over the dashboard of a Chevy Silverado somewhere in the wilds of Tamaulipas.

So, sure, the prosecutor told José's lawyer. We'll set his wife and daughter free, and we'll cut José a deal, too, on one condition: that he tell us what he knows about his brothers.

"You know that's a nonstarter," Finn told the prosecutor, and the prosecutor did know. They were headed to trial.

Now the trial was a week out. José was heading into Austin for a meeting at the courthouse. Finn was there, as expected. But so was Zulema and her lawyer. And so, to José's apparent surprise, was Alexandra. In a way, so was José's first grandchild. Alexandra was pregnant with a baby girl.

It quickly became obvious that this wasn't a strategy meeting, it was an intervention. With the trial looming, José's wife and daughter had finally pleaded guilty. Zulema had admitted to laundering Forty's drug money, which her lawyer told the press she did in the interest of supporting her young children. Alexandra had copped to failing to report a felony. Both would serve only a couple of years' probation. Neither would have to testify.

For José, this was great news. It was, it seemed to his lawyers, all he'd ever wanted. But now they were here, in this interview room, and it was becoming clear that more or less everyone there wanted him to cut a deal, too. He was right: Finn and the prosecutor had orchestrated the thing, in hopes of avoiding a trial for José. Even if José wouldn't testify, the prosecutors could ask the judge for a slightly reduced sentence if he pleaded guilty and accepted responsibility.

To Finn, cutting a deal was the only answer. Though he still considered his case strong—still believed the feds couldn't prove that José had laundered anything, knowingly or not—he'd come to realize that the Zetas would loom over the trial. Fond of metaphors, Finn believed that the mere mention of "cartels" would put prosecutors on third base to start. All they'd have to do to win was lay down a half-decent bunt.

Finn's plan was working, at least in that José soon found himself locked in conversation with his daughter, who urged him to cut a deal. Her voice rose and tears gathered in her eyes.

If I were on the jury, I would convict you, Alex told her dad.

I'm glad you're out of harm's way, José said. Then, before he said goodbye and they drove back to County—back toward, but never *to*, Tyler Graham and Tempting Dash—he told them, You know I can't plead guilty.

# CHAPTER TWENTY-SEVEN

## WE HIT THE FAMILY

AUSTIN, TEXAS
April 2013

Agent Lawson swiveled his chair toward the jury box and caught the jurors' eyes as they settled into their own stuffed leather. He greeted them each with a little half-smile—not too friendly, not too G-man, just a small facial move that looked to say, *Hey, we're all in this together, right?*

He was inside the federal courthouse in downtown Austin, a $125 million structure filled with floor-to-ceiling windows that allowed natural light to pour onto the modernist artwork inside. Funded largely by bailout money, it was an architect-designed reminder that the Great Recession—the very economic conditions that had allowed Forty and his Zetas to move so freely into the American quarter-horse business—had blown clear away.

When the prosecutor called his next witness, Lawson could feel the deputy marshals shifting, whispering into their wrists. He appreciated the extra security. He'd never felt especially unsafe working the border. But whatever fear his instructors and fellow agents had tried to instill in him back at Quantico, with their tales of cross-border shoot-outs and swinging corpses, had resurfaced as the trial approached.

He knew that Mexican drug gangs, even the Zetas, had no history of killing American agents on American soil. But he couldn't help recalling that he had shared an office building with Jaime Zapata, the one American agent who *had* been murdered by Forty's gang. And that the Zetas had followed and threatened American law enforcement. And that despite all the attention paid to the Zetas by the DEA, no other investigators had hit Forty quite as hard as he had. *We're the only guys who have ever kicked the doors in where their mom and brothers and nieces were sleeping,* Lawson thought on days when the paranoia felt justified. *We hit the family.*

He kept a low profile. Then he started to think that he'd watched too many gangster movies and decided the fear was all bullshit.

The government preferred Lawson's more cautious approach. Outside the courtroom, Homeland Security agents stalked the streets toting assault rifles, and K-9s sniffed their way around the perimeter. In the courtroom, the security was ostentatiously heavy from day one. Agents escorted witnesses to and from the courtroom. Another agent picked up the prosecutor and drove him to court in the morning and back home at night. That agent had done dignitary protection before but never when the threat was a group of elite military-trained warriors with a history of brazen killings in the United States. He found himself checking the trees.

By the time of the trial, the government had padded its original indictment to include a total of eighteen people. Six of them, including Forty, and Forty-Two, and some small-time players, were on the run in Mexico. One, Victor the Courier, was dead. Six, including José's wife and daughter, had pleaded guilty in hopes of reducing their sentences.

Carlitos was facing twenty years for money laundering, so he pleaded guilty, too. The Zetas' young horseman had come looking for a deal after he was arrested. He wouldn't testify, but in the months leading up to trial, he met with Lawson, Medina, and prosecutors at least nine times, answering their every question about José, Fernando, and the rest. He snitched on himself, too, admitting that he'd witnessed multiple murders, including Ramiro's. It hardly hurt him. Carlitos would see his sentence reduced to less than five years, and would be out of prison by early 2017. A Mexican national, he was expected to receive an S visa, a special immigration status reserved for witnesses and informants.

That left five people for the trial, each facing up to twenty years for money laundering.

José Treviño was the ringleader, prosecutors said. Along with sending José to prison, a guilty verdict would force him to forfeit any asset the government could tie to the quarter-horse business, most of which had already been seized. His assets included more than four hundred horses, which the Treasury Department had begun auctioning off, and a cache of farming equipment, including two horse trailers, several tractors, a John Deere Gator, a pallet fork, and cash. At the time of their arrests, José and Zulema had managed to push their businesses' bank account balances into the low six figures. They still only had seventeen hundred dollars in their personal checking account, the one from which they paid their mortgage, car payments, school-lunch, and ortho bills. The feds had already seized every penny.

Carlitos's sidekick, Fernando, went to trial. The government had seized his money, too, though it wasn't much of a haul. He had about $150, including $1.10 in his checking account. Most of the money he'd earned had been paid in cash in Mexico and never sniffed his American bank account.

Francisco Colorado, who had surrendered in Texas after learning of his indictment, went to trial. He and his oil company, ADT Petroservicios, had spent $10 million buying and caring for horses tied to Forty and his crew, making his alleged role critical: without Colorado as their bag man, the Zetas' drug proceeds would be worthless paper, the feds would argue. If convicted, he would forfeit millions of dollars in cash and both his private jets.

Informants, including Carlitos, told the government that Forty had paid Colorado back in cash, just as he used to with Ramiro. But the informants offered no proof of these cash deliveries. And something felt presumptuous about the American government threatening jail time over the business dealings of a Mexican company, which existed in a marketplace long before infiltrated by narcos and corrupt politicians, particularly when American policies helped fuel that corruption. Colorado's defense strategy was built from delicate strands of American money-laundering law by some of America's best lawyers, who argued that he'd spent his own money buying those horses out of fear for his life. A more compelling defense might have been *Hey, Uncle Sam, you try running an oil business in Mexico and saying no to Los Zetas.*

The last two men fighting for space at the defense table were Tempting Dash's trainer, Chevo Huitron, and his brother Jesus. Chevo hadn't done much training for the group after Tempting Dash left his stables, and he'd earned a fraction of what the trainer Paul Jones had. Still, Chevo had never left the government's radar. His older brother Jesus was a home builder who'd led their family from Mexico decades before, and whose thriving construction business had helped them get started in horse racing. The money Chevo had earned training Forty's horses had found its way into Jesus's business accounts.

The feds had added him to the indictment late, possibly as a way to pressure Chevo into pleading and talking. It didn't work. They were both here, lawyered up and ready to fight. There wasn't much cash on the line. The government had seized about thirteen thousand dollars from each brother; Jesus's was in the bank account of his home-building business, and Chevo's was in cash inside various drawers of his East Austin home. Most of it was in his son's bedroom.

Of the five of them, none was suspected of being a Zeta—of moving a kilo, of kidnapping a migrant, of killing or torturing. Still, many of the names on the government's witness list belonged to professed Zeta operatives who would talk about cocaine loads, gunrunning, and violence.

The defense lawyers saw a ruse. In their eyes, the witness list was part of a government strategy to confuse the jury into thinking that a bunch of horsemen were a bunch of gangsters. They viewed that army of agents in and around the courthouse—eyes shifting, lips whispering into their wrists—as role players in the government's stage show.

It didn't help that the jurors were mostly older and white, as most federal jurors are. That's a bug—or maybe a feature?—of the federal justice system, where jury summons often never find, or are ignored by, poor, working-class citizens, who move too frequently to receive them or are scared to miss work to respond to one.

Beyond the K-9s and wrist-whisperers, the government wouldn't have many chances to spook the jury with tales of grisly Zeta violence. Before the trial, the judge had warned the prosecutors not to spin needless tales of beheadings and bridge hangings. "The only effect testimony and commentary concerning alleged violent acts can have at trial," the judge wrote, "is to inject issues broader than what jurors need."

But the prosecutors would get their chances. They called Mamito, the original Zeta, who'd been caught in Mexico, extradited to D.C., and flown to Texas to testify. He spoke of Forty and the Zetas' love of horses, and about Forty's desire to move Tempting Dash into his "clean brother's" name. He also spoke of his own role in the Zetas' rise to power: about the thirty or more people he'd kidnapped, tortured, killed.

The most relevant tale of Zeta-inflicted violence came when Alfonso del Rayo walked into the courtroom. As the jury was about to learn, del Rayo was the Swollen Golfer—the mysterious Mexican businessman who had arrived beaten and bandaged at an Oklahoma horse auction, then overpaid for José's mangy horse. He looked fully recovered from his "golfing accident," strolling through the courtroom with beach-tan skin, wavy black hair, and a tailored business suit. Lawson braced himself, the wrist-whisperers settled down, and del Rayo told the jury his story.

Del Rayo was forty-six, a husband, father, and businessman. He'd been doing real estate in Veracruz for fifteen years, and in that time had amassed a fortune worth twenty million dollars. He was also politically active, an outspoken critic of the nationalist Institutional Revolutionary Party (PRI), which ruled Veracruz.

One night in December 2010, he went out drinking. Sometime after four in the morning, he was coming out of the restroom when a group of armed men grabbed him, dragged him out of the bar, and tossed him into a car.

Del Rayo knew immediately what was happening. Veracruz had been under the thumb of the Zetas for several years now, and not by chance. They'd spent millions of dollars bribing state officials from the nationalist PRI, allowing them to operate there undisturbed. Things had only escalated in the three years since Forty vanquished Z-14 from Veracruz as Carlitos and Fernando looked on. Journalists were hunted with impunity. Cops who refused to play along were killed; one was found dismembered, his limbs piled in a town square with a message: *"Esto es por faltarle a la letra Z."* "This is for disappointing the letter Z."

Political enemies of the PRI were also targeted. An outspoken supporter of the rival PAN party, del Rayo learned that the hard way.

His kidnappers drove him to a safe house. They pounded him with the butt and barrel of an assault rifle, breaking two fingers, busting his head, and rupturing blood vessels in his eyes. Then they made their request: They were Zetas, they said, and they wanted fifteen million pesos, or about $4.5 million, in exchange for his release. Otherwise, they would kill him.

He pleaded with them that he didn't have that kind of cash. His assets were in real estate; he couldn't just withdraw them from the ATM. After about nine days, they did something he never thought they would: they let him go.

Not long after, he got a call from a Veracruz state official. Despite their political differences, the official wanted to come by the house to talk about his kidnapping. Del Rayo agreed, hoping to be offered conciliation and answers. Instead, the official brought someone with him, a suave young operator who introduced himself as Carlos Nayen. Carlitos.

Carlitos and del Rayo had a friend in common, it turned out.

Upon hearing about del Rayo's kidnapping, that friend had pleaded with Carlitos to help. Carlitos obliged, calling Forty and urging him to set del Rayo free.

Now it was payback time. My boss helped you, Carlitos told del Rayo, and now you're going to help my boss. You're going to come to Oklahoma City to buy a horse.

Del Rayo was supposed to have surgery and pleaded for another solution. Carlitos told him to be on time. Otherwise, del Rayo explained to the jury, "I will be in problems again."

He had his surgery and was discharged just in time. He got his kids somewhere safe and flew from Veracruz to San Antonio to Oklahoma City. Carlitos and Fernando picked him up and drove him to a hotel. They all shared a suite, like frat bros at a bachelor party, and Carlitos and Fernando showed del Rayo the thick book filled with horses and statistics. Eventually, toward the end of the book, they came to Blues Ferrari.

This is the horse you will buy, they told him. You will raise your hand, letting them know that you're interested in that horse. Another buyer will bid higher. You will bid again, and keep bidding until it's yours. No matter how high it goes, they told him, you keep raising your hand.

"You gotta buy it."

Del Rayo studied the horse closely. It was Hip No. 1208, meaning 1,207 horses would be auctioned off before it. It was a bay colt, sired almost three years before by the champion stallion Corona Cartel. It was owned by Tremor Enterprises, the company of José Treviño.

Carlitos and Fernando escorted del Rayo to the auction house the next morning, he told the jury. The bidding started at $5,000. He pushed it to $8,000, and someone—it wasn't clear who—pushed it to $10,000. He went to $20,000, they went to $30,000. Up and up it went until someone bid $300,000. He hit $310,000, and the room went quiet.

After the sale, del Rayo approached the cashier with two checks: one for $150,000 from his account, and another for $160,000 from his wife's. That money would be promptly sent to José, who would deposit it in his account one day before the DEA knocked on his door. As for Blues Ferrari, del Rayo told the jury that he never saw the horse again. Apparently, it went right back to José's ranch.

Del Rayo's testimony absorbed all the stray energy from the courtroom; shuffling papers fell still at the lawyers' tables, and in the gallery, clandestine phone checking went momentarily dark. His testimony put a face on a scam that seemed to have grown beyond money laundering and into extortion: buy a horse cheap with drug money, slide its ownership into a legitimate-seeming American company, and then either rake in the winnings or force someone, under the threat of grisly violence, to take it off the Company's hands for a large sum of clean money. Lawson, who worried that the jury would get lost in the case's complexity, listened to del Rayo and thought, *I know they're feeling me now.*

From the moment del Rayo bought Blues Ferrari, Lawson had sensed something strange about his foray into horse buying. He just couldn't figure out what it was. The prosecutors had decided to indict him on money-laundering charges, simply in hopes of getting him over the border. They'd even brainstormed ruses to lure him across the border, so they could nab and try to flip him. Then one day, he'd called and offered to come on his own. Now he was a cooperator, a witness, against the gang that ruled his home state.

As the courtroom security agents shuffled, del Rayo stepped down from the witness box, slipped through the crowd, and headed home to San Antonio. His wife was there and his kids, too. They'd left Veracruz to come across with Dad, and they would probably never go back.


If Tyler Graham had ever felt like a rookie in the horse business, like a stuffed cowboy trying to fill his granddaddy's fading boots, he had never shown it. To his fellow quarter-horse men, he'd always belonged. To the Mexican newcomers who sought his counsel, he was a force to rely on and to reckon with. To Lawson, Tyler was a man who was going to get what he wanted by working for it—and by running through who- or whatever stepped in his way.

Certainly that's what Tyler showed when he pushed through the doors of the courtroom, prepared to reveal for the first time what he had done. He was twenty-nine now, seven years removed from his last days as an Aggie, and he'd spent three of those prime years doing this—whatever this was. He looked a little fuller in the face than when Lawson first came knocking, and a little thinner at the hairline, but he spoke with the same ease about the business he'd been living since he was old enough to toddle through a barn door.

The gallery was packed with defendants' family members, including a few of Forty's and José's sisters. Throughout the trial, they had been seen scribbling away as witnesses spelled their names and hometowns and places of employment for the record. No one knew what they were writing, but the agents involved suspected they were trying to intimidate the witnesses on the stand. Now here was Tyler David Graham, the prosecutor announced, and even spelled it for good measure: G-r-a-h-a-m. He stepped into the witness box in a dress shirt and leather cowboy boots.

Tyler had never asked Agent Lawson about the federal Witness Security Program but he probably could have gotten into it, had he wanted. He also never pressed Lawson to keep him off the witness stand. If he'd chosen not to testify, his existence could have been confined to court records and shrouded in mystery, ID'd by a code name like "Confidential Source 1." The government certainly worried about Tyler's safety: the day he was scheduled to testify, the feds sent a three-car convoy of agents to pick him up in Elgin and escort him to the courthouse.

But Tyler didn't flinch. He told Lawson that he didn't think his security was an issue. That he was "comfortable."

He looked it on the stand, as he calmly recounted how he'd come to do business with José: seeing the promise of Tempting Dash, recruiting José at the track and on hunting trips, and eventually luring hundreds of the group's horses to his ranch. But things shifted around the one hundred and twenty-fifth question asked by the prosecutor. Until then, his testimony had seemed like that of a passive observer, a quarter-horse insider who'd unwittingly become involved with the Treviños. Which he was. But he was also something more.

"Now, at some point were you contacted by Special Agent Scott Lawson over here?" the prosecutor asked.

"Yes, sir," Tyler said.

"And what was your understanding of your agreement with Special Agent Lawson and the government?"

"My agreement was that we just—they were informed on the, you know, operations of the horse business."

"Informed." There was that word. It was a short slip 'n' slide from there to "informant," which was a word Tyler didn't like. It felt too active, too official, as though he'd gone into the FBI offices and filled out an application, which he hadn't. To his mind, all he'd done was do his job, take Lawson's calls, and sign the forms that allowed him to keep taking Forty's money. But he couldn't keep himself from being attached to that word, "informant," especially once the government turned Tyler over to the defense.

Mostly, the defense lawyers tried to use Tyler to show that their clients were legitimate horsemen running legitimate horse businesses. He testified that he considered Chevo, Tempting Dash's trainer, a capable trainer and a friend. For all the conversations the government had recorded between Tyler and Fernando, never had they indicated anything but run-of-the-mill equine business.

José's second-chair lawyer, Christie Williams, used Tyler to fill in the portrait of José as an up-and-coming horseman. She elicited stories from Tyler about how hard José worked to learn the business and carve out a place in the world that Tyler's family seemed to own. She wanted the jury to believe that Carlitos and Fernando and, by extension, Forty were José's clients, not his co-conspirators.

Williams also knew that planting doubt required discrediting the government's witnesses. That was pretty straightforward when the admitted traffickers and murderers took the stand, testifying in exchange for sentence reductions. But discrediting Tyler was more delicate. The jury had heard about him by now, and knew him as a seemingly upstanding Texan and the grandson of a well-known vet. They could see by his outfit that he wasn't locked up, and they knew he faced no charges. With no jail time dangling overhead like mistle-toe, what motivation could he have other than the truth?

Williams tried anyway.

"How much money did Southwest Stallion Station make during the period of time that you were cooperating with the government from Carlos Nayen [and] José Treviño?" she asked Tyler. She knew Tyler hadn't been a "paid informant" in the classic sense; no tax-payer dollars had been exchanged for information, as it often is. But Williams thought she could perhaps use the money he'd made from José—under the terms of his and the FBI's Otherwise Illegal Activity agreements—to weaken his helpful-cowboy credibility.

"By cooperating?" Tyler asked. "What do you mean?"

"I mean that you signed an agreement with these agents that you were going to call people up, record your conversations, that you were going to go to Heritage Place auction, that you were going to go to races, that you were going to hang out and listen to conversations? During that period of time, from early 2010 to the date of José Treviño's arrest, how much money did Southwest Stallion Station make from keeping the horses that you've talked about here today?"

"Probably a few hundred thousand," Tyler said.

"A few hundred thousand?"

"Yes, ma'am."

"We heard about two hundred seventy thousand earlier, right?" Williams countered. "Do you remember that?"

"Yes."

"We heard about two hundred twenty-three thousand, right?"

"Right."

"So right there, that's five hundred thousand?" Williams asked.

"That's not net profit," Tyler said.

The line of questioning devolved without determining how much Graham's ranch had *profited* from its relationship with José and his brothers, but their respective points were made. For José, the point was that Tyler had some incentive to continue doing business with these guys, even after the FBI came around. For Tyler, the point was: We got paid for work we did.

That was true. But it was also true of every other horseman charged in the case, including José, Fernando, Chevo, and the others at the defense table. Like Tyler, they'd all done the legitimate work of horsemen. Like Tyler, they'd all been paid, at least in part, with money that started in an American cocaine deal and ended in a Mexican stash house. Like Tyler, they knew it was drug money when they did the work (albeit Tyler knew thanks to the FBI). Like Tyler, they perhaps could have guessed that they were in some small way helping someone launder that drug money, although they probably all knew that horse racing was better for losing money than for washing it. Tyler and the others were, in these respects and so many others, exactly the same. The difference was that Lawson had knocked on Tyler's door and not theirs.

The other defense attorneys took it easier on Tyler, but they worked along the same lines, always careful to label him as an informant. Tyler was always careful to push back.

"How did you come to be their informant?" one of them asked near the end of Tyler's second day of testimony.

"Once again," Tyler said, "I don't classify myself as an informant because that's not what they ever relayed to me that I was."

"OK."

"I would use another word maybe."

"What word did they use?"

"They never described me as anything. They never said you're this or you're that. Like I said, I don't even—I mean . . . 'cooperating citizen,' I guess you could say."

"OK," the lawyer said. "And do you think they just randomly pass out phones to other citizens and say, Here, record phone calls?"

The judge put an end to that. Before long, Tyler was pushing back through the courtroom doors, ready to catch his ride back to Elgin. It was the heart of breeding season, and he had a stud to tend to.


Compared with Tyler or Alfonso del Rayo, the man on the stand now, hunched and older, quiet and dressed in a prison jumpsuit, must have seemed to the jury perfunctory—his hour-long testimony like something that *Law & Order* could have covered with a well-timed *dun-dun*.

Lawson knew better. Lawson knew that better than any other witness or exhibit, this man could help satisfy his craving for a story the jurors could see—for that one cocaine twenty ending up in the hands of José Treviño. He listened closely, and hoped the jury would, too.

Lawson had met the man only right before trial, but their collision course had started way back in 2011, with a call from a colleague in Dallas. There was a whole crew of Zeta traffickers who'd flipped, the agent said. They'd turned on Forty, and Forty's men were blazing through Piedras Negras killing anyone who knew the snitches. So the snitches had fled to Dallas, where they were either locked up or holed up in hotels, spilling secrets to any agent who could get in the door.

Lawson called DEA Dallas and asked if he could debrief their sources. But DEA Dallas said no. Lawson hadn't let the DEA near Tyler, and the DEA wasn't going to let Lawson near these guys.

Lawson moved on, still hoping to find concrete proof of cocaine cash winding up in José's hands. Later, he received another call from a more collaborative DEA agent who had debriefed the same band of snitches. You *have* to talk to these guys, the agent told Lawson. They know it all.

So Lawson pressed. This time, he enlisted a manager. (Managers are often called upon to stamp out FMES-fueled fights among agents and agencies.) Finally, the DEA and prosecutor in Dallas relented. One by one, Lawson, Medina, and the IRS sat down with the informants.

It all started with Poncho Cuellar, the Piedras Negras trafficker who'd sipped beers under the palapa with José years before. In an interview at the FBI Dallas office, with Spanish-speaking Medina in the driver's seat, Poncho told them what he knew.

He told them about Ramiro. Everyone in the Company knew

that if you needed some good horses in the States, you sent Ramiro. He told them about the various Mexican businessmen whom Forty implored to buy horses in Mexico. He told them how one front man, a Veracruz customs broker, started to complain about the practice and wound up dead.

This was great intelligence. But it didn't scratch Lawson's cocaine-dollar itch. Then Poncho started talking about Carlitos.

Poncho knew all about Carlitos using drug money for the horse business, because Poncho had gotten the orders from Forty himself: *When Carlitos needs money for horse stuff, you pay him.* And Carlitos did, coming around every so often looking for cash to fund the growing horse business.

Poncho told them how he would be sitting in a safe house with Forty when Forty would get a text from Carlitos—usually a photo of the big board at the auction house showing a hip number, a horse name, and a dollar amount in the six figures. Poncho would then record the expense in the books.

Sometimes the expenses were for more ancillary costs. One day Carlitos called Forty with good news: He'd had dinner with some of the gate crew in Ruidoso, New Mexico. One of Forty's horses, Mr Piloto, was scheduled to run in the All American Futurity. The guys who handled the horses in the gate had told Carlitos that for three thousand dollars a head, they could do their best to give Mr Piloto the cleanest start.

No, Forty had said to Carlitos. You're not going to pay them three grand. You're going to pay them *ten* grand. Poncho arranged to have one of his couriers deliver the cash to New Mexico. The courier picked up $110,000 from Junior, the Company's Dallas distributor, hid it in a pressure cooker, and drove ten hours across the barren Southwest to Ruidoso, where he delivered the cash to an unidentified woman in a Walmart parking lot.

Lawson was riveted. He'd been at that race! It was better than that, though. One of the keys to a money-laundering case is what the agents shorthand as "SUA," or specified unlawful activity—basically a crime that was being furthered or concealed through money laundering. For the Zetas, the obvious crime was drug trafficking. But Poncho had just opened another door: the fixing of sporting events. If they could prove the Zetas were fixing sporting events in the United States, then the money derived from it could be considered laundered.

Along with Poncho, the DEA offered up a handful of other sources from the same Piedras Negras crew. One smuggler confirmed the piles of cocaine money spent on horses and recalled watching the big races in safe houses with Forty. The courier detailed his cross-country delivery of the bribe money. Junior, the Dallas cocaine kingpin, confirmed that he had delivered drug proceeds to Carlitos at various tracks and other locations around Texas.

It wasn't until the last informant showed up that the picture was complete. Because for everything these guys told Lawson and Medina—and, later, the jury—they didn't know much about José. They'd all heard Forty talk about his hardworking brother in Dallas who wanted nothing to do with the drugs. They knew he was involved with the horses, but they'd never delivered him money.

The guy on the witness stand now had a story about that.

José Vasquez Sr. was in his fifties, with graying hair more visible in his trim goatee than his closely shaved head. He wore his prison scrubs and leaned into the microphone, feet shackled, as a deputy U.S. Marshal lurked nearby. He spoke softly and told the jury his story.

He was technically Mexican but functionally American. He'd come to the United States when he was a baby, and by seventeen he was learning to lay bricks in Dallas, helping the city accommodate the flood of people. He'd been doing that for thirty-something years now, pulling down eight hundred, maybe a thousand bucks a week.

His son Junior was obviously making his money by less traditional means. Senior didn't ask about the details, but he knew much of what the jury now knew: that until his arrest, thirty-year-old José Vasquez Jr. was one of the Zetas' largest cocaine distributors in the United States. Every month, Junior imported about a thousand kilos of Forty's cocaine. He squirreled away about a million dollars in monthly profits, including the half a million he buried in his mother's fireplace. The rest got sealed and plopped into the gas tanks of SUVs, which he sent back south across the border.

Junior had been popped and flipped by a Dallas DEA agent, who, with Junior's guidance, even dug up the money in Mom's fireplace. But before all that, Junior asked his dad to help out a little. Mostly, Senior told the jury, he'd helped load the trucks with cash before sending them to Mexico. But occasionally he would deliver some of the drug proceeds himself. He took $120,000 in cash to some cowboy in Oklahoma, apparently to pay for a racehorse. He took another $120,000 to a guy named Carlitos at a hotel near the airport.

Lawson listened closely as the prosecutor asked about the last delivery. It had happened one evening a couple of years back, Senior said. His son Junior had handed him a bag stuffed with $100,000 in cash and asked him to deliver it to a guy in a Walmart parking lot just southeast of Dallas. Senior pulled into the lot. A guy stepped out of a rancher's pickup. Senior handed over the money. The guy walked away.

The prosecutors pulled up a photo.

"Did you make a delivery of cash to this individual?" the prosecutor asked.

Senior studied the photo of José Treviño, who lived about a mile from that Walmart, and said, "Yes, sir."

Lawson was the last of the government's fifty witnesses. His testimony hardly reflected everything he'd put into it. It was mostly a rote exercise in verifying the evidence he'd collected and putting a face on the investigation—showing the jury, *Hey, look, this goateed country boy is the one fighting for you here, folks.*

The most exciting part—to Lawson, anyway—happened during cross-examination. Fernando's defense lawyer had dug up some obscure U.S. code that outlined the "cash awards" agents could receive for making a big case. Lawson knew they were basically unicorns, and not particularly beefy ones; he'd never heard of anyone receiving more than a grand. But this defense lawyer asked Lawson to read through the code, which suggested that agents could make as much as twenty-five grand.

The lawyer asked Lawson outright whether he'd spent the last three-plus years working this case for a shot at that twenty-five grand. He had no evidence Lawson would even receive a bonus, but he left it there to hang in the jury's mind.

He also left the door open. After the defense lawyer finished, the prosecutor returned to the microphone.

"Are you doing this case for three years for a twenty-five-thousand-dollar cash award?" the prosecutor asked, obviously offended on Lawson's behalf.

"No," Lawson said, and it clicked just then what was happening: *I just got the green light to hammer these bastards.*

"Why are you doing this case?" Gardner asked.

"This case is important to me. I live on the border and—"

José's lawyer rose to her feet. She could sense that Lawson was about to veer into some soliloquy about the bloodlust of the Zetas, about the fear and violence they'd inflicted on both sides of the border. Williams knew it had nothing to do with José, and would only send the jurors into deliberations with the vague notion that they and Lawson were there to take down the Zetas together.

"Objection," she said. "Relevance."

But the judge had seen what the prosecutor had seen: that by suggesting Lawson was motivated by money, the defense lawyer had opened the door for Lawson to riff on what actually motivated him.

"He's entitled to respond," the judge said.

Lawson hadn't rehearsed a response, but he didn't have to think too hard about it. He'd been thinking about it nonstop for three-plus years now. He knew what he believed: that he was protecting America. America and Americans. American laws, too, and an American pastime, and American business, and American horses, the lifeblood of the state he now called home and felt duty-bound to protect.

"Since my time living on the border, I know what the Zeta cartel is capable of, how they entrenched themselves into the United

States," he said. "And also, I'm a fan of horses, so this was a case to show that the United States is not a place for them to come over and set up roots."

The government rested soon after.


All told, it took fourteen days spread over almost four weeks to explain all this to a jury of twelve Texans. The defendants, including José, put up almost no defense. He'd lined up dozens of witnesses—masonry foremen, family, friends, neighbors, and fellow horsemen, including Tyler Graham's dad and grandfather. All of them could tell the jury, their voices flooded with sincerity, how honest and hardworking José was in both of his careers.

José wanted badly for the jury to hear from them. But his lawyers knew that it was better to cut things off and hope the government had failed to prove its case. They also knew that the prosecutor had held back a few bits of salacious, if weakly supported, evidence, precisely to keep José from mounting a defense. If his lawyers put up witnesses vouching for his character, Lawson could testify that José had complained to his brother about Victor the Courier, implying that José was responsible for Victor's death; the jury wouldn't have to know that Lawson learned that from Carlitos, who *hated* José, and was desperate to appear useful to the government. The prosecutor could also call to the stand a snitch, code-named "Pitufo," or "Smurf." Pitufo had spent several years as a paid informant in Mexico, where he reportedly made five thousand dollars a month secretly testifying against his former cartel colleagues. He could apparently testify that he once worked with José Treviño to find stash houses in Texas, a fact that had somehow eluded the DEA agents on José's tail. His testimony in Mexico had proven reliably shaky over the years, and he would later be convicted in Texas of raping underage girls whom he was grooming to become prostitutes. But there he was, waiting to be deployed if the prosecutor needed him to finish José off.

The defense rested.

The judge's instructions were straightforward. To convict these five men, each juror needed to believe that the government had proved beyond a reasonable doubt that the men knowingly conspired to launder the Zetas' money. He drew their attention to "knowingly." "The word 'knowingly,'" he said, "means the act was done voluntarily and intentionally, not because of accident or mistake."

The closing statements were simple, particularly when it came to José. According to the government, everything he did was to help his family. "It's about establishing the legacy for your family," Prosecutor Gardner said. The jurors might have recognized that desire as natural, maybe even admirable. But Gardner used the crimes of José's brother to reformat that desire into something cheap, selfish, and criminal. "It is not built on sweat, ladies and gentlemen," he said. "It's built on the money from his brothers, family. Who do you trust more than family? That's why José Treviño has the horses."

His defense lawyers agreed that everything José did was to support his family, including buying Tempting Dash and everything that came after. "What reason has the government given you for why this man lived here since he's fifteen, worked hard, raised a family, worked at a hard job all his life, saved money, didn't do anything extravagant?" Christie Williams asked the jurors. "Why would he suddenly decide he wants to be a part of some Zeta legacy? Why would he decide that he wouldn't want his own legacy, his own personal hard work, bring your kids up the way they ought to be brought up? Why would he abandon that? Was somebody sick? Was somebody hurt? Was he in bankruptcy? Why would he abandon the life he had built for himself to become a part of this legacy of his brothers, this legacy of the Zeta cartel? Why would he want any part of that?"

It took fourteen days to get there, but at 3:54 P.M. on May 8, 2013, the judge sent the jury, along with thousands of pages of evidence in boxes and hundreds of hours of testimony in their brains, into the jury room to decide the fate of José Treviño and his four co-defendants.

They were back in less than a day.

The next afternoon, the men's families piled into the courtroom's wooden benches. They'd been huddled together for weeks now, sharing silent sympathies on their way into the courtroom each morning and words of comfort on the way out. Zulema was there, as were José's sisters and mom, who'd quietly sobbed throughout the trial. Plans, rooted in possibly naïve hope, were forged by some of the families to dine together after the verdict. Alex wouldn't be there. She was back in California, where she'd just given birth to José's first granddaughter.

The jury filed in and took their seats.

"Have you reached a verdict?" the judge asked.

"Yes, we have, Your Honor," the foreman said.

"Is it a unanimous verdict?"

"Yes, it is."

The clerk read their findings one by one. Jesus Huitron, the home builder whose brother had trained Tempting Dash, was not guilty. But his brother Chevo was guilty. So were trainer Fernando and moneyman Francisco Colorado.

When the foreman read José's verdict, a little extra air was sucked out of the room, probably because the room knew who his family was—his brother in Mexico, but also his wife and mom and sisters, who were crowded into the gallery as they had been for weeks.

"The verdict as to defendant José Treviño Morales," the clerk read. "Guilty."

José's wife, mom, and sisters sobbed. If he could hear them, he didn't show it. He listened stiffly as the judge asked the prosecutor whether some of the defendants should be detained while they awaited their sentencing hearings, which would take place in the months to come. But the judge didn't ask about José. It was understood that he would make the wait where he'd been waiting, locked up in rural central Texas, a short drive from Tyler's ranch and Tempting Dash. Here came the courtroom deputy now, to escort José on his way.

# CHAPTER TWENTY-EIGHT
## EXIT BENEFITS

LAREDO, TEXAS
July 2013

After the trial, Lawson settled into a more typical FBI-agent routine, though it didn't feel typical to him. He'd been on the job two months when he first drove north to meet Tyler Graham. He'd spent the next three years traipsing all across the Southwest, to places most rookie FBI agents never see—a mountaintop casino in New Mexico Indian country; a gilded hotel bar in Dallas; the thick mud of the backside at tracks all across the Southwest; and interview rooms, so many interview rooms, where he got to debrief some of the most knowledgeable narco operatives in American custody.

After that, his colleagues said, no case would ever live up. But Lawson wasn't so sure. He was proud of his work on the case and regretted nothing. Even if only José ended up serving more than a few years in prison, Lawson considered the outcome—José down for twenty and a strong message sent—worthy of the time invested by him and money by the government. Anyone who went into business with Forty deserved every minute of the max.

But he also was starting to realize how focused on achievement he'd been—how the initial allure of bagging the boss of a cartel, or even just disrupting the drug trade, didn't last much beyond trial. The Zetas were still the Zetas. The cocaine and the blood were still flowing. The result of a big investigation was more glorified, with high-profile targets, long trials, lots of media attention. That was fine. As he delved back into everyday cop work—the kind of work his dad had once done—he realized that while the result was different, the process was the same: talking to people, digging, putting the pieces together. Though he knew it would be hard in the FBI, where lengthy and complicated conspiracy cases rule, he began day-dreaming of a simpler caseload—responding to bank robberies, kid-nappings, and murders, and trying to solve them quickly, and quietly.

It was even easier to identify what he *didn't* want to do: move on to the next "drug lord." He'd run into a few of those agents, the career narco hunters whose self-mythology nearly matched that of the capos they hunted. He'd keep working dope; he wasn't naïve enough to think he could avoid it altogether. But he'd ridden the drug war's wave machine, and he would be happy to climb off.

There probably wasn't time to start something long-term anyway. Before long, he'd be leaving Laredo.

He'd come to love it there: the beer-swilling, two-steppin' camaraderie with the fellow rookies; his relationship with Medina, part big sister, part borderland emissary, and full partner-in-law; and the true multiculturalism of the border, even if its most alluring culture was across the river and off-limits. He would miss it all.

He'd even found himself a girlfriend, a Latina from South Texas. She worked in victim services. Like her predecessors in Lawson's romantic life, she didn't ooze ambition, which had once been a turn-off. But somewhere during his chase of the Treviño family, Lawson had shed some of his own careerism and found himself longing for the smaller life his parents had lived, however imperfectly—life where he found pride but not his entire identity in his work. He could even see making room in his life for children.

He just wasn't sure he wanted to raise them in Laredo, so far from his mom and from home. Which was why he'd been thinking about leaving. A lot of the agents were. As a "hardship" assignment, Laredo came with something called "exit benefits." After five years in a hardship office, agents could move more or less wherever they wanted. Even if they no longer viewed Laredo as a hardship, most of the agents took advantage of it. Lawson's DEA friend from Philly had his eyes set on home. Perdomo, the Cuban-American who'd trekked to Ruidoso with Lawson, was already back in Miami. Of his closest friends, only Medina would stay on the border indefinitely. She was already home.

Lawson would go home, too. The next year, he would transfer back to rural Tennessee, working in a small office outside Memphis. It was about an hour-long drive from his hometown, down a highway framed by oak trees and one-room churches. The last stretch of the highway before he hit Middleton had been renamed the Mike Lawson Memorial Highway, after his dad.

He would make the drive as often as he could, to see family or old friends, or to have lunch with his mom and chew on the details of his upcoming wedding. He would even find a way to reopen an unsolved murder from his hometown—an eighteen-year-old cold case that had once belonged to Lawson's dad, involving Mississippi drug dealers and witnesses more reluctant to talk than many narcos. He'd even consider one day running for county sheriff, a position one rung above where his father retired.

But before he left, some scraps of work remained on Lawson's biggest case. With appeals looming, he hadn't officially closed Tyler Graham as a Confidential Human Source, so he had to check in with Tyler occasionally, to make sure he was safe and hadn't heard anything the FBI should know about. However, it was a different source—a source in Mexico—who sent him and Medina fleeing the office one afternoon.

Mexican sources were still important to Lawson and Medina, because for everything they'd accomplished, Forty was still wreaking havoc across the border. Lazcano, the Zetas' leader, had been killed in a firefight with the Mexican Navy, leaving Forty as the boss. As far as the agents knew, he was hiding out in northern Mexico somewhere.

Unless he wasn't.

According to a source, Forty had been captured.

Lawson doubted it. They got these tips frequently, and they were always bogus. Between the agents' collective obsession with capturing Forty and the ballooning reward for whoever made it happen—it was now up to about seven million dollars, including five million from the United States government—informants loved to talk about Forty going down. It never happened.

A few minutes later, though, he heard the same thing from another agent, who'd heard the same thing from another source. Then another. They all contained the same broad outlines: Forty. Captured. Nuevo Laredo. Not a bullet fired.

Lawson called his DEA buddy, Agent Philly: "What are you hearing?" Philly reached out to his counterpart in Mexico and told him what they were hearing in Laredo. Was it true?

"They got him."

It would be a while before the details would be filled in. Even then they would be murky, as they always were when capos went down in Mexico.

Everyone seemed to agree that Forty had been in Nuevo Laredo visiting his newborn son. It was risky, he had to know, leaving the bunkered confines of his rural hideouts for an area near Nuevo Laredo, where his face, where his family, was known. But he apparently had done it, the same way his family had always done for him.

Forty had taken precautions, leaving under the cover of night and traveling through rural Tamaulipas with two associates and eight guns. He was headed back to his current hiding spot in Coahuila, the border state where his Zetas, in response to Poncho's disloyalty, had used the prison as a personal killing ground.

That's when a helicopter whooshed into view, carrying Mexican Marines, who'd been tipped off by American intelligence agents or a Mexican source, depending on which version you believe. Forty's truck stopped. He bailed and tried to run, but they caught up to him, and despite an armory of assault rifles, he didn't get off a shot.

He was carrying two million in cash, money he apparently planned on bequeathing the soldiers in exchange for their protection. They seized it instead.

Once the news became official enough, Lawson found his partner, Medina, and wrapped her in a bear hug. They drove to a sports bar not far from the office, a naturally dim place flickered to life by beer promotions and flatscreens. They ordered a round of tequila, hoisted their glasses, and drank.

Tequila burning their throats, they tried to process what Forty's arrest meant. He was one of only a few Mexican drug lords who'd struck fear in American agents on American soil. Lawson and Medina had to admit, his capture was a relief.

For their cases, who knew? Medina couldn't help daydreaming about what would happen if the Department of State successfully extradited Forty to the States. It was the longest imaginable shot, but maybe she could sit down across from him and ask where her still-missing kidnapping victims were. Where the bodies were literally buried.

Mexico would naturally resist extradition. It had to date declined to extradite notorious Sinaloa boss El Chapo, even after he'd escaped from the country's most secure prison. (His second escape, via tunnel, and eventual extradition were still years away.) American agents argued that it was a hedge against embarrassment—that the extradicted drug lords, looking for reduced sentences, would tell the world of the political corruption that allowed the cartels to flourish. The Mexican government gave a simpler explanation: that it preferred to prosecute its own citizens. Either way, as Lawson and Medina drank, they didn't have much hope for a speedy extradition.

Even if Forty was brought to the States, he'd likely never go to trial on the money-laundering charges. If he faced trial, he would be tried on charges of murder, kidnapping, and drug trafficking, almost definitely convicted, and sentenced to life in an American prison. Facing mountains of evidence in several jurisdictions, he might also plead guilty in exchange for a sentence slightly shorter than life, like his former Gulf boss Osiel Cárdenas had. But the government might be unlikely to offer such a deal, considering Forty's violent streak. Lawson and Medina tried to rule that prospect out, if only for their own sanity.

There were other questions for the agents to consider over celebratory tequila. What did Forty's capture mean for Mexico? For Nuevo Laredo? For the Zetas?

Would the Zetas survive without Forty? Was his brother Forty-Two the new boss? Would the violence dissipate with the decapitation of the outfit that redefined the rules? Or would it spike, as the Zetas' rivals scrambled to take control and the Zetas themselves splintered into less definable, but just as violent, groups?

Lawson, like many American counternarcotics agents, tended to see the answers across the border. Somehow, Mexico needed to regain its rule of law, although Lawson wasn't sure that was possible. He'd found himself following, even rooting for the *autodefensas,* vigilante militias taking up arms to purge the cartels from their communities. Better answers might lie in the halls of American power and influence—in the way drugs are regulated, drug users treated, drug traffickers sentenced. The solutions might lie in the way Americans' desire to get high, or get well, is exploited by vote-hankering politicians, their K Street puppet masters, and a collective refusal to acknowledge the racist history of drug laws, basic economic principles, and other causes.

Wherever the solutions were hiding, Lawson and Medina feared that nothing would change anytime soon. And they were right. For the rest of their time on the border together, they would watch the violence rage. The Zetas, splintered and weakened, would continue to spill blood across the river.

Forty's brother Omar would lead for a while, before being captured himself. After that, a new Treviño would take the helm. Though big brother Kiko was still in prison for marijuana trafficking, his sons had both risen through the smuggling ranks after he was sent away. One, Alejandro, had been killed already. But the other, Kiko Jr., would eventually accumulate enough power to lead a faction of the splintered Zetas. The young Treviño man's nickname was Kiko Kartel, and he was the next wave in an ocean that, no matter how many shoot-outs or takedowns or tequila shots, Lawson and Medina feared would never stop crashing.

As the agents drank that afternoon, a picture bounced its way across the Internet and into their phones. It was Forty. He was cleanly shaven but for some strategic stubble. He wore the events of the previous night, and maybe the years, on his tan face—a busted lip, a bruised cheek, and a scraped brow.

He was perp-walking through a justice center in Mexico City wearing a night-black polo shirt and camouflage pants, the clothes he'd apparently been captured in. He was surrounded by Mexican soldiers in heavy fatigues, as well as by news cameramen, invited there for a photo op of justice at work, of victory in a never-ending war against one of that war's most reviled combatants. He wasn't wearing handcuffs.

■ ■ ■

OKLAHOMA CITY, OKLAHOMA
November 2013

The sales books they lugged into the auction house in Oklahoma that morning were especially thick—655 pages of yearlings, mares, studs, and embryos still in utero, with many of those pages loaded with the heavy black type that made the cowboys reach for their highlighters. But if those cowboys were being honest, there were a handful of horses they wanted badly to see up close, either to bid on or just to bask in, to catch a whiff of an unraveling mystery.

It had been over a year since the feds crashed the gates at José's farm. Since then, many quarter-horse insiders had sucked down every droplet of fact and rumor they could find about the case—who was involved, what had gone down, and who had helped the feds wrangle their industry back from José Treviño and his brothers. Mostly, they wanted to know: What horses are we talking about here? What would happen to them?

After José was arrested, with his ranch in disrepair and horses falling ill and dying, he had agreed to allow the government to auction off most of the horses it had seized from the farm, knowing he could recoup the proceeds if he was acquitted. Later that year, contract cowboys hauled nearly four hundred horses to Heritage Place, the auction house owned by Tyler's grandfather, and sold them all over the course of a few days.

If nothing else, that first auction had proven how obsessed the Treviños and their associates had been with the sport's elite bloodlines. Twenty-nine of the horses had been sired by First Down Dash, despite the fact that First Down Dash had died a couple of years back, leaving behind a supply of frozen semen that was still considered among the best in the sport.

Thirty-six were sired by Mr Jess Perry, including All American–winning Mr Piloto. Corona Cartel sired forty-three. Breedings with both those stallions went for $35,000 a pop, which meant that in just three seasons, the group had spent $3.5 million in breedings from the sport's three top stallions. Thus, the immense interest in the fate of José's horses.

At that first sell-off, the government's biggest score had come from a two-year-old filly called Dash of Sweet Heat. Forty had paid $650,000 for her at an auction, buying her from Julianna Holt, the wealthy co-owner of the San Antonio Spurs. The filly had made only one start for Forty, but Holt was determined to get the horse back. She sent a team of people to the auction house with a singular instruction: "Bring the filly home." They delivered, buying back Holt's horse for $1 million. It was the most expensive purchase in the history of quarter-horse auctions, and the largest contribution to the Treasury Department's $9 million haul at that first auction.

But despite the volume, that first auction was more notable for the horses that were *not* sold. José had insisted that a handful of horses be held back—horses to which he had particular "sentimental attachment," as he put it in his plea to the judge—pending the outcome of the trial. Now, with José's conviction blurring in the rearview, the government had put those up for sale, too. Those were the horses the quarter-horse men were looking for as they lugged their dog-eared catalogs into the auction house that morning.

They found most of them in the outdoor barn out back. There, in one stall, was Dashin Follies, the chocolate-brown broodmare that had been the Treviños' first big, public purchase—$875,000 and not a penny more, thanks to José's compadre Tyler. There, in another stall, was Mr Piloto, the long-shot colt that had helped José capture the sport's biggest race and the million-dollar prize that came with it. And there, in that same cluster of stalls, was Separate Fire, the powerful filly that, along with the sport's best trainer, had allowed the Treviños to finally conquer Los Alamitos. As the clock ticked down toward the first gavel that morning, the crowd to see those horses grew so thick that even serious buyers had to stand in line to get a glimpse.

But those buyers could circle the stalls all morning and never come across the one horse everyone wanted to see, Tempting Dash. He was indisputably the government's most prized stallion—the horse that set Ramiro Villarreal on his deadly collision course with Forty; that lured José out of bricklaying and into horse racing; that carried Chevo into the feds' crosshairs; and that turned Tyler from stallion-hunting rancher into Confidential Human Source. But he was still infected with piroplasmosis, making it too risky to stable him among the hundreds of horses in the barns that morning. So he was right where he'd been all along, roaming a paddock in Elgin, Texas, the premier stud of the resurgent Southwest Stallion Station.

That, everyone figured, was where Tyler would like Tempting Dash to stay. But Tyler was going to have to pay for the pleasure, because while Tempting Dash wasn't in the auction house, his name, along with all the coveted black type that went with it, was in the sales book.

"Hip number one hundred seventy-five," the auctioneer bellowed in a voice that sucked like gravity on the place, pulling the crowd in toward the center. Tempting Dash was the first of the government's horses to go, and no one was quite sure what to expect. Rumors had swirled about what role the Zetas would play in the proceedings: they would send operatives to buy back their horses and bring them back to Mexico, or they would send muscle to intimidate buyers from bidding. No one was quite sure what to make of the rumors, including the feds. They sent a team of agents to monitor the proceedings.

The cowboys in the know wondered whether Tyler would even show up. He was a fixture at these auctions, but given his work as an informant—work that much of the industry had only learned about through newspaper coverage of the trial—no one would have been surprised if he had stayed home, especially given those return-of-the-Zetas rumors. But no, there he was, sucked to the center with the rest of them, finding his place in the line of sight of the bid-spotter perched high out back, where all the big-money cowboys liked to stand. Tyler could often be found here, watching the action, pulling on domestic drafts before flinging his empties into the trash. Today, though, he wasn't just watching. He was bidding.

Before the auction, it had become clear to the Graham family that if they didn't own Tempting Dash, or at least own a stake in him, the horse wouldn't continue to stand as a stud at Southwest Stallion Station. At least one of the people interested in buying him had already declared that he would move Tempting Dash to a different, more established breeding farm. If Tyler wanted Tempting Dash to stay home, he needed to own him.

"What about . . . how about . . . three hundred," the auctioneer was saying, and it didn't take long for everyone to realize that Tempting Dash was going to break someone's bank. Questions had always lingered about whether the horse's record run in Dallas, under Ramiro and then José, was legitimate. And his first official crop of offspring wouldn't hit the tracks until the following race season. His ceiling as a breeder was unknowable. So was his floor.

"One million," the auctioneer pleaded, and now it was getting quieter and louder at the same time, the scattershot chatter replaced by a static murmur, thousands of people all at once realizing they were about to witness history. Occasionally the auctioneer would get caught on a number, and the crowd would start to suck for air, and then, *boom,* the bid-spotter would point into the crowd, and the crowd would whoop for more.

Tyler kept catching the spotter's attention, determined to keep Tempting Dash right where he was in Elgin.

One point five, the auctioneer said, and one point six, and there was Tyler, still in it.

"Million seven hundred thousand, million seven hundred fifty, and . . ."

The gavel fell, high and loud like a storm's first thunderclap. "One million seven hundred thousand . . . We'll get the buyer's name in just a couple of minutes. And tell us where he'll be standing, please."

Weird thing about horse auctions: they don't say who the buyer is. Not at first. The auction house might not even know until they find the guy in the crowd and ask him to fill out his paperwork. In this case, the agents from the IRS had to sign off on it, too, to make sure everything was kosher. So for a while, the answer to everyone's question had to wait: *Who just bought Tempting Dash?*


The auction carried on. The cowboys hired by the Department of the Treasury trotted out the last eight horses in the government's stables, including two more of José's champion runners and four well-bred embryos. By the end of the day, the Treasury Department had brought in another $3 million, pushing the total value of the Treviño family's horses to more than $12 million. At least that was what they were worth when liquidated en masse at a fire sale.

In the midst of all that, the emcee's voice filled the auction house with the news everyone was waiting for: Tempting Dash, he told the crowd, had been bought by a rancher from central Texas, but not the central Texas rancher everyone expected. His name was John Simmons, and he planned to stand Tempting Dash at a place called Granada Farms—a stud farm with a little more recent success than Southwest Stallion Station. Simmons had outlasted Tyler in the end, agreeing to pay $1.7 million for the undersized stallion they once called El Huesos—more than any other quarter horse in history.

■ ■ ■

BRUCETON MILLS, WEST VIRGINIA
May 2015

There's plenty to spend money on inside the Hazelton Federal Correctional Institution, the medium-security prison tucked into the northeastern corner of West Virginia. Like at all federal prisons, there is a commissary inside the gray-brick fortress, where prisoners can buy coffee (Taster's Choice, $9.10), breakfast foods (strawberry Pop-Tarts, $1.95), soap (Neutrogena is a bank breaker), and two hundred or so other items. The most expensive item is a Sony Clear Digital Radio. It's popular with the prisoners. They use it to listen to music when they're freed from the prison walls and are left to explore the outdoor expanses of Hazelton's one-hundred-acre, one-thousand-bed campus, which cost the government $150 million. It's also popular with prison officials. They like its clear plastic body, which reduces contraband smuggling, and its $45 price tag, which increases commissary profits.

The most versatile item is the postage stamp. Since smoking was banned in federal prisons, the stamp has replaced cigarettes as the most common black-market currency. It's the paper you use to pay off the prison bookie, get a legal brief written by the in-house paralegal, or otherwise settle up.

Perhaps the most *valuable* thing a Hazelton prisoner can buy is communication. It's certainly how José Treviño chose to spend his small stream of money as he settled into his two-decade stretch at Hazelton, which counted among its inmates the former kingpin of Colombia's infamous Cali Cartel.

After he was sentenced, José's lawyers had pleaded with the judge to send him somewhere close to Dallas. There is a low-security federal prison in Seagoville, Texas, only a few miles from the family home in suburban Dallas—from the neighborhoods where José and Kiko had started laying bricks thirty years before, and from where José's wife and kids and sisters still lived. The judge said that while he didn't control where José would be ending up, he was sure that was where the Bureau of Prisons would ship him. "Tell them about your family," the judge had told José, "and I'm sure they'll get you to Seagoville very quickly."

They sent him to Hazelton.

Now, every month or so, someone in his family wired José a few hundred bucks. Most days, he spent three or five or ten bucks on phone calls.

For a while he had reason to call his lawyers. He had fired his original defense team, complaining to the judge that he was "misrepresented big-time"—that Finn, sensing a losing case, had passed the buck to his co-counsel and sleepwalked through the trial. (Finn denies this.) José had a new team now. Together with the lawyers of the other men convicted at trial, they were mounting an appeal.

In their lengthy briefs, the attorneys acknowledged that these horsemen had used the Zetas' drug money to fund their horse businesses. And they acknowledged that their business had the effect of hiding those drug proceeds from the government. But did the prosecutors prove that the men *knew*—had they been told, could they be sure?—that it was drug money? Did they prove that José and the others *decided* to help the Zetas conceal it from the government? That they *planned* to?

It was a good enough argument that the Fifth Circuit Court of Appeals, the country's most conservative appeals court, agreed to hear oral arguments, which it does in less than a third of cases. Once the case got there, the army of defense lawyers could collectively assault the bench with the government's failings.

It was quite an attack. When it came time to argue the case, the other defense attorneys yielded most of the time to the attorney of Francisco Colorado, the millionaire Mexican businessman. He'd brought in new lawyers for the appeal, and then hired a specialist for oral arguments: Alan Dershowitz, the famed O. J. Simpson defender and Harvard Law School professor.

Dershowitz spent most of his time arguing the finer points of his own client's case. But he made the case broadly and eloquently. "To be or not to be a money launderer," he said. "That Hamlet moment didn't happen in this case."

During the arguments, José's best hope could be heard in the voice of one of the judges. She sounded smitten with Dershowitz and his arguments. Late in the hearing, she rib-jabbed the government's own appeals lawyer to the point of embarrassment.

"Let me ask you something about José," the judge said, as the Justice Department lawyer tried to gather herself. "Your brief goes on and on about how he's the brother of these . . . known drug dealers. I find that disturbing. I don't think you're responsible for your brother. I don't have a brother, but if I did and if he were a drug dealer, I would not want to be accused because he's . . . you know."

The Justice Department lawyer started to apologize, but the judge went on.

"You put so much stock in that. I'm offended by that."

Besides, the judge said, there was more evidence that José *didn't* want anything to do with the drug business than there was that he did. What happened? "Did he just fall off the wagon?" the judge asked.

"I think he felt the horse business wasn't the drug business," the government's lawyer said.

"Is that intent to participate?"

"He knew where the cash was coming from."

"Knowing where the cash is coming from isn't enough," the judge said. "Even if it's your brother."

It took five months for the court to issue its ruling. When it did, it carried the same doubtful tone of the oral arguments.

The judges ruled that Chevo, the trainer of Tempting Dash, had done nothing other than train Forty's horses—that he'd never agreed or conspired to launder money. The court set him free. He'd be back at the track the next racing season.

They granted Francisco Colorado a new trial, largely on legal technicalities unwound by Dershowitz. In 2015, after another lengthy trial, Colorado would be convicted again, this time with Carlitos testifying against him. A ruling on his second appeal was expected in 2017.

The court upheld the conviction of Fernando, Carlitos's side-kick. But like Carlitos, Fernando would soon agree to cooperate with the government in its effort to reconvict Colorado. Like Carlitos's imprisonment, Fernando's thirteen-year sentence was eventually reduced to about five. Upon his release, he would be allowed to stay in the United States.

But however "offended" the appeals judge was by the government's case against José, it made no difference. The court dismissed his pleas in a few paragraphs, apparently deciding that he had known exactly what he was doing all along.

José fired his lawyers again after that. He managed to file a petition with the Supreme Court, likely with the help of an inmate-turned-paralegal. In the spirit of jailhouse petitions, José's twenty-seven-page brief was a little rambling and peppered with citations, but he made his point. He argued that he'd been failed by his lawyers, judge, jury, and the appeals court. The Supreme Court declined to consider it.

Guilty, twenty years, FCI Hazelton—it all stuck.

In the case's aftermath, José and his family made it clear that they had no plans to talk to the press. His wife and their youngest children returned to their brick house in Balch Springs. Zulema got a job working the five-to-eleven dinner shift at a fast-food restaurant. She told her lawyer to keep the press at bay, and when a TV reporter showed up at her home, the cops showed up soon after.

Luis and Alexandra stayed in California, and she, too, told her lawyer to keep the media away. About a year after she was sentenced to probation, she asked the court to release her, to make it easier to find meaningful work. She was studying photography and hoped to reenroll in college, but Luis had been deployed for several months of her first year. He'd just reenlisted.

Her probation officer supported her being released. The judge said no.

After the trial, I called and sent letters to José, Zulema, and Alex, asking them to share their stories. I didn't hear back for some time.

But one day, in 2016, I got a notification from CorrLinks, the third-party system that administers electronic mail for federal inmates. Inmates can't surf the Internet or use social media, although many use friends as surrogates to update their Facebook and Twitter sites. They can't use traditional email, either. But they can use CorrLinks, which allows them to communicate electronically through a clunky, monitored platform with people on their approved list of contacts. It costs them five cents a minute.

CorrLinks notifications buzzed in my pocket occasionally, and I never tired of getting them; for a journalist covering crime, they're little rockets of hope exploding in your inbox. But I wasn't expecting this one.

"INMATE: TREVINO-MORALES, JOSE," the subject line read. The body contained two automatically generated but welcome sentences: "The above-named person is a federal prisoner who seeks to add you to his/her contact list for exchanging electronic messages. There is no message from the prisoner at this time."

I hoped this meant he wanted to talk; I feared he wanted to tell me to screw off. Either way, I expected to hear something in the moments that followed. I didn't. So a few days later, I messaged him. He sent a message back right away, as cryptic as it was tantalizing.

"You will be hearing from me in a couple of days," he wrote. "I heard you tried to contact my wife."

I apologized for my pestering, but I continued to make my case, rattling off all the standard-issue rationales that journalists use to convince potential subjects and sources to talk, many of which we believe. I want the fullest picture possible, I told him. He didn't write back.

Time passed, probably not enough, and I emailed him again to check in. This time, he responded:

"Forgive me if I may sound skeptical (even cynical) but the past few years have shown me to trust no one. I would like for you to send me verifiable bonafides and 'clippings' before I go any further. You know who I am—or at least who the government portrays me to be. More so, if we are to begin a relationship it's better to begin with no concerns in the back of your mind. There is an extraordinary piece of evidence I'd very much like you to see that will shock you. How it slipped through the hands of the powers that be I won't guess but it's left them with their 'bonafides' hanging out. Let's begin in this manner and proceed accordingly. If all is as you say it is you might want to begin circling your sources in the Austin area for some explosive research."

I was at the post office the next day, sending him examples of recent reporting I'd done. After enough time passed for him to receive it, I began obsessively checking the website for CorrLinks, the inmate email service, even though I knew it would ping me if I had a new message. Nothing.

And then, something. I was in the kitchen. My phone buzzed. I checked it, and there it was: a message from CorrLinks with José's name. My heart pumped a little faster, and then my eyes caught up.

"The above-named inmate has chosen to remove your email address from his/her approved contact list and, therefore, cannot receive or send messages to your email address."

I wrote José twice more after that, but I never heard back. I circled my sources in Austin, too, just as he'd suggested. If there was explosive evidence that might mean something for José's future, they couldn't figure what it might be.

# KISS MY HOCKS

RUIDOSO, NEW MEXICO
July 2015

If you were looking for Tyler Graham, the Turf Club on a big race day would seem, at first, like something of a lost cause. It was, on this steamy July afternoon, toe-to-heel with cowboys who moved like geese from the bar to the betting window to their perches high above the track, slugging domestic bottles and honking about this jockey and that trainer and, *God damn, that was a helluva frickin' horse race.*

Who knew if Tyler was even here. If he even wanted to be seen, after sitting on a witness stand before judge, jury, and the family of one of the world's most wanted gangsters, and describing, in detail, his partnership with the FBI. A lot of people in the horse business couldn't believe he was alive. They feared for his life. Maybe he didn't want to be found.

Well, nope, there it was, wasn't it? A custom leather belt studded with gems that spelled out the name clear as can be: "Graham." Tyler pulled from a Coors Light.

It had been five years since Tyler was here with José and Carlitos and Fernando, watching their long-shot colt, Mr Piloto, take home the sport's fattest check. Five years since he'd lurked at the auction and celebrated at the casino, trading glances and texts with Lawson. None of that today. Today was simpler: Tyler had a horse. The three-year-old colt had been running well. He was the morning-line favorite to win today's big race, the $1.1 million Rainbow Derby. If the horse won, Tyler and his business partner would be a half million bucks richer. They'd also be in possession of a new high-dollar stallion for Tyler's ranch in Elgin.

The horse's name was Kiss My Hocks. Where most horse names paid homage to a horse's bloodlines, Kiss My Hocks's name ignored his, instead instructing some unnamed entity to kiss his hulking horse ass. Kiss My Hocks's dam was Romancing Mare, a solid mare that won or placed in twelve of her fourteen starts. His sire was one of the industry's rising young stallions: Tempting Dash.


No one was ever quite sure what to expect of Tempting Dash as a breeder, because no one was quite sure what to make of his brief, record-setting racing career—especially after the news broke of the Zetas and their industrious efforts to sway races. But his initial crop of offspring—foals from breedings that Tyler and José had sold and given away together—had shown promise. A colt named Hezadash-inbye won the Firecracker Futurity in Louisiana and took home $139,000 for his owner. A gelding named Tempting Destiny earned a spot in the finals of two of Ruidoso's biggest races and brought in $300,000.

But Tempting Dash's most promising offspring weren't from breedings Tyler and José had sold or given away. Nor were they from the many breedings Carlitos had arranged for Forty. They were from the breedings that Tyler Graham had arranged for himself.

One of Tyler's first free breedings yielded a short sorrel filly named Lovethewayyoulie, which won the biggest race of the year at Oklahoma's Remington Park and raked in almost a half million dollars. The second, and the best, was Kiss My Hocks.

As Tyler's daddy would say, that booger could *run*. First race out, in the 2014 trials of the big futurity in Houston, Kiss My Hocks, barely two by the calendar, broke a decade-old track record. Then, in the finals, he rode the rail and won Tyler and his business partner $225,000. That summer, they shipped him to Ruidoso, and he won the first leg of the track's Triple Crown and qualified for the All American Futurity.

Kiss My Hocks was named the two-year-old Colt of the Year, just like his sire, Tempting Dash. Tyler was named Owner of the Year. At the year-end awards banquet, Tyler was back on the stage at his grandpa's auction house to accept the award. This time, without José.

"It's just what everybody dreams of," Tyler said that night. "Especially having the opportunity to raise the horse, too—that just makes it a little more special."

Now Kiss My Hocks was three, and back at quarter-horse racing's mecca, in the mountains of New Mexico. If he could notch another big win, he would become even more valuable for Tyler as a stud horse. Things hadn't been the same since the Grahams lost Tempting Dash, the stud that could have made Southwest Stallion Station's name for years. To get back there, it was going to require a new colt winning big races like this one.

Tyler's brown hair was freshly cut and pushed away from his retreating hairline. He wore what seemed to be his Ruidoso race-day uniform: a paisley shirt, dark green and purple, tucked into loose-fitting blue jeans that hung over black skin boots. The day's program was rolled like a holy scroll and tucked into his back pocket, threatening but failing to obscure the gem-studded "Graham" on his black belt.

His race was up next. Tyler placed a bet at the window, strolled downstairs, and pushed through the crowd, near the spot where Lawson had snapped his pictures five years before. He walked through the cold tunnel that burrowed beneath the track and came up on the other side.

It was solemn again, that weird quiet that existed only on this side of the track, where no booze was allowed, and so, no booze numbed the violent reality of what was about to happen on the other side of the cracked plastic railing. Tyler stepped into the saddling paddock and ran his hand through the fine sorrel coat of his hulking quarter horse.

As the trainer prepped Kiss My Hocks, Tyler retreated to the viewing area, joining his family. His local-girl bride wasn't there; they'd divorced earlier in the year. His new girlfriend (and future wife) was there, though, and she offered the gentle hand of a knowing horsewoman on his back; she was a former champion rodeo competitor and champion horse owner. Farther back, Tyler's grandpa, a little hunched but still cutting a figure in his wide-brimmed hat, kept his distance, standing atop the knoll that overlooked the scene, ceding the moment to Tyler.

The jockey, a veteran named G. R. Carter, mounted Kiss My Hocks, led him out of the paddock and onto the track under threatening skies. Trainers, owners, breeders—they all have their spots from where they like to watch the race, but none is any good, a cruel irony of life on the track's inside. If you can see the starting line, you can't see the finish, and vice versa. If you're too far from the action, you can't feel it; but if you're close enough to feel it, you can't see what you're feeling.

Tyler's was maybe the best of all the bad spots—leaned against one of the metal beams that supports the jockeys' dressing room, shaded by a row of bushy trees. There was a flatscreen hanging on the outside wall. Tyler stared at it as the horses started loading into the gate.

He stood there, arms folded, stoic. There were people crowded around him, and yet he was totally, purposefully alone. His grandpa, his dad, and his girlfriend all lingered several yards away. A man in his zone, not to be bothered.

It was a weird kind of quiet, not the hush of a big golf shot but the breathless silence of a verdict, a diagnosis, of bad news about to be revealed. When someone clicked gingerly onto the rocks behind Tyler, looking for an angle, it pierced the silence like gunshots. "Just a plain race," someone said, lending words to the tension. "Everybody get out."

They were all loaded. Tyler's chest heaved, lifting and tugging his shoulders faster with each breath. The race announcer's voice sliced through the quiet, and that should have been the preamble to the tension's end, but then a lone gate rattled open. It was Kiss My Hocks, breaking through the starting line before it was time. Tyler shook his head. He knew. Horses don't overcome false starts to win. The rhythm was gone.

Then another horse busted through, as though it had caught Hocks's anxiety. The crowd groaned, knowing false starts can portend ugly races.

Finally, they broke, all at once. Hocks shot free, kicking up red dust. Tyler straightened up off the beam but kept a hand perched on his chin. His horse was in the lead, and as much as he seemed to want to keep it cool, the people around him—a lot of them wearing big, red kissing-lip stickers on their shirts—were not on board with keeping it cool.

"Come on, Hocks!"

"Let's go, baby!"

"Git you some, baby!"

"Come on, Hocks!"

"Take it down, son!"

Tyler's shoulders, up and down, up and down, as the thunder of his own horse passed *behind* him on the track. He stayed glued to that TV. These camera angles—even on the TV you couldn't see who was winning, not really, not until they pulled even with the camera and—

Hocks! As he neared the finish line, he was a half-length ahead, and it was clear, as clear as the feeling of the friend pounding on Tyler's shoulders, that this son of Tempting Dash had just won a half million dollars for his owners, and probably earned himself a rich, lazy life grazing the grasses of Elgin, Texas. One day they'd probably discover that he loved sunflower seeds.

Tyler whirled around and screamed into the wind, "Yeah!" He pounded a friend with consecutive high-fives and walked toward the track, into a ray of sunshine. He landed in a spot between the track and the winner's circle. He wrapped his arms tight around his girlfriend, and he waited—for the photo op, for the check, for Kiss My Hocks, the champion colt by Tempting Dash, to saunter back down the track and, eventually, back to Elgin, where, before long, he would be standing for $6,500 a breeding, hopefully for years to come.

"Call him home," someone yelled. Tyler and his girlfriend stayed locked in embrace, family, friends, and industry royalty swirling around them. Behind them all, way down the track, Tyler's horse was bouncing toward the winner's circle.

# REPORTING AND SOURCES

This is a work of nonfiction. It is based on interviews, documents, personal observations, and previous research by respected journalists and academics in the United States and Mexico. From start to finish, every fact is attributable to something. Here, I'll tell you a little more about those somethings.

I conducted several on-the-record interviews with FBI case agents Scott Lawson and "María Medina," who is the only person identified on these pages by a pseudonym. I also met with IRS case agent Steve Pennington, Assistant United States Attorneys Doug Gardner and Michelle Fernald, and dozens of other law enforcement agents, active and retired, across several agencies, who worked this and other cases involving Los Zetas. (Former agents Arturo Fontes and Al Peña were especially insightful.) Some spoke on the condition that they not be identified, although, mostly, their names were omitted for brevity, not by agreement. To the agents' credit, the only condition governing most of these interviews was that I not name confidential sources. The only informants identified here are ones previously made public by the government.

I attended several quarter-horse races and auctions, including trips to Ruidoso, New Mexico; Oklahoma City; Lone Star Park; and Los Alamitos, which were invaluable. On those trips and over the phone, people throughout the quarter-horse industry helped develop my understanding of the industry, the sport, the culture, and the people involved in this story.

I also interviewed a handful of Zeta operatives, about their involvement in this case or other drug-trafficking or money-laundering operations—all of those interviews granted on the condition that these sources not be identified, for reasons that are hopefully obvious. Their insights helped shape some of the details of how the Zetas operated behind the scenes. Their lawyers and other defense lawyers helped fill in gaps or corroborate their stories, as did public records.

There were a lot of records—thousands of pages of court transcripts, FBI and DEA interview summaries, surveillance reports, surveillance photographs, bank records, wiretap transcripts, intercepted emails, internal intelligence reports, employment applications, AQHA records, racetrack records, auction-house records, and thick sales books that I treated as gingerly as I could.

I never was able to interview José or his family. Their story is based largely on these records and interviews with friends, colleagues, attorneys, and law enforcement agents. I also did not speak with Tyler Graham, although his father, David, provided some insight into his family's businesses and the courting of Tempting Dash, including the descriptions of Chevo's visit to his store and Graham's visit to Chevo's ranch. Chevo declined to be interviewed, but his family confirmed that he and David Graham were friendly and had visited the ranch.

Most of the dialogue that appears in quotation marks was pulled directly from records, including intercepted phone calls, court testimony, and FBI and DEA reports. I also quoted conversations that were recounted by participants in later interviews. Dialogue recorded or recalled less precisely appears without quotation marks and is paraphrased.

I consulted dozens of books of journalism and history, but a handful contributed more directly to this one. For my understanding of the quarter-horse breed and its history, I relied heavily on *The Quarter Horse*, the 1941 book "penned up," as the book puts it, by researcher Robert Denhardt. *Smoke and Mirrors*, the journalist Dan Baum's political history of the drug war, was especially useful to understanding the role of the federal government in drug enforcement. Whenever possible, I verified Baum's and other journalists' reporting with primary documents—an easy task in Baum's case, thanks to his meticulous research and sourcing. *Wolf Boys*, by Dan Slater, and *Midnight in Mexico*, by Alfredo Corchado, provided the two most detailed portraits of Miguel Treviño that exist. Several books helped deepen my understanding of Mexico's war on the Zetas, and the Zetas' wars with El Chapo and the Gulf cartel. *The Executioner's Men*, by George Grayson and Samuel Logan; *El Narco*, by Ioan Grillo; *In the Shadow of St. Death*, by Michael Deibert; and *Narcoland*, by Anabel Hernández, were especially valuable.

I also relied at various times on the work of newspaper and magazine journalists, trying to verify their reporting whenever possible. That included stories by Ginger Thompson and several of her *New York Times* colleagues; the *Dallas Morning News*'s Corchado and Dianne Solis; *San Antonio Express-News*'s Jason Buch; Bloomberg's Alan Katz and Dakin Campbell; *Popular Science*'s Damon Tabor; *The Atavist*'s Mary Cuddehe; the unshakable staff of *Proceso*, the Mexican newsmagazine; and others, including many Mexican journalists who work anonymously out of fear for their lives.

# ACKNOWLEDGMENTS

If I'm ever allowed to write more books, I vow to do that cool veteran-author thing, where the acknowledgments are two sentences, over and out. But just in case I don't:

My mom taught me to read, write, and edit, and even those are pretty low on the list of gifts she's given me, through genetics and the sheer force of motherly will. My dad and his siblings showed me by example how to tell a good story, and by ridicule how to avoid telling a bad one. My sister quietly demonstrated how to live generously and fully.

At Santa Clara University, professors Gordon Young and Barbara Kelley helped me find my place in journalism. In Cleveland, Pete Kotz taught me to think, drink, talk, listen, and write, between shifts producing powerhouse works of his own. My colleagues at the *Dallas Observer* and Voice Media Group, where I worked when I first started this project, were the ideal partners in mischief.

Several other journalists have reported on this story, and they were always gracious when our paths crossed, including Jason Buch, Jazmine Ulloa, Melissa del Bosque, Cecilia Ballí, Alfredo Corchado, and Dianne Solis. Now at ProPublica, Ginger Thompson, who broke this story, was supportive and generous from the moment I decided to tell my own version of it.

I obviously couldn't have written this book if I couldn't report it, and reporting it required the intelligence and expertise of scores of people from the quarter-horse industry, law enforcement, the Texas legal bar, and other walks of life. There are too many to thank here, and many of them would rather not be called out anyway. That said, I do want to thank "María Medina" for her support and insight. And, obviously, I owe a great debt to Scott Lawson, for his generosity of time, spirit, intelligence, and wit. We didn't always agree but we did always get along, a feat that, nowadays especially, seems worth celebrating. I hope we get to soon.

Several families hosted and supported me in my travels, including the Bilanins, Kleinmans, Watkinses, and Nortons. I hope I left more beer than I drank. Other friends read early versions of this story, or otherwise helped me navigate the process of producing this book, including David Schechter, Justin Stenger, Obed Manuel, Gus Garcia-Roberts, Caleb Hannan, and Vince Grzegorek. The Salon and Marlin families offered bottomless love and support.

The teams at Stuart Krichevsky Literary Agency, Random House, and One World Books worked magic on this project and manuscript, including Cindy Spiegel, Julie Grau, Nicole Counts, Tom Perry, Greg Mollica, Andrea DeWard, Maria Braekel, Allyson Lord, Shona McCarthy, and freelancers Bonnie Thompson and Beverly Kennedy. In the United Kingdom, agent Felicity Rubinstein and Arabella Pike at William Collins shepherded this story gracefully.

From beginning to end, my agent, David Patterson, saw promise in this story, and in me, that I didn't always see in myself. My editor at One World, Christopher Jackson, saw that promise, too, and then worked tirelessly to bring it to life. Chris is truly brilliant, and fearless, and diligent, and kind, and hey: I wonder if I own the copyright to all the notes he wrote in the margins of my manuscript? I should look into that. They'd make a good little book themselves.

I had one son when I first started looking into this story. He was about ten weeks old. By the time this book was published, he was in kindergarten, and his little brother was three. They made their contributions, mostly ensuring that I never slept past six-thirty A.M. and occasionally hijacking my laptop to inject some *kasjg89;SX/jkqwd/jkbqwd* into the story. I'm so thankful to them for not deleting Daddy's horsey book. But mostly I'm grateful they were there, which was always enough to keep me going.

No one is owed more thanks than my wife, Melissa, to whom this book is dedicated. Writing it was literally her idea. Once she convinced me to pursue it, she encouraged me to write as she has always encouraged me to write, even when it wasn't especially clear how that writing would support or propel our family. She read pages, told me what to cut, endured my book-induced moodiness, and otherwise kept our lives together, all while running a business rooted in her lust to repair the world. If nothing else, I hope this book always reminds me of our earliest days as parents, and the beautiful grit with which she makes our life go.